Blowing the Whistle

Blowing the Whistle

Dissent in the Public Interest

WRITTEN AND EDITED BY
Charles Peters
AND
Taylor Branch

PRAEGER PUBLISHERS
New York • Washington • London

PRAEGER PUBLISHERS
111 Fourth Avenue, New York, N.Y. 10003, U.S.A.
5, Cromwell Place, London SW7 2JL, England

Published in the United States of America in 1972
by Praeger Publishers, Inc.

Library of Congress Catalog Card Number: 72-185768

Printed in the United States of America

Contents

Foreword

Among the articles we have selected for this book is one that appeared in the second issue of the *Washington Monthly*. Since then, whistle-blowing has been one of our main themes, scarcely a month going by without an article exploring some aspect of the question. Taylor Branch has provided settings for eleven of those articles assembled in these pages. He has also written the introductory and concluding chapters; a chapter on James Boyd; one on Charles Pettis, John McGee, and Jacqueline Verrett; another comparing Daniel Ellsberg and Otto Otepka; and has provided an interview with Ellsberg, printed here for the first time. The Branch material is uniformly brilliant and gives the book a coherence and unity that take it out of the realm of the usual collection. What emerges is an interpretation of whistle-blowing as a new American political phenomenon.

Why has whistle-blowing been so important to the *Washington Monthly*? In an early issue, I wrote:

> Of all the wrong decisions I have seen made in government, wrong ideas and information have played no greater role than the failure of the men with the right ideas and information to press their case courageously.

The government administrator should be zealous in reaching down into the bureaucracy for the information and ideas that don't get through the regular chain of command. When he fails, his subordinates must take risks to make sure that he is confronted with that information and those ideas, and, if he ignores them and the matter is important, they must be ready to go to the public. The mission of our magazine has been to encourage the risk-takers, the men and women willing, when it becomes necessary, to blow the whistle.

Government needs more people who are psychologically ready to resign or be fired—who, when vital issues are at stake, will stand up to their superiors and fight. Paradoxically, such readiness often means that they won't be fired or have to quit, as Suzannah Lessard, an editor of the *Monthly,* has written:

> It's rather like a troubled marriage in which the wife can't decide whether she really wants to leave or stay, but because she is so terrified of being alone, stays, never discovering that in the absence of terror she would have decided for positive reasons to stay. Such a marriage would limp along, slowly wearing down the partners. But if she felt ready to leave if necessary, and felt able, then having decided to stay, she could face the problems with confidence and work fearlessly to make something constructive out of the relationship. Paradoxically, by being willing to dump the marriage, she would make it worth saving. The same applies to a job. If, unafraid of being fired, you work courageously, with conscience and commitment, then the job is far more rewarding—worth staying in—than if cowed by the fear of dismissal, you yielded to all pressures in the effort to keep it.

This is why we are generally unsympathetic to guaranteed job security for the whistle-blower. There is one situation, however, in which absolute protection is needed. Employees whose responsibility is to protect the public health or safety must be free to go to the public whenever it is threatened by defective products or dangerous practices. Ironically, it is just this freedom that the law may deny. William Rehnquist has contended: "I think one may fairly generalize that a government employee . . . is seriously restricted in his freedom of speech with respect to any matter for which he has been assigned responsibility."* I urge the reader to consider whether Dr. Jacqueline Verrett's bureaucratic supervisor at the Food and Drug Administration should be able to fire her for her revelations about the danger of cyclamates. (See page *190.*)

But, with the Verrett exception, we believe that freedom to hire and fire without red tape is essential to good government and that potential whistle-blowers should not be promised a world free of risks. Of course, our society should offer everyone a cushion against catastrophic job loss in the form of a decent guaranteed annual income and free health care. Beyond that, we resist depriving life of adventure. In other words, if Dan Ellsberg had been working for the government at the time he released the Pentagon Papers, we think the government should have had the right to fire him. Similarly, we think that Dean Rusk should have had the right to fire Otto Otepka without question. (See page *242.*) Criminal prosecution of either man is, of course, another matter. It can only be called hideous. I have had the chance to get to know Dan Ellsberg and have found him to be an extraordinary intellect whose analysis of our errors in Vietnam is something that should be treasured by a society seeking to learn from its experience. Putting him in prison where he can't speak and teach is a stupid step toward repeating the errors of the past by silencing one who can help us understand them.

I also know two of the other whistle-blowers described in this book, James Boyd and A. E. Fitzgerald. Their cases are perhaps the most disturbing to me. I have always wanted to believe that one could function with honor in our government if one did so without holier-than-thouism, without abrasiveness, and with personal kindness and consideration for one's associates. Both Boyd and Fitzgerald filled my prescription perfectly,

* William Rehnquist, "Public Dissent and the Public Employee," *Civil Service Journal,* January–March, 1971. Among the important cases that have created the law of whistle-blowing are *Pickering* v. *Board of Education,* 391 U.S. 563; *Meehan* v. *Macy,* 392 F.2d 822; *Goldwasser* v. *Brown,* 417 F.2d 1169; and *Murray* v. *Vaughn,* 300 F.Supp. 1688.

and they were both fired. The United States Senate tried to blacklist Boyd. Even liberal senators were afraid to hire him. What did he do? He exposed a crook. The Air Force fired Fitzgerald only after a deliberation so thorough—both within the Department of Defense and in the White House—as to make the action totally contemptible. His offense: He told Congress the truth about the C-5A. So there really is no assurance that one can live with honor within this government. One can only try—and that is what this book is about.

CHARLES PETERS

Washington, D.C.
January, 1972

Blowing the Whistle

1 Old Muck, New Rakers

Strafing full spleen ahead, fueled by the demonstrable fact that there is graft in our politics, cruel greed in our corporations, and vermin still in our meat, muckrakers have returned to the American scene. In the years between 1907, when Upton Sinclair watched President Theodore Roosevelt sign the Pure Food and Drug Act, knowing that the bill had sprung from the rodent-flavored bologna he had portrayed so vividly in his muckraking novel *The Jungle,* and 1967, when Sinclair watched President Lyndon B. Johnson sign the Meat and Pesticides Act, the art of exposing graft and corruption and mismanagement was never really dead. But it certainly lay dormant for most of those sixty years.

The second coming of the meat bill resulted in large part from the efforts of Sinclair's kindred spirit Ralph Nader, symbol of the current age of campaigns in the public interest by typewriter and testimony. With the legendary Sinclair on hand, though confined to a wheelchair by age, the occasion had an air of rerun about it, a kind of drawn-faced solemnity, as if those present somehow resented the return to a stubborn old problem. How could everyone bask on the beachhead of progress, with Sinclair there to remind them that they were actually trying to mop up the failures of an old crusade?

A certain frivolity had enlivened the old days. People looked forward to the exposure of villainy here and there, and public outrage was tempered by the sheer entertainment value of such spectacles as prim Ida Tarbell dragging John D. Rockefeller through the muck in *McClure's Magazine*, starched collar, money, and all. Things may have been rough, but there was a sneaking admiration for the optimistic boldness of the villains in the writing of people like Lincoln Steffens—and an essential robustness to William Randolph Hearst's promise of "the most vascular and virile" horror stories ever revealed (written in Homeric prose and riddled with exclamation points). In the Nader era, by contrast, the scattered old potholes of corruption that were targets for Steffens and Tarbell and Sinclair have become one big swamp, covered by an oily film reaching almost everywhere. The generalizations and the patterns are plain and unmistakingly depressing; so, although Nader's attacks on specific outrages represent hope, it is a hope that struggles against the sagging weight of a very frustrated time. Unlike Sinclair, who represented diversion and bursts of progressive triumph, Nader is a promise of possible reform, a tentative hope aimed at the center of a pervasive national uneasiness. For that reason, Nader and his fellow muckrakers of the 1960's and 1970's give a somber cast to the nation's second period of major muckraking.

Alongside Nader looms something quite new in the history of American reform. This is the whistle-blower, the muckraker from within, who exposes what he considers the unconscionable practices of his own organization. Caught in the ethical dilemma between conflicting loyalties, the whistle-blower decides that he cannot merely leave—that he cannot remove himself from the problem while allowing it to go on. The advent of the whistle-blower, speaking out from inside institutions ranging from the U.S. Senate to the Lockheed Corporation, has raised new questions of what is permissible and what is positive, courageous dissent in the public interest.

The internal muckrakers are of two sorts. The pure whistle-blower attacks his institution while still employed there. The "alumnus" whistle-blower exposes what he finds as crimes against the public soon after leaving the service of the organization he accuses. Whether pure or alumnus, the muckraker from within, or whistle-blower, is understandably rare. And his emergence at this stage in history is remarkable.

Real and apprehended obstacles demand from the whistle-blower a quantum jump in commitment, far beyond what is demanded of an ordinary muckraker—who has no attachment to his target to make him hesitate. Even after conscience requires that a whistle-blower speak out, after his course becomes intellectually clear, he must face problems that never beset the muckraker on the outside. He must still cope with the stinging demands of loyalty, with the don't-make-a-big-deal-out-of-it feeling, and with the fear of retaliation. Furthermore, the act itself is unseemly and embarrassing, requiring the whistle-blower to "go public" in a way that looks soapboxy and cocky and messiah-bitten. Strong impulses counsel keeping things to oneself and learning how to get along while inching toward reform.

British history is marked by a phenomenon related to whistle-blowing: the Cabinet minister's resignation from the Government on principle. But a departing minister does not really blow the whistle on practices or new policies. He merely signals a policy disagreement with his Government, formalizing differences that are already known and legitimately voiced in Britain because of a tradition of individual ministerial responsibility. Compared with the American Cabinet, the British Cabinet is sufficiently collegial that a resigning minister is seen as one who disagrees with his colleague, the Prime Minister. Thus, Anthony Eden, when he resigned from Neville Chamberlain's Government prior to World War II, did what Walter Hickel or Robert McNamara might have done if the American Cabinet official were like his British counterpart. Instead, the secretary of an executive department in the U.S. Government has strong instincts of loyalty to a "team" led by his employer, the President.

The Teapot Dome Whistle

All things considered, the whistle-blowers of the late 1960's and the 1970's must be classified as a fresh species—first cousins to the outside muckrakers, perhaps, appearing alongside them in sour historical currents when reform is needed, but more courageous and complex. There is, however, a hint of whistle-blowing in the most famous scandal in American politics of the twentieth century, Teapot Dome. This affair, which took place in the administrations of Warren Harding and Calvin Coolidge, featured a government employee named Harry F. Slattery as whistle-blower. Slattery's performance is of insufficient purity to qualify him as a direct forbear of A. Ernest Fitzgerald (the man who exposed the $2 billion cost overrun of the C-5A contract in 1968). But the story of Teapot Dome itself—coming between the first era of muckraking at the turn of the century and the current period—illustrates a number of the changes in the circumstances of institutional fraud and deserves to be considered in that light. Some of the changes have helped bring forth today's whistle-blowers, while some have helped make whistle-blowing a more perilous task.

Harry F. Slattery was a minor bureaucrat and a disciple of Gifford Pinchot, one of the fathers of the conservation movement, cohort of Teddy Roosevelt, and a prime mover in the departments of Interior and Agriculture before Harding took office in 1921. Operating through contacts with colleagues still in the government, Pinchot and Slattery kept tabs on Harding's Secretary of the Interior, Albert Fall, whose record on conservation was far from sterling. Fall, a former senator from New Mexico, was known at the time for his claim to be the last person to wear six-guns on the floor of the Senate, and he received some recognition for the brassy frontier spirit in which he advocated the annexation of Mexico. Pinchot and Slattery found him environmentally suspect.

In the course of his duties as chief Fall-watcher for the small core of conservationists around Pinchot, Slattery began to notice the considerable enrichment of the Secretary of the Interior's real estate holdings in New Mexico—especially his acquisition of the huge Three Rivers Ranch, which seemed beyond the means of a Cabinet secretary of Fall's modest wealth even in the Roaring Twenties. Slattery's curiosity regarding Fall's sudden prosperity filtered back to Carl Magee, editor of the Albuquerque *Morning Journal*, who began to record his astonishment in almost daily editorials calling for an explanation. Harding's biographer Francis Russell, in *Shadow of Blooming Grove* (New York: McGraw-Hill, 1968), writes that Magee then "found himself boycotted by advertisers, his bank notes called, and his *Journal* harassed until finally it was forced to close down." Slattery himself got a foretaste of the whistle-blower's security problem when he was visited by a gunman named Baracca, in the employ of Fall, who attempted in John Wayne style to discourage further meddling.

Incensed, Slattery went to see his friend, Assistant Secretary of the Navy Theodore Roosevelt, Jr. The younger TR was outraged that Slattery could cast aspersions on Fall, who had been a Rough Rider with his Daddy. This argument presaged the whistle-blower's dignity gap, that inevitable but dismaying influence of stature and personal ties, which makes it difficult for the whistle-blower to get a hearing of his case. Slattery persisted, nevertheless, and managed to dig up enough facts to impress people who had less emotional commitment to Fall than TR, Jr.

It turned out that Fall, in poor health and desirous of retirement, had found himself too impoverished to secure the kind of life-style for his reposing years that he felt befitted a man who had been a senator and Cabinet secretary. So he took his liquidity problem to two wealthy men with whom he often came in contact—Harry A. Sinclair, president of Sinclair Oil Company, and Edward L. Doheny, president of Pan-American Petroleum and Transport Company. (Sinclair had met the Interior Secretary at the Kentucky Derby, long reputed to be a breeding ground of much iniquity among the rich.) Fall was interested in increasing his liquidity, and Sinclair was interested in the federal oil reserves at Teapot Dome in Wyoming, administered for the people by Secretary of the Interior Albert Fall. On April 7, 1922, Fall leased the entire Teapot Dome oil reserve to Sinclair in a closed, no-bid contract. This brought a huge windfall to Sinclair Oil, and Sinclair, encouraged by the prospect of future earnings, felt that he was in a position to "lend" Secretary Fall $300,000, which he did. (It was through deals like this that Harry A. Sinclair achieved so glittering a reputation for financial genius that the Albanians invited him to be their king for a while in 1924 to get them on a sturdier fiscal path. Sinclair declined, and the Albanians eventually came to rely on Mao Tse-tung in budgetary matters.) Doheny, meanwhile, was interested in obtaining a contract to build and operate emergency petroleum storage tanks for the Navy, whose utility was never clearly established but whose construction was so lucratively priced for Doheny that he was enabled to "lend" Fall $100,000, which went toward the purchase of the Three Rivers Ranch.

It was these two transactions that Slattery sniffed at, looking for hard evidence and aided somewhat by oil competitors of the lenders and by the efforts of Senator Bob La Follette the elder. The Teapot Dome lease was the prime suspect, known by government experts to be a criminal hoax on the public, but the intricacies of oil leases and emergency petroleum requirements were such that the public could not get aroused about the matter. Besides, Fall seemed definitely enriched, but the $300,000 loan was too dispersed to be traced back to Sinclair. Doheny's $100,000, on the other hand, went straight to Three Rivers, and the sleuths on Fall's tracks convinced conservative Senator Thomas J. Walsh that Fall could not account for the money. Walsh's reluctant investigation, based on the mysterious $100,000, was the breakthrough.

Most *cognoscenti* of scandal insist that Fall was not yet undone and that he could have ridden out the storm had he not panicked and prevailed upon his good comrade Edward B. (Ned) McLean to lie for him at the Walsh investigation by claiming to be the source of Doheny's $100,000. Dashing Ned, owner of the *Cincinnati Inquirer* and the *Washington Post*, was known to be rather dull-witted but certainly rich enough to have advanced the money to Fall. There were, however, holes in the hastily contrived story that Fall and McLean told the Walsh committee, and Slattery, Pinchot, La Follette, and others helped track them down. When Walsh announced his intention to hold further hearings, Ned retreated to his summer home in Palm Beach, Florida, and announced his unavailability for testimony. His battery of lawyers, led by retired Red-hunting Attorney General A. Mitchell Palmer, then advised him that, indeed, things looked bad. McLean installed the world's first hotline between Palm Beach and his offices at the *Washington Post*, over which he traced Walsh's movements with coded messages, while the senator threatened to take the hearing to McLean if McLean would not come to the hearing. This high drama finally attracted the press, the scent of scandal filled the air, and the Coolidge people escalated their references to the fact that the entire matter had taken place in the previous Administration.

In the end, Ned McLean admitted his perjury, and Albert Fall acknowledged Sinclair and Doheny as the sources of his loans. The former Secretary of the Interior stoutly maintained that the money had nothing to do with Teapot Dome or the storage tanks that became necessary when the reserves at Teapot Dome were sold off. But his efforts to cover up the matter had greatly diminished his credibility. Furthermore, Fall defended the covert manner in which the Teapot Dome lease was granted on the grounds that the national security implications of petroleum required both secrecy and a healthy oil industry. (Unfortunately, the judge at Fall's trial did not rule on this last argument, which even today provides a protective coating for much bigger dealings between the government and the oil men.)

Doheny also admitted his deeds before the Walsh committee, and the press savored every detail. Democratic senators on the committee, anxious to seize the rare media opportunity to flail the Republican Harding Administration for moral laxity, piously lectured Doheny on good citizenship and good government—

until the oil magnate spoiled things by remarking that he had also bought favors from four members of Woodrow Wilson's Cabinet and saw nothing wrong with it. "I hired them for their influence," he said drily, and the senators moved quickly to another line of questioning.

Through the entire Teapot Dome ordeal, Harry Slattery fulfilled his role as a kind of prenatal whistle-blower both by probing Fall's doings for elements of scandal and by interpreting the intricate regulations on national oil policy for the nonspecialist senators. The latter function, the sorting out of complicated material for the general public, foreshadows a prime task of the whistle-blower. In many ways he is a product of the increasing complexity of public affairs—unneeded in the old days when reform politics hinged on whether or not someone was a "crook," in the sense of obvious graft, but vitally needed when breaches of the public trust can be detected only with computers and the patience of a bureaucrat.

The whistle-blower, as insider, has crucial advantages for the job of cutting through the word curtains around policy decisions to get at the heart of the matter. He has enough inside information and familiarity with the issues involved to understand the real implications of policy statements—which too often strike the average citizen as mealy and confusing concoctions, suspicious but hopelessly snarled. Given these special skills, his test is whether or not he can present the facts in dramatic enough fashion to stimulate the chemistry of outrage in the media and the general public. Pressure from the public is the key to the tactics of exposure. The very idea of exposure, in fact, implies that someone will be there to become indignant and effectively active when the muckraker or whistle-blower throws back the shades that hide some gangrenous sore on the public weal.

Slattery and Pinchot had a strong case that, bribes aside, Secretary Fall's arrangements with Sinclair and Doheny were exceedingly detrimental to the public interest. Fall was leasing valuable government oil reserves to private businesses at a fraction of their worth—in effect, giving money from the taxpayers to particular oil interests. His deal included almost no provisions to guard against Sinclair's gushing crude oil over most of Wyoming and Colorado, a common and damaging effect of the sloppiness that plagued the early petroleum crusades. The list of charges against Fall was long, detailed, and convincing. But it did not make good reading, and nothing he did was imbued with enough overt evil to pump adrenalin through the voters in the street. Thus, Slattery, Pinchot, and their allies were licked by the very complexity of the case they were trying to make in behalf of the public, until given a boost by the publicity surrounding Fall's manipulations after he left office. While the people were generally unmoved by Fall's actions contrary to their interests, they became animated by roguish antics in high places, as Teapot Dome authority Francis Russell observed:

> Conflicting opinions on oil reserve drainage and offset drilling or the construction of storage tanks in relation to the strength of the Pacific fleet had been too abstruse to sway public opinion one way or another. But a rich playboy who had lied to a Senate committee, a mysteriously missing $100,000, a former Cabinet member who had arranged oil leases and now refused to talk—these were concrete elements of scandal comprehensible to any tabloid reader.

The conservationists were saved by the old epic style in which the four villains—Fall, Sinclair, Doheny, and McLean—operated: the direct methods like bribes, the romantic extravagance like lying for your friends, the straightforward effrontery like saying that you hired Cabinet members and were proud of it. They came from a time of black and white hats, big risks, and melodramatic conflicts of the heart, such as Fall's dilemma over whether to go straight and poor or crooked and comfortable. The stories were simple but purgative, as most people shared the tug of the temptations to which "poor Albert" fell prey—and he was a figure who attracted wide sympathy, although known for the record as the "man who sold out his country for cash."

Teapot Dome was transitional, because such high-steppers would soon give way to a more sophisticated breed, to people who would never speak of a bribe but who might have given Albert Fall the impression that he could expect a good shot at a lucrative and untaxing job after retirement if he gave enough consideration to their views. The direct bribe would be replaced by the campaign contribution to the Interior Secretary's boss, and the distinction between these transactions would have an enormous practical effect on scandal potential, despite the mental alchemy required to distinguish between the contribution and the bribe. The operatives both in and out of government would become more well-rounded and smooth, shying away from clear-cut illegality, and gravitating to the areas where money could be extracted amidst confusion. All this meant that the post–Teapot Dome whistle-blower's assignment would be made tougher by increasing complications in *modus operandi* on the part of the blowee. While growing layers of fuzziness around questions of public policy called for the whistle-blower's inside dexterity, the decline of easy targets like Edward Doheny made public drama a difficult art to practice.

Teapot Dome also illustrates a transition in the problem of suggesting solutions. For while everybody instinctively grasped the remedy for Fall's criminal deeds—jail—few people had a clue about the cure for the general oil policy ills demonstrated in the incident. At the very time of the Teapot scandal, President Coolidge quietly appointed an Oil Conservation Board, which later recommended:

> Federal legislation which shall (a) unequivocally declare that agreements for the cooperative development and operation of single pools are not in violation of the Federal Antitrust laws, and (b) permit, under suitable safeguards, the making in times of overproduction of agreements among oil producers for the curtailment of production.

This recommendation was acted upon, and, notwithstanding the public beacon that Teapot Dome placed on oil policy, the cartelization and subsidization of the oil industry proceeded apace. The depletion allowance was enacted in the 1920's; domestic quota systems were enacted in the 1930's to keep production low and prices high; and import quotas were established in the 1950's to maintain high domestic prices by keeping out inexpensive foreign petroleum. The critics of Albert Fall offered such vague or unconvincing proposals regarding the early development of oil policy that the successors of Harry Sinclair carried on without significant opposition, without even a good hearing of the case against them. Teapot Dome became known as an isolated moral failure on the part of individuals. Its critics failed the reformer's crucial test: to put forth specific and generally understandable measures of political reform at each crucial moment.

Moreover, the actual exposure of the plot was accomplished through nibbles and little shoves on the part of a whole menagerie of characters (including the oil companies that remained unblessed by Fall), not through the clarion call of a single muckraker. But the real fuel of the affair came from the personalities involved and from the foibles surrounding Ned McLean's lie—from the costumes and greasepaint of the players rather than from the underlying lessons of the play. Other Secretaries of the Interior would soon perform services to the oil industry like Fall's, in return for more legal and intangible fees than cash on the barrelhead, without a breath of stigma attaching to their names. Since Fall, they have been protected by the complexities involved in determining what constitutes a blood-boiling crime against the public interest and in finding workable solutions for messy societal ills.

Complexities of the Subtradition

There is considerable evidence that the early muckraking era faltered upon the problem of finding solutions and died because the rakers' craft was not suited to complication. They were at home, as Lincoln Steffens wrote in his autobiography, with "the great moral assumption which underlay all thinking: that political evils were due to bad men of some sort and curable by the substitution of good men. I was on the level with my time, my contemporaries, and our readers." This attitude, vintage throw-the-rascals-outism, was what imparted a kind of lighthearted air to turn-of-the-century muckraking—and the public appetite for the revelations was probably whetted not least because the means of public repair were readily at hand. Reform politicians cooperated wholeheartedly with early muckrakers. Teddy Roosevelt and Steffens were quite good friends, both when TR was commissioner of police in New York and when he was President of the United States. They often collaborated to roast people they considered pawns of the New York bosses or otherwise enemies of reform.

For Steffens, the bad man theory of public evil lasted through the beginning of his famous series on corruption in city government, published in *McClure's Magazine,* surviving through "The Shame of Minneapolis," in January, 1903, "The Shamelessness of St. Louis," in March of the same year, "Pittsburgh: A City Ashamed," in May, and "Philadelphia: Corrupt and Contented," in July. Not until he moved on to Chicago, New York, and the shame of the states—as he began to notice that the facts would not support his hopes of great change even after the rascals were thrown out, often more than once—did he begin to generalize, to appear to doubt the bad man theory, and to believe that many more people than a handful of bosses had a stake in the arrangement of public finance. Writing about the campaign of Joe Folk for Governor of Missouri in 1905 (after Folk had been so much of a reformer as prosecutor in Saint Louis that he was forced to seek a wider base), Steffens displayed his new cynicism:

We knew in our bones, and those addresses of Joe Folk to Missouri will show that we knew, that the voters of the State were in that stage of mental innocence which the voters of St. Louis were in when the disclosures of corruption began there. They thought they were innocent; they thought that bad men were deceiving and misleading them; they did not know that they themselves were involved and interested in the corruption. St. Louis found out. Missouri would find out some day, too. When that day came, as it did, then the people of the State would unite with the citizens of St. Louis to stop Folk and his interference with their business.

Steffens's writing changed much as a young journalist's might change today if he had grown up convinced that the SST was a conspiracy against the public on the part of Boeing's president, and then took a tour of Seattle and the various AFL-CIO offices across the country. But even Lincoln Steffens, the brightest of the muckrakers, could not formulate exactly what he thought of politics after he lost faith in the bad man theory. In a crunch, he would come out for the democratization of the economy, but he usually reserved for himself the role of wry commentator on public morals. Other less erudite muckrakers, too, gave up prescribing cures for political wrongs—generally sticking to spicy diatribes while they still sold—or fell into clumsy new utopian theories. (Thomas W. Lawson, an ambitious muckraker who specialized in the stock market, was an early identifier of the problem as "the System," rather than the bosses. His ideas about what to do, however, were so vague and contradictory that he lost his readers in the bewilderness. Whereupon he returned to his former occupation as a stock speculator, furious at the stupidity of the people, whom he called "gelatin-spined shrimps" and "saffron-blooded apes.")

The increasing complication of the solution problem recommends the use of the whistle-blower, who is often alone in having enough knowledge in a field to show the way out of a dilemma, to cipher the government's fog, and to help create excitement about the positive effects his reform plan will spread among the populace. He must also be ready to cope with the extremely adroit countertactics that his opponents are likely to employ. These opponents will hardly admit their error sheepishly, head for the hills, or do anything else that carries the kind of honest guilt frequently encountered when old-style crooks were caught red-handed. Instead, a whistle-blower's antagonists will probably do something like the following: hand the press a 2,000-page, computer-blessed study by experts in support of their position; cite national security, job protection, or economic emergency as the justification for their actions; impugn the person with the whistle as an unqualified, self-seeking, disloyal, and moderately unbalanced underling who just doesn't understand the complexities that converge at the top; call for further study of the problem; and retire to dinner with their lawyers. In such a spot, the whistle-blower invites failure if he responds with a vague or perplexing reform proposal.

The likeness is imperfect, but it is tempting to compare the decline of confidence among muckrakers in the second five years of this century to the frustrations and complications that beset New Frontier activists after about 1965. Yet enough new whistle-blowers have emerged in the last ten years to establish the beginnings of a subtradition within muckraking, which has even achieved a measure of public legitimacy. Ralph Nader sponsored a conference in honor of whistle-blowing, and nine of its practitioners, in January, 1971. Those honored included A. Ernest Fitzgerald, who was fired by the Pentagon for exposing the cost overrun on the C-5A, and Jacqueline Verrett, a biochemist with the Food and Drug Administration who exposed her agency's tolerance of cyclamates in the face of overwhelming evidence that they cause birth defects.

The Fitzgerald and Verrett episodes took place in 1968 and 1969, but the new variant of dissent in the public interest has slightly earlier roots. Conservatives may come to date whistle-blowing from 1963, the year in which Otto Otepka was fired by Dean Rusk for giving classified documents to a Senate subcommittee to support his case that the Kennedy Administration was harboring security risks in the State Department. Otepka defended his actions on grounds of a "higher loyalty" to the nation and its protection from Communist influences. Liberals, scorning Otepka, may come to see the first true whistle-blower as James Boyd, who, three years later, and after prolonged and agonized debate with himself, exposed the corruption of his boss of twelve years, Senator Thomas Dodd.

Most subsequent whistle-blowers have felt more of an ideological affinity with Boyd than with Otepka, but there is still some doubt about whether whistle-blowing is generally a conservative call to lost principles or a liberal summons to the task of institutional change. The cases are mixed. The campaign against Army surveillance of civilian politics, first exposed by former intelligence officer Christopher Pyle, was taken up primarily by Senator Sam Ervin, a classical conservative. On the other hand, the cause of Daniel Ellsberg—who became the nation's most celebrated whistle-blower upon the publication of the Pentagon Papers in June of 1971—has rested predominantly with political liberals.

This book seeks to explore the phenomenon known as blowing the whistle in an effort to explain, among other things, why such a novel approach to organizational decay has arisen. The phrase itself causes a certain noticeable discomfort to people who have learned to appreciate the myriad interdependencies that tie us together and the thousands of subtle environmental factors that converge upon each decision in the public realm. It suggests that facts revealed still speak for themselves without needing the interpretive services of a professional task force. More importantly, it suggests a clear division between right and wrong, with no hedged bets. In short, it seems like a throwback to simpler bygone days.

This awkwardness in expression is partly a failure of language. The time-worn words of contempt for those who traffic back and forth between opposing camps with loyalties awaiting the highest bidder—words like "turncoat," "traitor," and "scab," have a strength that has persisted into a time when loyalties are necessarily more muddled, when conflicting loyalties are assured for people who choose to see them. Their persistence obstructs new words that might recognize the courage of those who expose from within when they have a good case that their employing organization is inflicting unconscionable harm upon the public. "Whistle-blowing," drafted by default into this word vacuum, suffers from the flippant image of its origin: the caricature of the bulbous-cheeked English bobby wheezing away on his whistle when the maiden cries "Stop, thief!" Daniel Berrigan once complained that the term "nonviolence" clumsily covers another verbal crevice in our language—one growing out of the bellicose survival requirements in most of human history, when it was too dangerous to ascribe much virtue to the idea of not killing people. "Nonviolence" falls as far short of capturing the power of the peace philosophy as "nonhate" of love, or as "noncowardice" of courage. Similarly, "whistle-blowing" fails to capture the anguish and higher loyalties of the act.

It is perhaps fitting that the nomenclature of whistle-blowing strains so much to avoid the treason tag that it errs on the side of oversimplification—seeming to overlook the complexities involved in figuring out what the public interest is, and thereby inviting the derision of savants in publico-legal affairs. The strain is fitting, because revulsion against any whiff of treasonous conduct poses a bigger threat to the concept of inside exposure than the problem of complexity. While the intricacies of detecting crimes against the public interest in the modern age make exposure a murky intellectual field indeed, the stigma of treason is aimed right at the solar plexus of the whistle-blower. Complexity may have helped slay the early muckrakers and created a challenge to the special skills of the whistle-blower, but the treason problem is the most distinctive obstacle to general acceptance of the need for whistle-blowers.

The paramount importance of the loyalty issue is not surprising, because the loathing of tattlers and turncoats has been almost universal for centuries, while the idea of a positive, even vital, brand of turning in the boss is comparatively fresh. One can scour literature and mythology for examples of people who achieved a pleasant reputation for having exposed their army or prince or company to the public—and find scant encouragement, if any, for such a role. In fact, whistle-blowing is severely hampered by the image of its most famous historical model, Judas Iscariot. Martin Luther seems to be about the only figure of note to make much headway with public opinion after doing an inside job on a corrupt organization.

Of course, this detestation for the traitor entrenched itself under conditions entirely different from those prevailing in the recent whistle-blowing period. It arose when exposing your team aided only an "enemy" team and endangered your comrades in time of warfare—whereas now exposing your team, say the Department of Labor, to the public is intended to aid the public. Since any department of government is supposed to serve the public as a constituent part, not make war on it, the distinction is logically clear in most cases, but victims of whistle-blowing usually attempt to interject "enemy" terminology into the dispute, seeking to call forth the musty tribal instincts against the whistle-blower, getting the public to slant its ears back and rally against the rat as if in time of direst external threat.

In addition to the martial kinds of loyalty, the whistle-blower must overcome a more recent kind of institutional loyalty, one that has its roots in a rational calculation of where one's future interests lie. If there is anything that parents have rightfully presumed to teach their children about the future in the last thirty years or so (roughly the period during which the future itself has been somewhat in doubt and rapid changes have made practical tips from Grandma obsolete overnight), it has been that the child's future lies in learning how to get along with others. The little ones have been taught how to get along in a group and be "other-directed," because they are overwhelmingly likely to earn their livings in an organization, where such skills are put to work on a practical basis as the adults scramble to get ahead. In his book *The Organization Man* (New York: Doubleday, 1956), William H. Whyte catalogued these cooperative tools. He wrote that the independent American yeoman was being snuffed out inexorably by the "team player"—that an increasingly intertwined mesh of large institutions was closing off opportunities for the individualist like a zipper across the lips. Henceforth, he said, the ambitious man would labor to build a broad network of esteem, good will, and obligation within any organization by emphasizing the amiable side of conformity and the flexible side of enthusiastic intelligence. This network would become the playing field upon which he would put things together, accumulate seniority, innovate at the margins, and otherwise strive to become a captain of the team. When a nostalgic modern man tried to "stand on his own two feet," he would find them helplessly dangling in the air, because the organization provided both his security and his advancement. When he tried to take a stand on principles or ideals, he would learn how to give and take. These realities have of necessity seeped into our folkways and pedagogy. Getting loyally along is now so vital a social command that a child's flesh learns to crawl early at the thought of a tattletale or weirdo, however noble his purpose. And an adult knows instinctively that he who slanders his institutional home will wear the mark of Cain.

The loyalty issue has been by far the most important new ingredient of whistle-blowing, causing problems that the muckrakers never had to face. Each potential whistle-blower has had to come to terms with some form of Judas fear before the big plunge. The threat is usually a mixture of the old traitor syndrome—being treated as an outcaste or alien in the mold of Benedict Arnold—and the he-could-do-it-again liability, in which one gains a reputation as an unreliable employee.

Both the complexity problem and the loyalty issue have paradoxically mixed effects on whistle-blowing. Complexity means that an employee's inside information and interpretive services are a prerequisite of successful reform, and it also makes the issues more confusing and more difficult to generate public outrage about. Loyalty inhibits whistle-blowing and also introduces many extraneous questions that can sidetrack debate, yet the very power of the loyalty feelings on both sides helps the whistle-blower attract attention to his message. And attracting the attention of reporters, who look to established figures for their news, or of the public, which often reads only the headlines in haste, is where the whistle-blower meets one of his chief obstacles.

The loyalty issue does not come into play as dramatically with "alumnus" whistle-blowers as with pure ones, because people in the former group leave their organization before they expose it. Alumni whistle-blowers are not usually free of fear, however, because they know that criticism of their former employer may saddle them with the reputation as troublesome employees. The chapters that follow deal with alumnus whistle-blowers and with pure, with the personal and general problems, and with the extremely difficult ethical judgments involved in muckraking by insiders. Readers who are primarily interested in the anguish of whistle-blowing, or in the arguments surrounding the concept itself, may want to concentrate on the pure whistle-blowers by skipping from the Boyd chapter to the Greenberg chapter. Those who are more concerned with the kinds of unique information that a whistle-blower alone can bring to the analysis of a public issue may want to focus on the alumni whistle-blowers in chapters 3-9.

If exposure from within becomes a significant tool for opposing institutional inefficiency and corruption, a literature of whistle-blowing needs to be built. Citizens who may be faced with the dilemma of institutional loyalties that clash with a sense of public responsibility stand to learn not only from the tactical mistakes of the early whistle-blowers but also from the various ways in which they resolved the conflicting pressures upon their integrity.

2 Whistling Down Tom Dodd

One of the most important examples of internal muckraking in the recent mini-era of such events, the exposure of financial corruption on the part of Senator Thomas J. Dodd, had its beginnings in the summer of 1965, when two of Dodd's former assistants pilfered incriminating documents from his office in the Senate. Knowledge of the corruption reflected in these documents had led to their disenchantment with the Senator after the 1964 election. Intensive preparation of the case against Dodd spanned the winter of 1965–66 (that same winter when Ralph Nader's *Unsafe at Any Speed* [New York: Grossman, 1965] was published, launching his career of public-interest advocacy) and culminated in a long series of Drew Pearson–Jack Anderson columns based on information given them by James Boyd.

Boyd, the principal exposer of Dodd, had worked for twelve years for the man on whom he blew the whistle. He was far more successful than most people who have tried to bring to public attention the gross deficiencies in the whole ethical foundation of the U.S. Congress and the campaign finance practices of its members. His success is due largely to the fact that he had the goods on a particular member of Congress, including who gave money to his campaigns and what these donors were likely to require in return.

Although Dodd was peculiarly indiscreet about taking campaign contributions from representatives of organizations that had business before his Senate committees, he was probably not very unusual. The community of interest within the Senate against a public airing of ethical standards concerning money and gratuities received from private sources acted, like Gardol, to create an enormous protective shield around Dodd, as the senators sought to ignore the scandal and thereby prevent an investigation. A similar disclosure of campaign funds, amounts, and correspondence indicating the wishes of the donors would scorch most occupants of Senate seats today, even many who marked the doings of their Connecticut colleague and voted to censure him. Not until the pressure became too great to ignore did Dodd's colleagues lift their practiced voices to speak of him as if he were highly unusual in his sins and definitely not representative of the Senate as a whole.

The timing of the Pearson-Anderson columns was a crucial element in building the necessary pressure. They were spaced out over a period of more than three months, one tidbit at a time—adding to public indignation with their cumulative weight, and often catching Dodd in error regarding his denial of the previous column.

In many ways, the Boyd-Dodd case is whistle-blowing at its most classic. Boyd went through a long period of agonizing over the decision to go public with the evidence against his boss, some days leaning one way, some days the other, like a border state man sweating out his decision about the Civil War when personal ties pulled him both ways. He knew he was right in his conviction that Dodd was ethically too cavalier a man to serve under any longer, but he did not have great confidence in his decision to expose him. Was it the morally right and practically effective way to proceed? Should he resign and hold his tongue, knowing but not telling the uses the Senator was making of the campaign contributions? Should he resign and take his case quietly to the proper authorities—in this case, the Senate Committee on Rules and Administration, whose indolence in such matters is well known on Capitol Hill? Boyd finally made the difficult decision that his vague but theoretically supreme obligations to the people who elected Dodd, and who paid both Dodd and Boyd himself through taxes, were greater than his very strong obligations to Dodd. In the end, he won on the merits of his case, but the entire episode was lamentably typical in the price it required Boyd to pay for his view of the right course in a situation without clear guideposts.

Boyd's period of trial by conscience began during the 1964 re-election campaign. Some big cash donations—$2,000 from Robert Blinken of the Mite Corporation and $8,000 from A. N. Spanel of International Latex, for example—seemed irregular, especially since Dodd was known to perform political favors for these generous men. Boyd and a secretary in the Senator's office named Marjorie Carpenter (whom he later married) resolved to leave Dodd's employ after the campaign. The white-maned, Communist-fighting Senator was hard enough to serve because of his unpredictable choler. The strong smell of corruption now made him intolerable—enabling Boyd to sever the ego-umbilical cord that develops between a senator and his dependent aides.

But Boyd still planned to leave quietly and loyally—until Senator Dodd's election dealings culminated in the report on the successful 1964 campaign, filed under Connecticut law on December 3. Although the political war chest for 1964 was known by Boyd to have exceeded $400,000, the report listed contributions of only $167,497.67. Moreover, Dodd claimed a *deficit* of nearly $7,000. Boyd reasoned that about a quarter of a million dollars must have been siphoned off for private purposes. And when the Senator announced a $1,000-a-table dinner, complete with an address by Vice President Hubert H. Humphrey, to cover the fraudulent deficit with further profit—Jim Boyd and Marjorie Carpenter decided that Dodd was incorporating every available figure of stature into a monstrous lie that not only enriched his pockets but also helped to slant his senatorial position and *quid pro quo's* toward vested interests. They began to consider making a public disclosure of what they knew, and they maneuvered to get their hands on hard evidence.

Detecting their disenchantment and signs of snooping in the records, Senator Dodd fired both plotters before they had firmly resolved to expose him and flexed his political muscle to deny his former principal aide employment elsewhere in Washington. Then he tried to tame Boyd and lure him back, to make him incapable of causing trouble. Alternating moods rapidly—now the talented spinner of yarns about the good old days, now the stern taskmaster, now the benevolent father-figure pained by his son's betrayal—Senator Dodd labored to exercise his personal power and reclaim a chastised assistant. This, on top of the Humphrey dinner and the campaign report, was the final act required to assure his public exposure by his once loyal staffers.

"We didn't want to fight him," recalls Boyd. "I had been very close to him personally over a period of years, and the loyalty thing is one of the strongest of the Hill's ties. Also, being an administrative assistant is a nice life in many ways. I mean he did what I asked him to 90 per cent of the time, and that makes you feel significant. You *are* significant. The campaign fund diversion in 1964 was bad but it took Dodd's malevolence to make his actions real—not abstract. I felt small and like I was being toyed with for the first time since I was in the Marine Corps. He was really hurting people and then abusing his power over me to cover up his abuses of the public. Still, there was nothing ennobling in the decision to sink my teeth into Dodd and hold on until one of us lost. It was one of those times when you know you are right but you still feel horrible."

For a full six months, Jim Boyd and Marjorie Carpenter vacillated over whether to expose Dodd and, if so, how. "We shifted from day to day," he says. "We kept wondering, 'Who are we to take him on?' And there was always a fear of looking naive—of summoning up a burst of moralism and then having everyone laugh and say that's just the way things are done." Finally the conspirators told their story to newspaperman Jack Anderson, who encouraged them with his muckraker's fervent argument that the public had a right to know if there was evidence of foul deeds behind Dodd's senatorial pomp.

On Saturday afternoon, June 11, 1965, the Boyd-Carpenter team pulled a caper in the old style—complete with hallucinations of capture, open-valved perspiration, and unmitigated fear. They removed, in this and subsequent raids, about 7,000 documents from Dodd's office for xeroxing. These formed the basis for a series of twenty-three Pearson-Anderson columns, the first of which appeared on January 24, 1966. The whistle was formally blown, although not in the press of the nation's capital. The *Washington Post* got off to a late start by suppressing the first two columns and then running edited versions of the others only after Drew Pearson pressured the *Post* into lifting its embargo.

The impact of the exposure took a long time to really hit Senator Dodd, who sought to ride out the storm in silence. But a backlash hit the conspirators with lightning speed. Terry Golden, another former Dodd secretary and an accomplice to the plot, was fired by her new employer, U.S. Court of Appeals Judge David Bazelon, after a visit from an old Dodd acquaintance named Jack Fleischer. Michael O'Hare, another inside accomplice, would suffer almost two years of intermittent joblessness before Drew Pearson helped him secure a position with a civic organization called Big Brothers of the National Capital Area. Marjorie Carpenter received support from her new employers, the Lawyers' Committee for Civil Rights Under Law, but she resigned when her new fame produced strain and apprehension within the organization. And Boyd quickly lost his job as a part-time speechwriter for a House subcommittee under Representative John Blatnik. Blatnik, while sympathetic, explained that he had no choice because his staff budget had been cut one position's salary by Committee Chairman George Fallon —reportedly at the behest of Speaker John McCormack, who may have been moved by the treachery against his good friend Tom Dodd. Boyd's only employment between the Blatnik assignment and the writing of his book *Above the Law* (New York: New American Library, 1968) in late 1967 was a brief stint as an *ad hoc* speechwriter for Franklin D. Roosevelt, Jr., of the Equal Employment Opportunity Commission. Roosevelt soon ceased buying the speeches (whether because he did not like them, was apprehensive of the association with Jim Boyd, or possibly feared that a habit of disclosure might lead to revelations that he traveled about the country giving speeches paid for by taxpayers and written by a man he had never seen will never be known). In any case, Boyd ghosted no more, and he did not find full-time employment until maverick foundation man Phil Stern hired him to head the Fund for Investigative Journalism in September, 1968—almost four years after he left Dodd and almost three years after the first Pearson column.

While the case against Senator Dodd was being methodically detailed in Pearson-Anderson columns, official Washington demonstrated how much it matters who you are in a conflict of the whistle. Boyd offered 7,000 documents to the FBI for a possible investigation of a variety of charges against Dodd, ranging from larceny and fraud to the acceptance of bribes and double-billing the taxpayers for junkets. The Bureau declined that investigation and launched a probe of Boyd, not excluding his private life. The supply of rumors was ample, most prominently stories that the conspirators were sex offenders and that they had been paid by Pearson (or Dodd's political enemies) to unearth their volumes of dirt.

No angle was overlooked in the effort to discredit the source. Although the personal attacks were logically irrelevant to the validity of the charges against Dodd, their spiciness facilitated an *ad hominem* two-step around the issue by those who were uncomfortable with a spotlight on congressional ethics. Within Congress, the cohesion was remarkable. Liberal Senator Birch Bayh wrote Dodd, "We're all with you on this yellow attack by Pearson." And conservative Russell Long remarked, "I'll support you all the way on this, Tom, even if you're guilty." Congressmen and senators united around their community of interest—that is, their universal fear of having facts about themselves exposed by rebellious staff members—to focus scorn on the "stool pigeon" question and on the character defects of such traitors to the Congress.

Outside the government, the silence was equally loud. In April, after nearly three months of exposure in seventeen "Merry-Go-Round" columns of voluminous evidence of a major scandal, no Washington newspaper had called for an investigation. Of all the major U.S. papers, in fact, only the *Los Angeles Times* had done so. The networks were mute.

Finally, Senator Wayne Morse called for an investigation on the floor of the Senate, and the iron jaws of authority slowly began to masticate a member of the club. Dodd's transgressions were so numerous and raw that the Senate investigation whittled them down to a chosen few for the censure motion—leaving only those sins that seemed more Dodd's alone than applicable to the Senate as a whole. (A broader indictment might have provoked a public cry for congressional reform, an issue best left to its rhetorical home.) After a fifteen-month period of delay and investigation, the Senate censured Senator Dodd on June 23, 1967. By this time, the unemployed whistle-blowers were relatively obscure, and the press had risen from its former protective silence to assume a proper tone of sanctimony regarding the errant senator.

The Dodd episode was certainly not remunerative for Jim Boyd and his colleagues, nor did it win them great public appreciation. Neither did their exposure provoke a general reform movement in the Senate. Dodd's honor was thoroughly soiled, but he retained his committee posts and his seniority, served three more years in the Senate, and ran for a third term in 1970. In short, Boyd and his friends paid a high price, and the public really gained little of an immediate nature.

Boyd is not sorry. "It was the greatest liberating experience of my life," he observes. "It cut away all sorts of restrictions and taboos that kept me from saying what I think honestly. What a Senate aide does is to promote the image of a politician, selling out little by little in rational, absolutely essential steps. I didn't realize what twelve years like that can do to you, even after we decided to expose Senator Dodd. It was the fight itself that opened my eyes to all this."

These are strange feelings for a man of modest origins in Connecticut—a nonideologue and nonmovement person who seized an opportunity to work up through the grime of politics in the 1950's after starting as a stamp-licker and errand boy. He utilized no class analysis, no new politics, no alienation theory, nor any other currently invoked rationale for his actions. The ethical standards by which he measured Dodd are relatively commonplace, although seldom applied to an institution like the Senate. What Boyd supplied was a willingness to appear presumptuous, moralistic, treasonous, and ridiculous in the eyes of his colleagues on Capitol Hill. What he accomplished by way of general ethical reform in the Congress may have been limited. But he can fairly be credited with causing the downfall of Senator Dodd—who was almost a shoo-in for the 1970 reelection before the Boyd disclosures, and an extreme long-shot after them. By felling Senator Dodd, Boyd upset a lot of people who had been feeling snug in their special privileges in the Senate's ethical playground. After the Dodd episode, there will always be a nagging fear of a repeat. It can also be said, in retrospect, that Boyd blew a sharp blast on a whistle that many other insiders, perhaps unconsciously emboldened by his example, were to pick up and use after him in the years immediately following.

And he says he would do it again.

3 Only the Right People

Adam Hochschild is a free-lance writer and a former reporter for the *San Francisco Chronicle* and *Ramparts* magazine. Hochschild became an alumnus whistle-blower on the U.S. system of back-up military forces with his "Reserves and Guard: A More Selective Service," published in the January, 1971, *Washington Monthly*.

He wrote:

In the Civil War days, if you didn't want to be drafted, you could "buy a man" for $300 to take your place in the Army. You can also avoid the draft today, though things are more indirect—instead of paying $300, you can join the Reserves or the National Guard. As long as this escape valve exists for a million privileged men, most of President Nixon's reforms to democratize the draft are meaningless.

The Reserve and the Guard are much easier to be in than the regular Army. First, they usually don't send you into combat; second, you're on full-time active duty for only four and one half months, which disrupts your marriage, career, and friendships far less than being drafted for two whole years. For these reasons, when I was 21, I enlisted in the Army Reserve rather than wait to be drafted.

An enlisted man must join the Reserve or the Guard for a six-year hitch. After those initial few months of active duty training, you go to a two-week camp each summer, and to weekly drills during the year. Theoretically, the weekly drills in your hometown Reserve or Guard unit keep up your training. In practice, they are more like a mechanical toy I remember reading about a few years ago. The toy was a square black box of machinery with a switch on the side. When you flipped the switch, the cover of the box opened slowly, a mechanical hand came out, turned the switch off, and then retreated slowly inside the box. The toy had no use aside from grinding away and eventually turning itself off. My Reserve unit was like that.

When I first joined, I spent several of those drills being processed, paid, and promoted. All around me the same was happening to most of the unit's other 500-odd officers and men. I somehow thought this was a deliberate lull to catch up on administrative paperwork, and that the regular program would start in a few weeks. But it never did. Eventually I realized my Reserve unit did virtually nothing but administer itself.

Each drill began with recorded bugle calls played over a loudspeaker, and then sundry saluting and marching about on the small San Francisco Army base where we met. Then the 500 soldiers, with much shouting of commands and waving of clipboards, were sent indoors and divided up for work into more than a dozen different "sections," for what was called "on-the-job training."

One section checked through the sign-in rosters and sent threatening letters to people who missed meetings (if you miss five meetings, you get sent to active duty); another promoted people; another issued everybody's paychecks; a truly enormous section with yards of desks and typewriters kept the personnel files in order. Still another section processed men into the unit, while a subgroup processed them out. A section of Military Policemen patrolled the building to make sure no one escaped from all this. (They weren't always successful. One evening three friends and I got out, saw a movie downtown, and came back to the drill in time to sign out. Others, still bolder, did this kind of thing regularly.) Another section dispensed paper and typewriters and mimeograph ink; another prepared coffee and doughnuts for the refreshment break. As the unit grew new jobs flowered: One section set up interoffice telephones, and another provided a messenger service to carry papers between all the sections.

A number of mechanisms used up excess time. One was

lesson plans. Every time somebody gives an Army class, he must turn in a "lesson plan"—a long outline, in a special format, of what he said. However, in my own section of the unit, and I believe in most of the others, there were no classes: Everyone was too busy either doing the administrative paperwork or trying to get out of it. But regulations called for classes, so we had to write out lesson plans each week—outlines of classes never given. We turned in the lesson plans quarterly to another section, which kept people busy tabulating them. Visiting generals could then be shown proof of all the training we were getting.

There were also the movies. Unit members who could not be kept busy in the sections were sent to a large auditorium. There, they were usually shown Army films, with the same film often shown many times over the years. Occasionally there were movies on things like first aid or safe driving, but most were much farther afield. I remember one documentary about Greenland (huskies, ice, fjords, and freedom-loving Eskimos), and one ancient Air Force film, in an extraordinary reddish-brown no-man's-land between black and white and color, about "Survival in the Tundra."

For all its insanity, going through this charade each week is preferable to Vietnam, which is why Reserve units have huge waiting lists. (Each armed force has its Reserve; the most important are the Army Reserve and the Army National Guard, to which nearly 700,000 of the country's one million paid Reservists belong.) Men whose draft notices are about to arrive are sometimes so desperate to join the Reserve that they pay. In New York City alone, there have been half a dozen cases in recent years where Reserve or Guard officials have been arrested and accused of accepting bribes to enlist people. One Chicago National Guard sergeant was charged with letting men into his unit at a price of over $500 apiece.

Competition to get into the Reserve and Guard is heavy, and the privileged usually win. Most Reserve and Guard units are exclusive institutions, with the flavor of country clubs, fraternal societies, or comfortable restaurants where you know the other patrons. Defense Department figures show the percentage of college graduates among Army Reserve enlisted men is nearly *three times* as high as among draftees and enlistees of the regular Army, who do the fighting in Vietnam. In my own unit, most members were attorneys, stockbrokers, insurance agents, students, or executive trainees. A number of people had been fraternity brothers in college. At drills men talked about ski trips, stock tips, and M.B.A.'s.

All of this is far different from the World War II Army, where the Hollywood myths had a little truth and rich and poor actually sometimes did fight together. Now the split between the Reserves and the regular Army intensifies the class divisions in this country rather than lessening them.

Besides being unjust, all this matters politically. If the sons of the influential were being killed in Vietnam at the same rate as the sons of black people and the often pro-war white working class, pressure to stop the war would be enormously stronger. An antiwar movement of upper-middle-class college students has already put something of a dent in two administrations' war plans. If this class of men had been forced to do the actual fighting, instead of being able to join Reserve units, their protests might well have stopped the war. The Pentagon must be grateful for the Reserves and Guard, a system that keeps so many of these men out of Vietnam.

(Like regular Army soldiers, a good many Reservists and National Guardsmen are publicly protesting the war now. The way they do so often reflects their affluence: Recently, large groups of Reservists and Guardsmen in Boston and Washington, D.C., called press conferences and announced that they were giving their military pay away to peace organizations and candidates. The Army was furious, but couldn't find any regulations against this. Legal actions are also popular, since thousands of Reservists and Guardsmen are lawyers or law students. The Army has been hit with lawsuits over every conceivable issue, ranging from its right to send Reservists to war to its right to make them cut their hair.)

Reserve and National Guard units are not supposed to have such an elite clientele. With some exceptions, the law says units are supposed to enlist new members first-come, first-served. Theoretically you can't get in until your name comes to the top of the long waiting list. But in practice, it doesn't work that way. As with all things in the military, it takes lots of paperwork to enlist somebody. So you just speed up the paperwork when you want to get a friend in or, when you want to keep someone out, you slow it down until he gets drafted.

I know this often happens, because I'm guilty of having taken advantage of it twice. When I joined my unit, I was able to jump over the heads of a sizable backlog of other applicants because a friend of a friend knew a high-ranking officer. A year later I was able to get a close friend into my unit in a hurry. I was told quite frankly: "We wouldn't do it except that he's a friend of yours."

Most Reservists and National Guardsmen are guilty of the same practice. In almost every unit, sons, brothers, in-laws, and former college classmates abound. There are also lots of certain kinds of people whom everybody wants to know—such as professional athletes. We had several San Francisco Giants and Forty-Niners; a 1967 survey disclosed 360 pro athletes in Reserve and Guard units around the country.

Another way the Reserve's and Guard's class nature shows is that they are virtually all white. San Francisco is roughly one-seventh black, but except for pro ballplayers, my unit had only three Negroes out of 500 men. The unit I was in before that drilled a few blocks from downtown Oakland, one of the largest Negro ghettos in the western United States, yet we had no black members at all. In the National Guard, things are worse: the proportion of Negroes in the Guard actually *declined* during 1969 from 1.18 to 1.15 per cent.

This escape valve for upper-middle-class draft-avoiders is not only unjust but colossally expensive. In 1969, my old unit cost the U.S. taxpayers over $300,000 in salaries alone. Nationally, this adds up. The total Reserve and Guard budget is $2.5 billion a year. There are also certain additional costs, such as the hefty pensions paid retired Reservists and Guardsmen. And altogether the two organizations own approximately $10 billion worth of real estate, armories, airplanes, tanks, guns, ships, and other equipment.

The Reserves and Guard help draft-avoiders and help the Army by keeping such men out of Vietnam, but they have no other military use whatever—either for defense or for our adventures in Southeast Asia, the Dominican Republic, and elsewhere. The best proof of this is that the United States is fighting the fourth largest war in its history, Vietnam, almost without them. Approximately 35,000, many of them fliers, were mobilized briefly after the *Pueblo* incident, but they are all home now. Otherwise there have been no Reserve or Guard units in Vietnam.

Of course, the National Guard does sometimes rescue people from avalanches, tornadoes, and the like, and no one can argue against that. People who believe that demands of students, blacks, and strikers should be answered with armed force probably would say there is a "need" for the National Guard there, too (though not for the Army Reserve, which in recent years has not been used in domestic disorders, except for the New York mail strike). But even then, huge parts of the Guard establishment are excess by anyone's definition: Even George Wallace doesn't advocate putting down ghetto rebellions with long-range artillery. In fiscal year 1969, less than one out of every seven Army National Guardsmen in the country was called up for what the Pentagon likes to call "civil disturbances." And the Guardsmen sent into battle at Kent State and elsewhere have created many additional disturbances of their own.

Though the Reserves and Guard provided a good deal of manpower for World War II, in the 1970's America does not need a reserve land army of 700,000 men for its "defense." And in the days of ICBM's and ground-to-air missiles, the Air National Guard's expensive jet fighters, manned round the clock at twenty-two bases throughout the country, are about as necessary as horse cavalry.

One interesting and little-known Reserve operation is the Civil Affairs program. The idea, based on World War II experience, is that Army Reservists be trained to administer the daily, civilian affairs of countries the Pentagon may be occupying. There are currently over 5,000 officers and men in the Reserve Civil Affairs units. Judging from the countries they are studying, it looks as if the Pentagon has contingency plans to run most of the world.

Generally, each unit specializes in running one country, or a group of small countries in one area. A large unit in the Bronx is trained to set up a government anywhere in Africa; a smaller San Francisco unit reportedly concentrates on Southern Africa; a San Pablo, California, unit spent its last summer camp learning about South Korea; a group of South Carolina units specializes in the Balkans.

Some units train each man for a specific job—running the

railways of Bolivia, the museums of Czechoslovakia, or the bus lines of Sofia, Bulgaria.

The Civil Affairs units often write booklets on "their" countries—long tracts not unlike diligent high-school papers, full of statistics from almanacs and encyclopedias. There are such Reservist-written books on Greece, Bulgaria, Romania, and Azerbaijan-Armenia-Georgia.

It is hard to find out much about the Civil Affairs units. The Pentagon is not eager to publicize them. But a clue to the way the Army plans to use these men comes from the "scenario" of a recent training exercise done by eighty men of the 450th Civil Affairs Company of Riverdale, Maryland. Several other East Coast Reserve units appear to have drilled with the same war-game-on-paper.

The scenario was this: It is June, 1970. An anti-Castro revolt breaks out in the Las Villas province of Cuba. Great food shortages. Exile groups (apparently supported by the United States) send raiders. Castro flies to Moscow for instructions. He flies back and declares martial law. Peasants join the invading exiles. The rebels set up a provisional government. "Anarchy" is in sight, so the provisional government requests 20,000 OAS troops. The troops are to "maintain law and order." The United States will provide only air cover and noncombat support troops; other OAS nations will supply the rest (Vietnamization catches on fast).

The exercise goes on to say which Reserve units are to administer which areas—the 352nd and the 300th in Camaguey and the 450th near Santa Clara.

Unable to get rid of the ungainly and ill-trained reserve forces, the government from time to time asserts that there really is a need for them after all. Defense Secretary Laird recently announced that in the future Vietnam-type wars would be fought with mobilized Reserve and Guard units, not with draftees. It is not yet clear whether he really means what he says. At present his words mean nothing, for there are no Reserve and Guard units among the 300,000-plus Americans in Vietnam, and there are no plans for sending any.

Defense Secretary McNamara had enough technical common sense to know the Reserves were military surplus. In 1964 he proposed that the Army Reserve be cut down drastically, and that what remained be merged into the National

Guard. His plan suffered a resounding defeat by Congress and no administration has dared try anything like it since. Reserve and Guard strength has remained the same. McNamara had run up against one of the most powerful and least known lobbies in Washington.

The Reserve and Guard, of course, provide an inexhaustible market for tanks and guns and planes, the same way the rest of the armed forces do, and no doubt the big war contractors like this. But the most powerful lobby behind the Reserve and the Guard is its members. I'm not talking here of draft-avoiders like myself who leave as soon as their mandatory six years are up, but of the men who stay in voluntarily beyond them. Most Reserve and Guard officers above the rank of captain and most enlisted men above staff sergeant are making a part-time career out of the military. The pay is excellent. A colonel, for instance, can earn over $90 for a single day's drill. Twenty years' service earns you a pension of up to several hundred dollars a month—not bad for a one-evening-a-week job.

These "twenty-year men" are a mixture. Some are decent people who just need the money. Others are lonely men, often divorced or unmarried, who seek in Reserve or Guard units the kind of fellowship they can't find elsewhere. And some are the type anyone who has been in the Army knows too well: men who get a visible, almost erotic pleasure out of snapping salutes and shouting commands, who would like to see the whole world in uniform. For these militarist types, the Reserve is sometimes a Walter Mitty fantasy momentarily come true: The busboy by day becomes a sergeant major by night; the insurance clerk flies jet fighters on weekends.

These career soldiers are well organized. They have two efficient pressure groups, which even Hanson Baldwin, the hawkish former military writer for the *New York Times*, calls "powerful lobbies," the Reserve Officers Association and the National Guard Association. The roots of these groups go back a long way, and their histories are full of fascinating lessons in lobbying technique. (The lobbying prowess of the National Guard Association is the subject of a full-length book by a Harvard political scientist.) Shortly after World War II, for example, the Air Force wanted to merge the Air Force Reserve and the Air National Guard for obvious efficiency reasons. The NGA stopped the plan cold by quietly threatening to use its influence to get a congressional investigation of liquor sales at certain air bases.

The most remarkable thing about these pressure groups is that, unlike most lobbies, they don't just influence Congress: Their members are *in* Congress. About 130 senators and representatives are in the Reserves, plus a similar number of their staff. A good many of these Reservist-congressmen are also active members and office-holders of the two associations. Senator Strom Thurmond, an Army Reserve major general, is a former national president of the Reserve Officers Association.

This strange combination of outside pressure groups and congressmen has stopped all attempts to change the Reserve structure. Its most stunning victory was over the 1964 McNamara plan, but unlike the Reserves the ROA is always ready for battle. In 1970 the Nixon Administration tried to cut a few thousand men from the small Coast Guard Reserves as a minor economy measure. The ROA swung into action, vigorously, effectively, and rather dishonestly (it instructed its Coast Guard members to fire off protest letters to congressmen and the President *without* saying they were Coast Guard Reserve officers). Reservist-congressmen joined the fray, and the plan was swiftly killed in committee. As former White House assistant Douglass Cater wrote a few years ago: "These citizen soldiers are so solidly entrenched politically that no one in Washington dares challenge them frontally."

The links between Congress, the Reserves, and the two lobbies make one big family. The ROA's Washington office is headed by Colonel John T. Carlton, former administrative assistant to ex-Senator George Smathers of Florida. The former head of the NGA's office was once a staff member of the House Armed Services Committee. Committee chief counsel John Blandford is a Marine Reserve brigadier general, scheduled for promotion to major general. A few years ago, the Committee's chief clerk was an Air Force Reserve brigadier general.

No one seems to mind that soldier-congressmen are Reservists under the command of armed forces for which as senators and representatives they vote money. Or that a Reservist-Senator could vote to call—or not to call—himself to active duty. (A group of antiwar Reservists I belong to recently brought suit charging that this situation is unconstitutional.) This conflict of interest simply strengthens the military bloc; the chance to do things like fly jets on weekends (remember those pictures of Air Force Reserve Major General Barry Goldwater from the 1964 campaign?) makes these hawks still friendlier toward the military budget.

Momentum also comes from the Reserves' lavish public relations program, which is currently getting a major step-up. (I know a little of this firsthand, because I spent much of my own recently ended six years in the Army Reserve writing press releases.) A good example of how this works was provided in 1968, the Army Reserve's sixtieth anniversary. Information officers in the nation's Reserve units were sent neatly packaged red cardboard "kits" of propaganda for their local news media. Among other things, each kit contained slides and scripts for TV and radio commercials and a selection of newspaper advertisements in different sizes. The largest ad was worded as if written by someone other than the Army: ". . . they're always there when we need them. So now we'd just like to say thanks. And happy sixtieth anniversary to the men and women of the U.S. Army Reserve." There was a blank space at the botton where a local newspaper or business could print its name. The kit also included a prepared speech about the Reserves for delivery "before such groups as the Lions, Rotary, and Kiwanis, etc.," a statement for your mayor to sign to proclaim Army Reserve Week and a memo with an unnerving suggestion: "Check with your local television stations . . . to see if they would show one or more 'war' movies during the anniversary week as a special salute to the Army Reserve."

The National Guard handbook for unit information officers includes a prepared prayer to give local clergymen: "Almighty God . . . we thank Thee for those noble patriots who in times past didst rise up to deliver our nation out of the hands of the enemy." When talking to mortals, the handbook urges officers to stress the Guard's pork barrel aspect: "Your unit . . . represents a 'hidden' industry for your town. Your Chamber of Commerce or other civic newsletter will be glad to know this. . . . The fact that the extra pay earned by Guardsmen during the year and at field training is spent with local merchants is a good selling point."

The National Guard, especially, goes in for publicity in a big way. Its public relations office at the Pentagon has a

$450,000 annual budget, and besides this there are information officers at hundreds of Guard units around the country. The Guard employed a big ad agency two years ago and has gotten the late Senator Everett Dirksen, John Wayne, and others to tape radio and TV commercials. Supposedly all this hoopla is necessary for "recruiting," but the Guard now has a waiting list of over 100,000 men hoping to get in. In fact, these publicity campaigns are really to help persuade the public to keep the Guard and Reserves alive at all.

Finally, the Reserve-Guard lobby gets strong support from another unexpected source—state governors. A number of them can always be counted on to testify before Congress if Guard appropriations are under fire. The main reason is that governors appoint National Guard officers, and no politician wants to lose that valuable patronage network.

The end result of all these pressures is that Congress methodically votes more money for the Reserves and Guard than the President asks for. In 1967 Congress wanted to continue certain Air Force Reserve and Air National Guard units the Pentagon wanted dropped, and the House Appropriations Committee wrote into the defense bill provisions for 20,000 more Army Reservists than the Pentagon wanted. President Johnson blew his top: "While similar restrictions have been included in the Defense Department appropriations bill in recent years, I am becoming increasingly concerned about them because of the undesirable rigidity they impose on our military structure." When even Johnson complains about military appropriations being too high—and this in the middle of the Vietnam build-up—then things are really out of control.

The cost is one reason for ending the Reserves and the Guard; Vietnam is the other. It is a sorry system: The poor and the blacks fight the war; the courageous of all classes go to jail as draft resisters; the privileged join the Reserves or the Guard. Eliminating that escape valve from the draft would not only be just, it would help end the war. People with power in America have shown themselves little moved by the deaths of Vietnamese and of U.S. troops there now. If their own sons were there, things might be different. Now, the sons of senators and corporation presidents are more likely to be in Reserve or Guard units than on patrol in

> Vietnam. It is harder to talk calmly of just "slowly winding down" the war if your own boy is in it. This alone should make elimination of the Reserves and the Guard an urgent goal for all who care about stopping this war and preventing the next.

Hochschild's central thesis—that the Reserve system is at least 99 per cent useless—represents a special kind of exposure, which might be called the "ultimate" whistle. In such cases, the writer does not object to specific practices conducted by an otherwise useful institution, but rather exposes the entire apparatus, complete with its solemn statements of purpose, as frivolous. Since it would be patently illogical to propose reforms for the organization Hochschild describes, a wry, often sarcastic, humor emerges as the only way to respond to the ludicrous charade of reserve meetings—or the $2.5 billion in annual supplemental income received by the week-end soldiers while people are hungry. Ultimate whistle-blowing has enough truth in it to be revealing of situations that seem truly upside-down—not only a sham but a scrambled sham, with values inverted in a nearly surreal way.

Hochschild made the additional sharp moral point that the Reserve system has operated as a kind of safety valve against opposition to the Vietnam war. People with influence are likely, on average, to go into the Reserves, while people without influence are likely to go to Indochina. If the reverse were the case, he says, the war might have ended long ago.

He also offered a concrete reform proposal—that members of Congress should not be permitted to serve in the Reserves while they also vote on Reserve appropriations and decide whether the Reserves should be called to active duty. Such a conflict of interest has long existed for some 130 senators and representatives, and Hochschild said it should be ended. He did more. In April, 1971, three months after the article was published, the Reservists Committee to Stop the War, of which Hochschild is a founding member, won a judgment in Federal District Court that Reserve commissions are unconstitutional, a violation of the principle of separation of powers. On November 3, the Justice Department filed an appeal brief in the U.S. Court of Appeals for the District of Columbia, arguing that the ruling is an "interference with the system of armed forces reserves established by the Executive."

The case is still in litigation as of this writing, and no commissions have yet been resigned as a result of the suit, but Hochschild's conflict-of-interest charge is the kind of clear factual nugget with which whistle-blowers have been most successful.

4 The Case of Christopher Pyle

Christopher H. Pyle, a Ph.D. candidate in political science at Columbia University, completed two years as an Army Intelligence captain in 1969. Using information he had gathered as an officer and instructor, he wrote an article in the *Washington Monthly* for January, 1970, about the U.S. Army Intelligence Branch for the Continental United States, acronymed CONUS, and its surveillance of civilian politics.

Pyle's charges touched a raw nerve in a wide-ranging coalition of people—from conservative, civil-libertarian, constitutionalist Senator Sam Ervin to liberals who were instinctively opposed to any growth of power for the Pentagon. This broad-based opposition had enough supporters in the press to create a nationwide controversy over military surveillance of domestic political groups, with the Army decidedly on the defensive. In the face of headlines and harsh criticism from a substantial number of senators and representatives, the Army announced that it would discontinue the improper activities.

However, Pyle returned to print in July, 1970, with a second article in which he charged that surveillance was continuing despite deceptive announcements to the contrary.

Pyle's two articles provide a narrative of events, as well as an anatomy of the surveillance apparatus and a tightly reasoned case that most of the Army's activities in this field were unconstitutional. They also reveal his style and technique, which most observers think contributed heavily to his effectiveness and consequently to the over-all success of concerted efforts to end military surveillance.

The January article follows:

CONUS Intelligence: The Army Watches Civilian Politics

For the past four years, the U.S. Army has been closely watching civilian political activity within the United States. Nearly 1,000 plainclothes investigators, working out of some 300 offices from coast to coast, keep track of political protests of all kinds—from Klan rallies in North Carolina to antiwar speeches at Harvard. This aspect of their duties is unknown to most Americans. They know these soldier-agents, if at all, only as personable young men whose principal function is to conduct background investigations of persons being considered for security clearances.

When this program began in the summer of 1965, its purpose was to provide early warning of civil disorders that the Army might be called upon to quell. In the summer of 1967, however, its scope widened to include the political beliefs and actions of individuals and organizations active in the civil rights, white supremacy, black power, and antiwar movements. Today, the Army maintains files on the membership, ideology, programs, and practices of virtually every activist political group in the country. These include not only such violence-prone organizations as the Minutemen and the Revolutionary Action Movement (RAM), but such nonviolent groups as the Southern Christian Leadership Conference, Clergy and Laymen United Against the War in Vietnam, the American Civil Liberties Union, Women Strike for Peace, and the National Association for the Advancement of Colored People.

The Army obtains most of its information about protest politics from the files of municipal and state police departments and of the FBI. In addition, its agents subscribe to hundreds of local and campus newspapers, monitor police and FBI radio broadcasts, and, on occasion, conduct their own undercover operations. Military undercover agents have posed as press photographers covering antiwar demonstrations, as students on college campuses, and as "residents" of Resurrection City (the 1968 encampment in Washington, D.C., led by the Reverend James Abernathy following the death of Martin Luther King). They have even recruited civilians into their service—sometimes for pay but more often through appeals to patriotism. For example, when Columbia University gave its students the option of closing their academic records to routine inspection by government investigators, the 108th Military Intelligence Group in Manhattan quietly persuaded an employee of the Registrar's Office to disclose information from the closed files on the sly.

Typical of the hundreds of reports filed by Army agents each month are the following, taken from the unclassified intelligence summary for the week of March 18, 1968:

> *Philadelphia, Pa.:* A. The Philadelphia Chapter of the Women's Strike for Peace sponsored an anti-draft meeting at the First Unitarian Church which attracted an audience of about 200 persons. Conrad Lynn, an author of draft evasion literature, replaced Yale Chaplain William Sloane Coffin as the principal speaker at the meeting. Following a question and answer period, Robert Edenbaum of the Central Committee for Conscientious Objectors stated that many Philadelphia lawyers were accepting draft evasion cases. The meeting ended without incident.
>
> B. Rev. Albert Cleage, Jr., the founder of the Black Christian Nationalist Movement in Detroit, spoke to an estimated 100 persons at the Emmanuel Methodist Church. Cleage spoke on the topic of black unity and the problems of the ghetto. The meeting was peaceful and police reported no incidents.
>
> *Chicago, Ill.:* Approximately 300 members of Veterans for Peace and and Women for Peace held a peaceful demonstration at the Museum of Science and Industry protesting an exhibit by the U.S. Army. Several demonstrators entered the building in spite of warnings by museum officials and 6 were arrested on charges of disorderly conduct, resisting arrest and criminal trespassing. Five of those arrested were juveniles.

To assure prompt communication of these reports, the Army distributes them over a nationwide wire service. Completed in the fall of 1967, this teletype network gives every major troop command in the United States daily and weekly reports on virtually all political protests occurring anywhere in the nation.

The Army also periodically publishes an eight-by-ten-inch, glossy-cover paperback booklet known within intelligence circles as the "blacklist." The "blacklist" is an encyclopedia of profiles of people and organizations who, in the opinion of the Intelligence Command officials who compile it, might "cause trouble for the Army." Thus it is similar to less formal lists that the Department of Health, Education, and Welfare has maintained to exclude politically unpopular scientists from research contracts and consultant work.

Sometime in the near future the Army will link its teletype reporting system to a computerized data bank. This computer, to be installed at the Investigative Records Repository at Fort Holabird in Baltimore, eventually will be able to produce instant print-outs of information in ninety-six separate categories. The plan is to feed it both "incident reports" and "personality reports." The incident reports will relate to the Army's role in domestic disturbances and will describe such occurrences as bombings, mass violence, and arms thefts. The personality reports—to be extracted from the incident reports—will be used to supplement the Army's 7 million individual security-clearance dossiers and to generate new files on the political activities of civilians wholly unassociated with the military.

In this respect, the Army's data bank promises to be unique. Unlike similar computers now in use at the FBI's National Crime Information Center in Washington and New York State's Identification and Intelligence System in Albany, it will not be restricted to the storage of case histories of persons arrested for (or convicted of) crimes. Rather, it will specialize in files devoted exclusively to descriptions of the *lawful* political activity of civilians. Thus an IBM card prepared many months ago for the future computer file of Arlo Tatum, executive secretary of the Central Committee of Conscientious Objectors, contains a single notation—that Mr. Tatum once delivered a speech at the University of Oklahoma on the legal rights of conscientious objectors.

Because the Investigative Records Repository is one of the federal government's main libraries for security clearance information, access to its personality files is not limited to

Army officials. Other federal agencies now drawing on its memory banks include the FBI, the Secret Service, the Passport Office, the Central Intelligence Agency, the National Security Agency, the Civil Service Commission, the Atomic Energy Commission, the Defense Intelligence Agency, the Navy, and the Air Force. In short, the personality files are likely to be made available to any federal agency that issues security clearances, conducts investigations, or enforces laws.

Headquarters for the collection and coordination of this information is a wire-mesh "cage" located inside a gray metal warehouse at Fort Holabird. The official designation of the office is "CONUS Intelligence Branch, Operations IV, U.S. Army Intelligence Command." CONUS is the Army's acronym for Continental United States. Direction of this program is in the hands of Major General William H. Blakefield, head of the U.S. Army Intelligence Command at Fort Holabird. Established in 1965, the Command coordinates the work of a number of counterintelligence "groups" formerly assigned to the G-2 offices of the major stateside armies. It is here that reports from agents are received, sorted, and retransmitted. Because its staff is small and the volume of reports large, the CONUS Intelligence Branch (also known as "Ops Four") rarely has time to verify, edit, or interpret the reports before passing them on to "user organizations."

Daily recipients of this raw intelligence include all of the Army's military intelligence groups within the United States, riot-control units on stand-by alert, and the Army Operations Center at the Pentagon. The Operations Center, sometimes called the "domestic war room," is a green-carpeted suite of connecting offices, conference rooms, and cubicles from which Army and Defense Department officials dispatch and coordinate troops that deal with riots, earthquakes, and other disasters. Recipients of weekly CONUS intelligence summaries, also prepared at Fort Holabird, include not only those on the daily distribution but such unlikely organizations as the Army Material Command, the Military District of Washington, the Air Defense Command, and Army headquarters in Europe, Alaska, Hawaii, and Panama.

What is perhaps most remarkable about this domestic intelligence network is its potential for growth. Uninhibited by congressional or Presidential oversight, it has already expanded to the point where it in some ways rivals the FBI's older internal-security program. If the Army's fascination with the collection of domestic intelligence continues to grow as it has in the recent past, the Intelligence Command could use military funds to develop one of the largest domestic intelligence operations outside of the Communist world. Before this happens, the American public and its elected representatives ought to demand a say in the development of this program.

Intentionally or not, the Army has gone far beyond the limits of its needs and authority in collecting domestic political information. It has created an activity that, by its existence alone, jeopardizes individual rights, democratic political processes, and even the national security it seeks to protect.

There is no question that the Army must have domestic intelligence. In order to assist civilian authorities, it needs maps and descriptions of potential riot or disaster areas, as well as early warning of incidents likely to provoke mass violence. Before trusting its employees or prospective employees with military secrets, it has to look into their past behavior for evidence of disloyalty or unsuitability. The Army also must investigate train wrecks, fires, and other disasters which may disrupt its lines of supply. And where ultra-militant groups seek to attack military installations, destroy files, or abuse soldiers, it has the right and obligation to keep informed about the groups' specific objectives, plans, and techniques.

The Army needs this kind of information so that it can fulfill long-established, legitimate responsibilities. But must it also distribute and store detailed reports on the political beliefs and actions of individuals and groups?

Officials of the Intelligence Command believe that they must. Without detailed knowledge of community "infrastructure," they argue, riot-control troops would not be able to enforce curfews or quell violence. To support this contention, they cite the usefulness of personality files and blacklists in breaking up guerrilla organizations in Malaya and South Vietnam. One early proponent of this view was the Army's Assistant Chief of Staff for Intelligence during 1967–68, Major General William P. Yarborough. At the height of the

Detroit riots of 1967, he instructed his staff in the domestic war room: "Men, get out your counterinsurgency manuals. We have an insurgency on our hands."

Of course, they did not. As one war room officer who attempted to carry out the general's order later observed: "There we were, plotting power plants, radio stations, and armories on the situation maps when we should have been locating the liquor and color-television stores instead." A year later the National Advisory Commission on Civil Disorders reached a similar conclusion about the motives of ghetto rioters. "The urban disorders of the summer of 1967," it declared unequivocally, "were not caused by, nor were they the consequence of, any organized plan or 'conspiracy.'"

But even if there were some evidence of conspiracy, the Army's case for personality files and blacklists would remain weak. The purpose of these records, according to counterinsurgency manuals, is to facilitate the selective arrest of guerrillas and insurgents. However, within the United States the Army has no authority to round up suspects the moment civilians take up arms. The seizure of civilians on suspicion of conspiring or attempting to overthrow the government by unlawful means or of inciting people to crime is, and continues to be, the responsibility of local and state police and of the FBI. The President may order Army units to help state or federalized National Guard troops keep the peace or fight guerrillas, but the Army does not acquire authority to arrest civilians unless and until civilian law enforcement has broken down and a declaration of martial law puts all governmental authority in the area of conflict in the hands of the military. In that highly remote circumstance, the Intelligence Command might have some need for personality files and blacklists on criminally inclined, politically motivated civilians. By then, however, it certainly would have full access to the more extensive and up-to-date files of the civilian agencies and thus would not have to prepare its own.

The Army's need to keep its own dossiers on the politics of law-abiding citizens and groups makes even less sense. So long as there is a possibility that peaceful protests may get out of hand, some surveillance undoubtedly is in order. But must the Army conduct it? Are its agents and record-keepers more competent than those of the FBI or of the police departments of the cities in which large demonstrations typically occur? Are the civilian law enforcement agencies so uncooperative that the Army must substantially duplicate their efforts?

More extraordinary still is why the Intelligence Command each week alerts military headquarters in Alaska, Hawaii, Panama, and Europe to stateside nonevents like the following:

> *Miami, Fla.:* A spokesman for the Southern Students Organizing Committee announced plans for a demonstration to be held on the campus of the University of Miami in the morning. According to the spokesman, a group of anti-war/draft supporters will participate in the demonstration.
>
> *Philadelphia, Pa.:* Members of the Vietnam Week Committee composed largely of professors and students of the University of Pennsylvania, will conduct a "sleep-in" to protest the scheduled appearance of Dow Chemical Company recruiters on campus. The next day, 19 March, the same organization will sponsor a protest rally on campus.

Perhaps the best answer to all of these questions is that much of the CONUS intelligence program serves no military need at all. But if this is so, then where does the Army get the authority to run it?

According to the Nixon Administration, authority for this kind of program comes from the Constitution. So, at least, the Justice Department claimed in June, 1969, in a brief defending the FBI's failure to obtain search warrants before tapping telephone calls of what were then the "Chicago Eight." The Justice Department argued that Article Two of the Constitution authorizes the President and his agents to engage in whatever "intelligence-gathering operations he believes are necessary to protect the security of the nation" and that this authority "is not dependent upon any grant of legislative authority from Congress; but rather is an inherent power of the President, derived from the Constitution itself." Thus, the Department contended, "Congress cannot tell the President what means he may employ to obtain information he needs to determine the proper deployment of his forces."

Fortunately, the "inherent powers doctrine," as this theory

is called, has few supporters. The courts have never accepted the proposition that Congress is powerless to prescribe how the President shall exercise his executive powers. Indeed, in 1952, the Supreme Court rejected President Truman's claim to inherent power to seize the nation's steel mills to avert a strike that threatened the flow of equipment and supplies to American troops fighting in Korea. If there were no constitutional Presidential power to meet that emergency, it is unlikely that one exists to authorize the intelligence powers that the government claims today.

It is far more probable that the courts would endorse a conflicting view: that the Army's authority to collect domestic intelligence is limited by, and can only be inferred from, those laws which traditionally mark off the Army's responsibility for law enforcement from that of other agencies. These include not only the statutes that restrict the Army to a back-up function in times of riot, but the laws that assign surveillance of unlawful political activity within the United States to the FBI and the Secret Service. Other sources of the Army's authority include the Uniform Code of Military Justice, which permits investigation of unlawful political activity within the armed services, and those laws and federal-state agreements under which the Army governs many of its installations. These rules, and not the vague provisions of Article Two, are the legitimate sources of the military's domestic-intelligence powers.

Yet even if the current Administration's claim to an inherent constitutional power to watch lawful political activity were to be accepted by the courts, the surveillance itself probably would be forbidden by the Bill of Rights. The reason is the chilling effect that knowledge of surveillance has upon the willingness of citizens to exercise their freedoms of speech, press, and association, and their right to petition the government for redress of grievances.

Ten years ago, the federal courts would not have accepted this contention. Then the courts were hesitant even to accept constitutional challenges to the government's collection of political information when the plaintiffs could prove that the investigators had no other purpose than to deter them from exercising their rights under the First Amendment. Recently, however, the courts have begun to accept the proposition that vague and overbroad laws and administrative actions are unconstitutional if they inhibit the exercise of those rights, regardless of whether that effect was intended.*

Beyond the Army's need for the present CONUS intelligence program and its authority to pursue it lies the matter of its impact upon the public interest. In particular, there is its effect upon the rights of individuals, the democratic process, and the nation's security.

The impact that the program can have upon the exercise of political rights needs no further explication. The threat it poses to job rights and privacy, however, may not be so apparent.

Like the freedom from inhibitory surveillances, the job rights threatened are rights in the making. As yet no one has established a legal right to a job that requires a security clearance or to a security clearance essential to a job. Nevertheless, in recent years the courts have begun to recognize that those who already hold federal jobs and security clearances have a right not to be deprived of either without just cause or, at the very least, without the rudiments of fairness. The impending marriage of the CONUS intelligence wire service to a computer could nullify even this protection by filling security-clearance dossiers with unverified and potentially erroneous and irrelevant reports. These reports would then be used to determine who should, and who should not, receive security clearances.

* Typical of this growing body of constitutional interpretation is the 1965 case of *Lamont* v. *Postmaster General.* There the Supreme Court struck down a federal statute that authorized the Post Office to suspend delivery of unsolicited mail which the government agents regarded as "Communist political propaganda" until the addressee returned a reply card declaring that he wished to receive the mail. The Court, in a unanimous opinion, held that the effect of this practice, whatever the government's purpose, was to abridge freedom of speech by inhibiting the right to read.

Even more on point is the decision of a New Jersey Superior Court ...ast August declared most of the state's domestic intelligence sys... ...stitutional. In *Anderson* v. *Sills,* a suit filed by the American ... Union on behalf of the Jersey City branch of the NAACP, ...t files that would be maintained as a result of this ...nherently dangerous, and by their very existence ... would advocate . . . social and political

If the men and women who adjudicate security clearance were competent to evaluate such unreliable information, its inclusion in security files might be less cause for concern. Unfortunately, they are not. The most highly trained adjudicators—civilians employed by the stateside army commands—receive only nine days of job instruction on loyalty determinations at the Army Intelligence School. Moreover, this training does not even touch upon the subject of suitability, although almost 98 per cent of all clearances denied today are ostensibly rejected on that ground. The least-trained adjudicators—intelligence officers assigned to field commands—receive exactly two classroom hours on loyalty and two on suitability while being trained to become investigators. It is not unusual for an adjudicator to conclude that a person arrested in connection with a political protest is not suited for a security clearance, regardless of the circumstances of his arrest, the legality of his detention, or his innocence of the charges.

The adjudicators' lack of training is compounded by security regulations that permit—indeed, seem to require—the denial of clearances on less evidence than would support a magistrate's finding of "probable cause." In other words, it is a question not of whether reliable evidence indicates that the individual cannot be trusted with state secrets, but of whether the granting of the clearance would be "clearly consistent with the interests of national security." No one really knows what this ambiguous phrase means, but in practice it frequently is used to justify findings of guilt by association. For example, soldiers and civilian employees of the Army with foreign-born spouses are virtually blocked from jobs requiring access to especially sensitive intelligence. Their association with a spouse who once "associated with foreigners" is taken as proof of their vulnerability to recruitment by foreign agents. Moreover, in nearly all other cases, adjudicators usually have to make their decisions without knowing the source of the evidence, without hearing the accused confront his accusers, or without hearing the accused defend himself with knowledge of their identity.

Given the tenuousness of the right to due process under these conditions, the influx of CONUS intelligence reports can make the system even more unjust than it is now. At the present time, little information on political activity is developed in the course of most background investigations. Army investigations, in particular, tend to be superficial; in some sections of the country shortages of personnel, caused by the war in Vietnam, have forced the Intelligence Command to abandon interviews of character references in favor of questionnaires-by-mail as its main means of inquiry. But if these questionnaires were to be supplemented by CONUS political reports, the number of clearances unjustly denied would skyrocket. These injustices would occur not only within the military; they would reverberate throughout all federal agencies with access to the Fort Holabird data bank.

The Army's domestic-intelligence program also imperils numerous expectations of privacy, some of which enjoy the status of legal rights. It does so by exposing Americans to governmental scrutiny, and the fear of scrutiny, to an extent to which they have never been exposed before. Even the Budget Bureau's ill-starred proposal to consolidate the federal government's statistical records into a National Data Center would not have brought together so much information about individual beliefs and actions.

Once citizens come to fear that government agencies will misuse information concerning their political activities, their withdrawal from politics can be expected. This withdrawal can occur in a variety of ways. Some people may decline to become involved in potentially controversial community organizations and projects. Others may go further and avoid all persons who support unpopular ideas or who criticize the government. Some may refuse to object to the abuse of government authority, especially when the abuse is committed in the name of national security. Others may even stop reading political publications, out of fear that the government might learn of their reading habits and disapprove. Indeed, an adjudicator of security clearances once asked me if she could lose her clearance if she allowed her daughter to subscribe to the *National Observer*!

Inhibitions generated by awareness of extensive domestic surveillance are likely to be strongest at the local level. This is where most citizens participate in politics if they become involved at all. The withdrawal can be expected to occur all across the political spectrum, although the strongest objections to surveillance will undoubtedly come from the Left. Those most likely to be deterred, however, are not the extremists of the Right or the Left, whose sense of commitment runs deep, but the moderates, who normally hold the balance of power.

A less immediate but no less serious danger lies in the potential for misuse inherent in the Army's extensive files on individuals and groups. It is frightening to imagine what could happen if a demagogue in the Martin Dies–Joseph McCarthy tradition were to gain access to the computer the Army seeks now, or if a General Edwin Walker were to take charge of the Intelligence Command.

Such speculation assumes, of course, that the Army cannot guarantee the inviolability of its files. The assumption has some validity. Only last year, information from the Army's confidential service record on New Orleans District Attorney Jim Garrison was leaked to the press. Officers at the Investigative Records Repository at Fort Holabird (which functions as the Army's lending library for such files) suspected that the leak came from a civilian agency in Washington. They were helpless to do anything about it, however, because they had no system of records accountability by which they could fix responsibility. When asked why such a system did not exist, one officer told me: "We probably couldn't stop it [the leaks] if we tried."

Finally, the unregulated growth of domestic intelligence activity can have the paradoxical effect of undermining the very security it seeks to protect. It can do so in at least two ways. First, by increasing the "cost" of lawful political activity, it tends to force extremist groups to go underground. Second, by intruding too closely into the lives of government employees (or prospective employees), it tends to inhibit them from applying for jobs requiring security clearances or from exercising initiative and imagination in those jobs. The direct consequence of programs that deny this freedom is to impair the quality of secret work and the caliber of the men who do it. As John Stuart Mill warned over a century ago:

> A state which dwarfs its men, in order that they may be more docile instruments in its hands, even for beneficial purposes, will find that with small men no great thing can really be accomplished.

If the Army has exceeded the limits of its needs and authority to establish a domestic intelligence program that endangers numerous public interests, what steps should be taken to curb its excesses?

An obvious first step is a court challenge of the Army's authority to possess information for which it has no substantial need. The main target of such a lawsuit should be the personality files and blacklists describing the *lawful* political activities of individuals and groups. A second target should be the collection and storage of information on individuals and groups suspected of participating in *unlawful* political activity—except where that information is essential to an "early warning" system, or where the persons involved are associated with the armed forces, or where the information is collected in the course of security investigations.

The lawsuit's argument should be twofold: (1) The Army has no substantial need for either kind of information, and (2) the very existence of the program inhibits the exercise of First Amendment rights. Such a suit should seek a court order declaring the Army's possession of both kinds of information to be unconstitutional; it should also ask the court to enjoin future collection and storage of such information and to direct the destruction of all existing personality files and blacklists.

While such a lawsuit stands a good chance of success, it could take years to litigate. Moreover, a favorable decision could be ignored or evaded for many more years. Thus, while the symbolic value of such a decision would more than justify the time and expense, an effective challenge of the intelligence program will require the development of legislative and administrative remedies as well.

Whoever attempts to devise these remedies should be prepared to undertake subtle analyses of competing interests and values, for while the excesses of the program must be permanently curbed, the Army's ability to fulfill its responsibilities must not be impaired.

The congressional power of inquiry should be exercised first. Few Americans—and not even most members of Congress—know anything about the activities and plans of the *domestic* intelligence community. Many do not even realize that the growth of formal and informal ties among law-enforcement, intelligence, and security agencies has made it necessary to think in such terms.

For maximum effectiveness, Congress should hold open

hearings, not only to inform itself and the public, but to remind the intelligence community in general, and the Army in particular, that their authority to spy on civilian politics must be construed strictly, in accordance with such established principles as civilian control of the military, Presidential control of the bureaucracies, state and civilian primacy in law enforcement, compartmentalization and decentralization of intelligence duties, and obedience to law. Where it is not, corrective legislation should be promised.

A special effort should be made in the course of these hearings to inform the domestic intelligence community that Congress does not accept the Justice Department's position that "Congress cannot tell the President what means he may employ to obtain the information he needs."

Congress should also exercise its appropriations power so as to encourage major reforms in the Army's program. Specifically, it should block all funds for the planned computer unless and until the Army agrees to:

1. Instruct its agents to limit their collection of CONUS intelligence to reports of incidents, except where the reports describe violations of the Uniform Code of Military Justice or of Army regulations. This would dry up the source of most blacklists and personality files.
2. Forbid the Intelligence Command to convert incident reports into personality reports, except where they relate to criminal or deviant activity by persons subject to military law or employed by the military. Thus storage of information about named civilians unassociated with the armed forces would be doubly foreclosed, should such information be reported by mistake or as an essential element of an incident report.
3. Establish effective technological, legal, and administrative safeguards against the abuse of individual rights in the process of collecting, reporting, storing, and disseminating domestic intelligence or personnel security information. For example, the Army should forbid its agents to infiltrate civilian political groups. (If it fails to do so, Congress should make such infiltration a federal crime, just as it is now a crime for a local military commander to order his troops to serve in a sheriff's posse.) Computer storage systems also should be encouraged, since they can be equipped with more

effective safeguards against misuse than is possible in document storage systems. However, these safeguards must be carefully designed, regularly tested, and reinforced by laws and regulations to deter those who might seek to circumvent them.

4. Establish separate headquarters, preferably in separate cities, for the CONUS-intelligence and personnel-security staffs. So long as the two programs are located at the same headquarters (they now share the same room and some of the same personnel), the danger of informal leakage of CONUS intelligence material to the adjudicators will remain high.

5. Request that the United States Judicial Conference or some similar body nominate a civilian advisory board to review and report annually on the sufficiency of the Intelligence Command's procedures for safeguarding individual rights. Such a board could satisfy both the public's need for a regularized system of independent scrutiny and the Army's need for friendly critics capable of alerting it to the legal, moral, and political implications of its domestic intelligence program. How successful such a board can be is open to question; much depends upon how skillfully its members can be chosen so as to assure both military and public confidence in their capacity for balanced and constructive judgments.

6. Improve the professional quality of Intelligence Command personnel and security-clearance adjudicators. In the final analysis, the Army must be the front-line defender against the dangerous consequences of its own actions. Thus, among other things, the Army should be encouraged to end the overcrowding and understaffing of its Intelligence School, to revise and expand the curriculum of its agents' course, and to transfer the training of security-clearance adjudicators to an accredited law school or the Practicing Law Institute, a nonprofit organization well known for its practical courses for lawyers and laymen on specialized legal subjects.

Needless to say, each of these reforms should be initiated by the President or the Army without waiting for congressional encouragement.

Implementation of these reforms can do much to bring the Army's domestic intelligence practices in line with its legitimate responsibilities. But it is not enough to reform only the Army. The Intelligence Command is only one member of a huge, informal community of domestic intelligence agencies. Other members of the community include not only the FBI, the Secret Service, the Air Force, and the Navy, but hundreds of state and municipal police departments. Some of the latter are surprisingly large. The New York City Police Department's Bureau of Special Services, for example, employs over 120 agents and has an annual budget in excess of $1 million.

Each of these organizations now shares with the Army the capacity to inhibit people in the exercise of their rights, even without trying. By collaborating, they could become a potent political force in their own right. Thus as the Army, the FBI, and the Justice Department strive to coordinate these agencies through the establishment of wire services, hot lines, and computerized data banks, it is essential that the American public and its representatives be equally energetic in the imposition of checks and balances. In particular, special efforts should be made to prevent needless concentrations of information. The United States may be able to survive the centralization of intelligence files without becoming totalitarian, but it most certainly cannot become totalitarian without centralized intelligence files. The fact that we may trust the current heads of our investigative agencies is no guarantee that these agencies will not one day come under the control of men for whom the investigatory power is a weapon to be wielded against political and personal foes.

Six months later, Pyle wrote:

CONUS Revisited: The Army Covers Up

The Army still watches civilian politics. Despite over fifty congressional inquiries, the threat of House and Senate hearings, and a lawsuit by the American Civil Liberties Union, more than 1,000 plainclothes soldier-agents continue to monitor the political activities of law-abiding citizens.

Some reforms have occurred since this blanket surveillance was first revealed. The Army has admitted that its CONUS (Continental U.S.) intelligence program exceeded its needs in preparing for riots and has agreed to cut it back. It has also promised to destroy two widely circulated "blacklists" on dissenters and to scrap its computerized data banks containing records on the membership, ideology, programs, and practices of virtually every activist political group in the country, from the violence-prone Weathermen to the non-violent Urban League. Important as these reforms are, however, they are deceptive.

When reporters asked for a response to the charges against the CONUS program made in the January *Washington Monthly*, the Pentagon's Office of Public Information refused to comment. Reporters were told to submit their questions in writing. From its headquarters at Fort Holabird in Baltimore, the Army Intelligence Command flashed orders to each of its intelligence groups limiting the collection of domestic intelligence to only the most "essential elements of information." Agents were forbidden to discuss any aspect of the program with newsmen and were warned that any who did would be prosecuted for breach of national security. From his office on the second floor of the Pentagon, Robert E. Jordan III, Army General Counsel and Special Assistant to the Secretary for Civil Functions, suspended all replies to congressional inquiries. In violation of its own regulations, the Army even refused to acknowledge receipt of them.

By the end of the month, however, the rising tide of criticism could not be ignored. Recognizing this, the Army issued, on January 26, the first in a series of partial admissions. In the jargon of the spy trade, such admissions are known as "plausible denials," because they are invested with just enough truth to mask an essential falsehood. Thus the Army confirmed the existence of the nationwide intelligence apparatus (true), but said that it collected political intelligence only "in connection with Army civil disturbance responsibilities" (false). "Civil disturbance incident reports are transmitted over [an] automatic voice network teletype system to the U.S. Army Intelligence Command headquarters" (true) and "information on incidents by types and geographical location is placed in the data bank from keypunched cards" (also true). But: "This is incident information only and does not include individual biographies or personality data" (false).

The statement also acknowledged that the Army "does publish an identification list, sometimes with photos, of persons who have been active in past civil disturbance activity" (true), but failed to mention that the list (actually a booklet) also contained detailed descriptions of persons and organizations never involved in civil disturbances.

Finally, the Army admitted in a backhanded way that its agents had infiltrated civilian political groups: "For some time there has been a special prohibition against military persons undertaking such activities as undercover operations in the civilian community." Of course, it did not say when the order was issued, or whether it was being obeyed. (It is not.)

The "plausible denials" satisfied no one. Inquiries directed to Secretary of the Army Stanley R. Resor poured forth from both houses of Congress. Legislators of such diverse persuasions as Senators Williams of Delaware, Hart of Michigan, Dole of Kansas, Brooke of Massachusetts, Percy of Illinois, Fulbright of Arkansas, and Cook of Kentucky demanded to know if the charges were true and, if so, by what authority and for what purpose the Army was spying on law-abiding citizens.

Congressman Cornelius E. Gallagher (D-N.J.), Chairman of the House Invasion of Privacy Subcommittee, and Senator Sam J. Ervin, Jr. (D-N.C.), Chairman of the Senate Subcommittee on Constitutional Rights, led the attack. Gallagher wrote to Secretary Resor on January 26: "I am deeply concerned about the implications of collecting dossiers on Americans who are pursuing constitutionally protected activities, especially when they are to be imbedded in immediately available form in a computerized data system."

Senator Ervin, a member of the Armed Services Committee and a former judge, was more outspoken. "The Army," he said in a Senate speech on February 2, "has no business operating data banks for the surveillance of private citizens; nor do they have any business in domestic politics."

When the Army continued to avoid inquiries during the month of February, however, members of Congress expressed annoyance at being ignored. Congressman Gallagher, usually a staunch friend of the military, was especially fed up. After waiting over two weeks for the Army to acknowledge his letter, he threatened to hold hearings.

Still the Army stalled for time. It had good reason. Like Congress and the public, its civilian hierarchy first learned of the Intelligence Command's unbridled curiosity from the press. Unable to learn more from the Assistant Chief of Staff for Intelligence, who greatly downplayed the CONUS system's capabilities, the civilians resolved to conduct their own inquiry. This reached a point of revelation sometime in mid-February, when Army General Counsel Jordan went to Fort Holabird and watched as the computer bank on dissidents disgorged a lengthy print-out on Mrs. Martin Luther King, Jr.

On February 25, Jordan dispatched the Army's first reply to more than thirty congressional critics. Each received the same letter, regardless of the questions he had asked. It opened with a lengthy defense of the Intelligence Command's library of security-clearance dossiers—never at issue—and closed with a brief confession: "There have been some activities which have been undertaken in the civil disturbance field which, on review, have been determined to be beyond the Army's mission requirements.

"For example, the Intelligence Command published . . . an identification list which included the names and descriptions of individuals who might become involved in civil disturbance situations." And: "The Intelligence Command has operated a computer data bank . . . which included information about potential incidents and individuals involved in potential civil disturbance incidents."

Jordan assured members of Congress that both the identification list and the data bank had been ordered destroyed. "Thus," he concluded, "the Army does not currently maintain the identification list referred to above. No computer data bank of civil disturbance information is being maintained."

Again, the denials were both plausible and deceptive. Jordan's seemingly candid letter failed to mention that, in addition to the Fort Holabird computer (an IBM 1401) and the Intelligence Command's identification list (published in over 330 copies), the Army also maintained:

1. *over 375 copies of a two-volume, loose-leaf encyclopedia on dissent entitled "Counterintelligence Research Project: Cities and Organizations of Interest and Individuals of Interest" but popularly known as "the Compendium."* Compiled by the domestic intelligence section of the Counterintelligence Analysis Division (CIAD), a Pentagon-based unit responsible for briefing high Army officials like Jordan on protest politics, the Compendium contained descriptions of

hundreds of organizations and individuals, including the John Birch Society, the Urban League, the Fifth Avenue Peace Parade Committee, Negro playwright LeRoi Jones, and the late Rev. Martin Luther King, Jr.;

2. *a computer-indexed, microfilm archive of intelligence reports, newspaper clippings, and other records of political protests and civil disturbances at CIAD headquarters in Alexandria, Virginia.* The index to this data bank is a computer print-out, fifty lines to a page, a foot-and-a-half thick. It catalogs microfilmed documents relating to such groups as Young Americans for Freedom, the Southern Christian Leadership Conference, and the Center for the Study of Democratic Institutions. Individuals listed include Rear Admiral Arnold E. True and Brigadier General Hugh B. Hester (war critics), Georgia State Representative Julian Bond, and folk singers Joan Baez, Phil Ochs, and Arlo Guthrie.

3. *a computerized data bank on civil disturbances, political protests, and "resistance in the Army (RITA)" at the Continental Army Command headquarters, Fort Monroe, Virginia.* The civil disturbance–political protest side of this data bank was developed because the Continental Army Command hoped to recapture supervision of its riot control troops from the Pentagon's special 180-man Directorate for Civil Disturbance Planning and Operations.

4. *noncomputerized regional data banks at each stateside army command and at many military installations.* In addition to the usual agent reports, incident reports, and newspaper clippings, these records include booklet-size "CONUS intelligence summaries" published each month by the 1st, 3d, 4th, 5th, and 6th armies, and the Military District of Washington.

5. *noncomputerized files at most of the Intelligence Command's 300 stateside intelligence group offices.* These records on local political groups and individuals are similar to, but more detailed than, the records at Fort Holabird that the Army promised to destroy. The political files of the 108th Military Intelligence Group's Manhattan offices, for example, take up five four-drawer file cabinets and require a full-time custodian.

Congressional reactions to Jordan's admissions, omissions, and denials were mixed. Congressman Gallagher—although fully aware of the omissions—seemed pleased. Without withdrawing his threat of hearings, he announced to the press that the Army would no longer keep tabs on peaceful demonstrations or publish a list of individuals who might be involved in a riot. His announcement, repeated in interviews over the weekend, became the basis of widespread and erroneous newspaper reports. The *New York Times* of February 27 was typical: "Army Ends Watch on Civil Protests." Gallagher got the credit for the apparent victory.

Other members of Congress were slower to react, and before they did Morton Kondracke of the *Chicago Sun-Times* reported on February 28: "The Army acknowledged yesterday that it maintains files on the political activities of civilians other than the computerized political data bank it told Congressmen it was closing down." Kondracke, a thorough reporter, listed them all.

The following Monday, Senator Ervin expressed his dissatisfaction with Jordan's letter. In a letter to the Secretary of the Army he reiterated his demand for a complete report to Congress, and in a Senate floor speech denounced the surveillance as a "usurpation of authority." "The business of the Army in [civil disturbance] situations is to know about the conditions of highways, bridges, and facilities. It is not to predict trends and reactions by keeping track of the thoughts and actions of Americans exercising first amendment freedoms.

"If there ever was a case of military overkill," he added, "this it is. . . . I suggest the Army regroup and define its strategic objectives, lower its sights, and reidentify its enemy. Under our Constitution that enemy is not the American citizen."

Within the Army, much regrouping was already going on. A letter received by Congressman Gallagher from sources close to the 116th Military Intelligence (MI) Group at Fort McNair in Washington, D.C., described what was happening at the lower echelons:

> On the morning after news reports about the dismantling of the CONUS system first appeared in the Washington papers . . . members of 116th were . . . informed that their unit and its operations would be unaffected. . . . They were told that the only major effect of the Congressional and press criticism would be destruction of the national data bank and related files that were kept at Fort Holabird. Files kept by the re-

> gional M.I. Groups (which were the basis for the Fort Holabird file and contained more information) would remain intact, and members of the M.I. Groups would continue their operations of surveillance, infiltration, and reporting as previously.
>
> In addition, all files and operations of the 116th were to be classified to prevent the release of any information about them; disclosure of such information would subject people who released that information to court-martial or prosecution in civilian court for violation of national security.
>
> At the present time, the files of the 116th M.I. Group consist of a 5x7 card file on several thousand persons in the Washington area. On these cards are a picture of each person, his name and address, occupation, background, a record of political groups with which he has been affiliated, notes on political meetings, rallies, and demonstrations which he has attended, and summaries of his views on political issues.
>
> To gather such information, the 116th routinely assigns some 20 of its men as full-time undercover agents to infiltrate political groups and observe politically active persons. . . . Some of these officers have grown beards and long hair to pass as students on local college campuses. In addition, other members pose as members of the working press to obtain pictures of those involved in political activities; concealed tape recorders are also commonly used to record speeches and conversations at political events. Until very recently the 116th's standard equipment also included a full TV videotape camera and sound truck labeled "Mid-West News," which was used to record major demonstrations.

Higher up the chain of command, officials at Fort Holabird also balked at carrying out the new policy. Questioned by Joseph Hanlon of *Computerworld* on March 10, an Intelligence Command spokesman refused to say whether the computer tapes there had actually been erased or merely placed in storage. He admitted, however, that the "input" to the bank (presumably the key-punch cards) had not been destroyed.

Higher still, the civilians supposedly in charge of the Army struggled to find out what their military subordinates were doing. Robert Jordan, surprised by the *Washington Monthly* article and by his pilgrimage to the Fort Holabird computer, was taken aback once more on February 27 during a conference with Congressman Gallagher. Asked why his letter made no mention of the microfilm archives at CIAD, he replied: "I'll have to check into that."

To help Jordan out, Secretary Resor wrote to the Army Chief of Staff, General William C. Westmoreland, on March 5: "I would appreciate your asking all commanders in CONUS, Alaska, and Hawaii down to the installation level to report whether their command has any form of computerized data bank relating to civilians or civilian activities, other than data banks dealing with routine administrative matters."

The results of this canvass have not been made known, but on March 20 Under Secretary of the Army Thaddeus R. Beal wrote long letters to both Ervin and Gallagher. He claimed: "The only other 'intelligence files' concerning civilians maintained by the Army consist of the files maintained by the Counterintelligence Analysis Division."

No reference was made in either letter to: (1) the Continental Army Command's computer files at Fort Monroe, about which Gallagher had made specific inquiries; (2) the regional data banks kept by most of the 300 offices of the Army Intelligence Command; or (3) similar records maintained by the G-2's (intelligence officers) of each stateside army command and of many Army posts.

The microfilm archives at CIAD, Beal went on to say, contain only "limited files concerning political activity" in keeping with that unit's responsibility "for identifying factors which affect civil disturbance potential." He did not mention that these files take up over 200 rolls of microfilm, at 500 frames a roll. Nor did he acknowledge that the unit's domestic intelligence section, which is larger than any of its foreign intelligence sections, had charged its "left wing," "right wing," and "racial" desks with maintaining detailed card files on dissident individuals and groups. These files are in addition to mounds of current FBI and Army reports and newspaper clippings that are coded on key-punch cards (for the computerized index) and recorded on microfilm.

The Under Secretary's claim that the archive was used only in connection with civil disturbance planning was similarly misleading. According to former CIAD employees, one of the principal uses of this file—if not the main reason for its existence—has been to satisfy the curiosity of the Pentagon's brass. A not unusual assignment carried out by one domestic intelligence expert was to write an unclassified report on SDS for a general to send to his daughter at an exclusive Eastern women's college.

In addition to these "plausible denials," Beal also admitted that CIAD had compiled "an identification list . . . on individuals and organizations associated with civil disturbances." "This list," he contended, "was last updated in late 1969 [true] and is available to a limited number of Department of the Army organizations with civil disturbance responsibilities [false]." According to persons who helped compile it, the Compendium went out to over 150 Army intelligence and troop units, plus the FBI, the Justice Department, Naval and Air Force Intelligence, the CIA, and U.S. embassies in West Germany and Canada.

More important, Beal conceded that "the lists are now out of date, are not considered necessary [and] are being . . . destroyed." In addition he promised that the Army would: (1) henceforth limit its curiosity to "incidents where there is a high potential for violence or disorder growing beyond the capability of state and local police and the National Guard to control," and (2) destroy all existing *computerized* data banks on civilian politics.

No new computerized data banks, he said, would be established without the approval of both the Secretary of the Army and the Chief of Staff after "consultations with concerned committees of Congress."

The concessions were substantial. To Congressman Gallagher, they were sufficient. "In view of the Army's commendable action in reversing its former policy," he announced, "I see no further need for a congressional hearing at this time."

To Senator Ervin, on the other hand, Beal's assurances were plainly inadequate. Only the press of other matters, such as preventative detention, bail reform, and the Government Employees' Privacy Bill, kept him from calling his subcommittee into session for a full-scale review of all government political data systems, starting with the Army's.

While congressmen and senators struggled with the Army's evasions and deceptions, the civilian intelligence program was being attacked in the courts. On February 17, 1970, the American Civil Liberties Union filed suit in Federal District Court in Washington, D.C., against the Secretary of Defense, the Secretary of the Army, the Army Chief of Staff, and the

Commanding General of the Intelligence Command. The suit charged that the surveillance, data banks, and blacklists violated the Bill of Rights by reason of the chilling effect that knowledge of their existence can have upon the willingness of citizens to exercise their freedoms of speech, press, and association and their right to petition the government for redress of grievances.

Even before filing suit, the ACLU was aware that a cover-up might be attempted at the lower, as well as higher, echelons of the Army. This suspicion was confirmed by the letter describing the activities of the 116th MI Group and by former intelligence agents who warned that many units would hide copies of blacklists and personality files, regardless of what their civilian superiors told them to do.

In an effort to prevent this, the ACLU asked the District Court on March 12 for a preliminary injunction ordering the Army to cease its destruction of the records and to deliver them (along with inventories, receipts, and certificates of destruction) to the court for safekeeping, pending the outcome of the suit. Then, if the plaintiffs were successful, the court would be in a position to assure complete destruction of the records.

A hearing on this request, and an opposing motion by the Army asking that the entire suit be thrown out for failure to show that the program violated anyone's constitutional rights, was convened in Washington on April 22 before U.S. District Court Judge George L. Hart, Jr.

Judge Hart, a graduate of Virginia Military Institute and a battlefield colonel during World II, was openly hostile to the ACLU's contentions. He began the proceedings with an announcement that he would not hear testimony.

In effect, this announcement meant that Hart had prejudged the ACLU's claims. Few, if any, judges would consider issuing an injunction against the government on the basis of affidavits (written statements by persons not present to testify). To do so, of course, would deny the government the opportunity to cross-examine the witnesses against it and would be regarded quite properly as an abuse of judicial discretion.

Hart's reasons became clearer as the hearing progressed. For example, when Frank Askin, the ACLU's chief counsel at the hearing, argued that it would be all right for members of Army intelligence to follow accounts of protest politics in the newspapers, but that they should not be permitted to maintain computerized files on the political activities of specific individuals, the judge scoffed: "It's all right if they remember it, but they can't take note of it. . . . Isn't that ridiculous?"

Nor could he understand why citizens should fear the military's surveillance any more than they should fear reporting of political activities by the news services. "Newspapers don't have guns and don't have jails," Askin responded. "Nobody is afraid that one of these days the newsmen are all going to sweep into town and come to arrest the troublemakers."

But the judge was unimpressed: "There is no threat that the Army is going to come in and arrest you." "If it does," he added, "we still sit here with the writ of habeas corpus."

"But, your Honor, then why are they keeping these lists of people, that's the issue at stake. . . . They have no need for this."

"It may help them know what persons are likely to cause trouble [in civil disturbances] and thereby keep an eye on them," Hart replied, apparently forgetting that the Army had agreed to withdraw the lists precisely because they were not needed for that, or any other, purpose.

The ACLU's other contentions—that the surveillance had exceeded the Army's civil disturbance responsibilities, that riot control troops do not need blacklists to enforce curfews or clear streets, that the CONUS intelligence operations encroached upon the authority of civilian law-enforcement agencies—were also rejected. Even Askin's offer to present a former intelligence agent who had infiltrated a coalition of church groups was brushed aside with the question: "Did they have a sign saying 'No Military Personnel Are Admitted'?"

"What . . . the plaintiffs are complaining of here," Hart decided, "is that the Army is keeping the type of information that is available to the news media in this country and which is in the morgues of the newspapers . . . and magazines. . . . They show no unconstitutional action on the part of the Army; they show no threat to their rights." Accordingly, he refused to confiscate the records. Instead, he dismissed the suit.

The likelihood that the CONUS intelligence program will be cut back soon is low. The ACLU has asked the Court of Appeals for a prompt hearing and reversal, but that court has yet to act. With summer here, chances of a hearing before fall are dim.

Chances are better that Judge Hart's decision will be overturned on appeal, but even that depends on which members of the relatively liberal Court of Appeals are assigned to review it. The panel could turn out to be as unsympathetic as Judge Hart, in which case the plaintiffs would have to take their appeal to the Supreme Court and suffer still more delays.

Thus, it will be many months at best before the witnesses testify, and perhaps years before a final judgment is rendered. Meanwhile, as the delays multiply and Army security restrictions tighten, the ACLU will find it increasingly difficult to keep its evidence up to date.

Odds for congressional hearings are also poor. Representative Gallagher appears to have left the field, while Senator Ervin and his subcommittee staff are swamped by work on other matters. And although many members of Congress have expressed their personal concern about the surveillance, no other congressional committees have taken up the fight.

Inside the executive branch, prospects are even worse. The Army's civilian leaders have said nothing since Beal's letters of March 20, while Pentagon press officers continue to evade inquiries with the excuse that to answer them would prejudice the ACLU lawsuit. Moreover, the Justice Department has reasons of its own to put up a stiff legal battle to keep the Army contributing to the expanded surveillance of dissenters ordered by President Nixon. Were the Court to end all military domestic intelligence operations, the FBI would have to run the civil-disturbance early warning system—a politically risky and tedious task which it does not want—and the FBI and the Secret Service would have to find new alternatives to what has been a free source of supplementary manpower.* In addition, the Justice Department would be

* During the 1968 Democratic National Conventional in Chicago, for example, Army agents posed as TV camera crews, a naval intelligence agent tape-recorded speeches in Grant Park, and two plainclothesmen from the staff of the Army Assistant Chief of Staff for Intelligence occupied assigned seats within the convention hall. All of this assistance—and more—was given despite the Counterintelligence Analysis Division's correct prediction that federal troops would not be needed.

deprived of the Army's political wire service, upon which it depends to feed its political computer and to produce, each week, a four-volume guide to coming events on the political circuit.

No matter how discouraging the prospects for reform may seem, however, efforts to curb the CONUS intelligence program must go on. The initiative remains with Congress—particularly with those committees of Congress that have jurisdiction to hold hearings.*

Without the threat of hearings, the Army's civilian leaders are not likely to end their evasions and deceptions, admit the full scope of the program, or reconsider its needs or consequences. They are the crisis managers of their bureaucracy. Threats, not suggestions, determine their agenda.

But while hearings may command their attention, only skillful questioning can move them toward reform. Once the full scope of the program is established, the Army's officials must be pressed to concede what in effect they acknowledged by their promises—that blacklists and dossiers do not contribute to the prediction or control of riots. Having conceded that, they will be hard put to justify the continued pursuit of personality and organizational data in light of its cost, its effect on the willingness of people to participate in politics, and the mischief that could result were the records to fall into the hands of blackmailers, demagogues, or security clearance adjudicators.

Whether or not the hearings produce legislation, they should attempt to establish a consensus on what the lines between permissible and impermissible conduct for Army intelligence should be. The difficulty will come in determining (1) the extent to which military intelligence units in the field should be permitted to watch controversial political figures on the theory that "agitators" cause riots, and (2) the extent to which the Army, through CIAD or similar units, should be expected to analyze the political and social aspects of civil disturbances. There are strong reasons for leaving

* Besides Senator Ervin's Constitutional Rights Subcommittee (of the Judiciary Committee), these include Senator Edward M. Kennedy's Subcommittee on Administrative Practices and Procedures (also of the Judiciary Committee), Senator John Stennis's Armed Services Committee, Senator Abraham Ribicoff's Committee on Executive Reorganization (of the Committee on Government Operations), and Congressman Robert W. Kastenmeier's Subcommittee No. 3 (of the House Judiciary Committee).

> both of these functions up to civilian authorities. On the other hand, the domestic intelligence section of CIAD has a fairly good record for common sense and has more than once persuaded hard-nosed generals that demonstrators and rioters are not "the enemy," "insurgents," or part of "the Communist conspiracy."
>
> Wherever the lines around the Army spy program are finally drawn, however, action on them should begin promptly. Incredible though it may seem, the Army has already assembled the apparatus of a police state. That apparatus must be disassembled before it falls into the hands of those who would deliberately or inadvertently misuse it.

Pyle's second article appeared to provoke a strong reaction in the Congress, where critics of military surveillance had generally been satisfied by the Army's announcements that the problem would be eliminated. The congressmen were moved to act not only by the continuation of the domestic intelligence activity but also by the deceptive statements on the part of high Defense Department officials (although there is considerable evidence that these officials actually did not know what was going on at the scattered lower echelons, where the CONUS intelligence bureaucracy was entrenched). On July 27, 1970, Senator Sam Ervin announced that his Constitutional Rights Subcommittee would conduct hearings on military surveillance in the United States. The hearings were originally scheduled for October, 1970, but were later postponed until the spring of 1971 for unspecified reasons that probably centered on campaigning in the 1970 elections.

In the courts, progress against the surveillance was not so swift. The ACLU appealed Judge Hart's April, 1970, decision to throw out its suit without even hearing evidence or witnesses. On April 27, 1971, the U.S. Court of Appeals ruled in favor of the ACLU and directed Judge Hart to gather evidence on the matter, indicating that the Court felt that the ACLU would probably have a case for the unconstitutionality of surveillance if it could establish the validity of disputed facts. The government, however, has appealed the decision of the Court of

Appeals to the Supreme Court, and Judge Hart will not be required to hold hearings, that is, to *begin* the substantive litigation of the case, unless the Supreme Court sustains the Court of Appeals, by which time the matter may be moot.

The ACLU initiated a second lawsuit, *ACLU v. Laird,* on December 21, 1970, in Chicago. This suit followed the disclosure by another former intelligence agent, John O'Brien, that the 113th Military Intelligence Group had been monitoring and building files on Illinois political figures such as Senator Adlai Stevenson III, and Representative Abner Mikva. The 113th was also building a file on the Rev. Jesse Jackson, a black Chicago leader then head of the Southern Christian Leadership Conference's "Operation Breadbasket," and Gordon Sherman, former president of Midas Muffler and benefactor of antiwar groups and Ralph Nader. On January 5, 1971, Judge Richard B. Austin threw out the suit, arguing in effect that the Army's apparatus was so inept that it was incapable of violating anyone's constitutional rights by scaring or intimidating them and that the practice constituted no threat to civilian government. The ACLU has appealed.

Secretary of the Army Stanley Resor issued a statement on December 17, 1970, denying that the Army maintained any files on Stevenson and Mikva. This denial was retracted in March, 1971, by Assistant Secretary of Defense Robert C. Froehlke, testifying at the Ervin hearings, which finally began on February 23, 1971. Discrepancies such as this one had made the Defense Department look awkward and indirect in its handling of the domestic intelligence issue, and a steady flow of minor disclosures and newspaper and TV stories on surveillance kept the pot boiling for more than a year. Among the stories was an hour-long treatment of Army surveillance that appeared on NBC's "First Tuesday" in December, 1970. The cumulative pressure of media coverage and congressional hearings led to Assistant Secretary Froehlke's announcement on March 2, 1971, of Defense Department regulations that prohibit military involvement in civilian affairs. Froehlke told Ervin that the regulations would be strictly followed and that huge quantities of improper intelligence material had already been destroyed.

Pyle, who in the course of his involvement with surveillance acquired a large number of informal contacts within the intelligence services, says that Froehlke is right. The destruction of intelligence records is in fact taking place, and the surveillance bureaucracy is being dismantled.

"It is fair to say that today the Army no longer monitors civilian politics directly," Pyle observed in September, 1971. Nevertheless, he believes that legislation is necessary to prevent a relapse. At the time of Pyle's statement, Senator Ervin was drafting a bill to give the Defense Department regulations the force of law, providing a statutory ban on the activities now proscribed only by an administrative regulation.

Chris Pyle has been one of the more effective whistle-blowers —unusually successful in comparison with the others described and quoted in this book. A number of factors seem to have contributed to his impact. For one thing, Pyle charged that the Army was violating a specific principle of constitutional and traditional history—the subordination of the military to civilian rule and the required abstention of the armed forces from domestic political affairs. He did not criticize the military for general political obstinance or for ideological differences, but rather pointed to specific acts and practices that violated the values of most American citizens on both Left and Right—and seemed to violate the law as well. The clarity of these violations, and Pyle's precision in describing them, gave critics a handle for dealing with the surveillance issue. The Army's improper activities were precisely separated from its proper ones, keeping vague indictments of the entire Pentagon out of the argument.

If the problem was well-defined, so was the solution—as Pyle kept his attention focused on the next logical step toward ending military spying. These concrete, methodical steps gave people objective standards with which to measure progress, or lack of it, in the reform campaign. Simply calling for an abolition of the program at each juncture might have failed. Big goals for solving big problems, like "reordering national priorities," seem to sink into the public mist surrounding the problems themselves. Calling for simple steps worked. People gained a sense of where the effort was, where to focus the pressure at different times, and they could take heart when a small victory was won.

Pyle's technique also required him to keep out of the forefront of the surveillance debate. He testified at the Ervin hearings, appeared on the NBC "First Tuesday" program, and was the subject of a *New York Times* profile—but he was never a figure of controversy, and his name never became closely associated with the campaign against Army spying. He generally worked quietly with congressional staffs and with intelligence agents who made contact with him because of his role in first exposing the surveillance. He spent most of his time helping new people keep things simmering with additional disclosures and keeping up with the Army's performance on its promises, but seldom making statements himself and never calling press conferences.

Pyle's behind-the-scenes approach was, of course, easier because he had left the Army and was not embroiled in a fight over employment or breaking regulations. This approach enabled him to keep maximum attention on the surveillance issue instead of on himself. One consequence was that there was no backlash into support of Army spying from individuals who, for one reason or another, happened not to like Chris Pyle.

It is impossible to pin down the exact size of the contribution made by Pyle's technique. In the elimination of surveillance, he had a "good" issue—on which the majority of the population could be expected to support his position on the face of the facts, without needing persuasion in some murky debate. Many people have a deep personal fear of a large spying apparatus of any kind, or any other step that might lead to a supergovernment or police state. Also, influential figures like Senator Ervin came forward to lead the attack, allowing Pyle to go on collecting information in the background. Moreover, the Army itself was in a bad position—supporting a program that caused it great embarrassment for little real gain. The surveillance bureaucracy was tenacious but so dispensable to the military in a crunch that several spokesmen complained of being unable to unload the few legitimate functions on other agencies, which found spying not worth the trouble.

Still, it is not difficult to believe that surveillance would have continued unchecked had it not been for Pyle's first and follow-up articles.

Pyle himself regarded blowing the whistle on domestic intelligence-gathering as merely the first step in a continuing personal fight against a bureaucratically entrenched program. Such long-range commitment is perhaps the first requirement of successful whistle-blowing. Pyle might not have gotten anywhere without the salience of the issue, but clearly his approach worked well enough, and seems logical enough, to set a standard of effectiveness.

5 Inside OEO

This chapter and the two that follow it illustrate the unique opportunities, and special limitations, of alumnus whistle-blowing when the issues involved do not elicit the broad public concern evident in more celebrated cases, such as the Army surveillance of civilians revealed by Christopher Pyle. These issues are not necessarily less important than those raised by other alumni whistle-blowers or pure ones like James Boyd. On the contrary, their cumulative impact may be far more important in the long run. These three chapters deal with the remodeling of the OEO Legal Services program for the poor, with the operations of helicopter gunships in Vietnam, and with the quality of information generated by the Pentagon's Defense Intelligence Agency.

The "inside" perspective they share helps the reader understand how bureaucratic pressures often seem to build policies with a life of their own. But this perspective, while it illuminates policy formation and may be useful to students of government, is a hindrance to the effectiveness of the whistle-blowers. The authors' disagreements with current practices emerge from inside disputes over policy or program direction. Such disagreements are the grist of government, but as described for the outsider they do not lend themselves to the kind of black-and-white contrast of right and wrong or the exciting identification of villains that facilitates a whistle-blowing campaign. The dispute often seems too diffuse and academic for the public, with the charges hitting like spray rather than like bullets. Nevertheless, since implementing the reforms that the authors recommend requires political shifts *within* the government, this kind of whistle-blowing may well have a crucial, though publicly unspectacular, effectiveness.

The article on the OEO Legal Services program bears a special relationship to whistle-blowing not shared by any other chapters in this book. For the Legal Services program of the Office of Economic Opportunity is, like whistle-blowing itself, a unique new approach to the task of reforming decayed and corrupt institutions. The "poverty lawyers," as they came to be called, used the law and the courts to force government agencies and corporations to follow both their own regulations and the statutes that govern them. The need for such pressure was obvious. The institutions of power had coagulated so much that neither competition nor representative government nor bureaucracy protected the rights and opportunities of the poor. Instead, these institutions tended to protect themselves and their employees in ways that were manifestly illegal in the eyes of the courts.

The Office of Legal Services supported suits against government agencies both local and federal—police departments, welfare boards, state bureaus, the Department of Labor, HEW, and so on. Using very conservative standards—that is, the legality or illegality of government practices by existing statutes—the lawyers brought about enormous changes in the operation of government for the poor. And this was accomplished without the creation of additional expensive and tiresome bureaucracies to monitor the inefficiencies of the old ones.

Naturally, the government representatives on the receiving end of Legal Services lawsuits were not pleased with the program, and they reacted against it in much the same way as other management officials have reacted against whistle-blowers. They maneuvered successfully to reduce the power of the Office of Legal Services and stifle the pressure.

An article by "Clark Holmes" was published in the *Washington Monthly* of June, 1970, seven months before the article reprinted below, at a time when the program was still, by all outside appearances, going strong. The author's name was a pseudonym for two former employees of OEO who left Legal Services but not the government. The pseudonym provided some protection from reprisals for the two, who drew on their experience and inside information to predict a major political offensive against the Office of Legal Services and its Director, Terry F. Lenzner.

In November, 1970, OEO Director Donald Rumsfeld fired Lenzner and Deputy Director Frank N. Jones, causing an explosive controversy in the legal world and giving some weight to the validity of the "Holmes" prediction. Lenzner and Jones proceeded to speak out publicly against what they regarded as the gutting of the Legal Services program, blowing the whistle on the Nixon Administration's efforts to respond to political pressures by requiring the poverty lawyers to refrain from taking "controversial" cases—especially those that offended officials of local governments. The infighting that led to the Lenzner-Jones dismissal is described in editor Taylor Branch's article, first published in the *Washington Monthly* of January, 1971. Using a great deal of internal OEO material, it probed for reasons why Lenzner and Jones felt they had to blow the whistle—rather than leaving with a McNamaran silence—and also for the reasons why Rumsfeld fired them.

The Ordeal of Legal Services: How Poor People Won in Court but Lost in OEO

On his first day of unemployment, November 21, Terry Lenzner publicly accused the Administration of watering down the Legal Services program to please the political powers who opposed it:

> We believe that poverty lawyers must provide the best advocacy possible—advocacy that is unconstrained by fear of antagonizing powerful interests. We believe that the poor deserve lawyers who protect their rights with the same vigor

and concern that is expended by private lawyers on behalf of corporations and the well-to-do.

Frank Jones made his point in the straightforward, right-on style that symbolizes the chasm between Rumsfeld and his former employees:

> There is something dishonest, immoral, and possibly illegal about pretending to be concerned about the poor as Mr. Rumsfeld does, on the one hand, and using his position and resources as Director of OEO to further his own political end and the careers of politicians whose interests are diametrically opposed to those of the poor.

These charges were echoed in the unanimous protest statement of the ten Legal Services regional directors and the national staff—an unusual show of solidarity in a government agency, where survivors usually muzzle themselves to protect a shot at the spoils. And Senator George McGovern told the Senate on November 23 that Rumsfeld had squeezed one of the last pockets of social commitment from the Administration, leaving only a few people and large doses of public relations to smooth over the power politics.

Rumsfeld is rumored to have been both surprised at the intensity of the reaction to his gear-shifting in OEO and angered by the piercing accusations of insincerity directed against him. In response, he stressed the enormous progress of the Legal Services program under his guidance and denied any political compromises of its independence.

Rumsfeld also went on the political offensive by emphasizing through his aides the details of three cases in which he charged that Lenzner and Jones disobeyed his orders by supporting controversial programs that were in violation of OEO guidelines. Each case had a political message beyond the administrative technicalities, as the Legal Services programs were linked to the representation of the Black Panthers and SDS in New Orleans; the "voluntarily poor," hippie-type distributor of an underground newspaper in Dallas, which once featured the photograph of a nude male; and a group of middle-class, non-poor government employees in Los Angeles. For those who were not convinced of the guideline violations or of the evil of representing these people *per se*, a more sophisticated argument was advanced, namely, that Lenzner and Jones were blind to the political delicacies involved in selling the legal services idea to the masses. The firers characterized the firees as a bit swim-headed, naive, and full of that save-the-world-quick purity which plagues good government.

It must have been difficult for Rumsfeld to "go public" with detailed allegations against one of his own programs, in view of the obvious risk that the spicy stories would promote political sniping from all directions—the kind of publicity that hurts appropriations. He could have protected the Legal Services program by maintaining that the firings rose simply from a personality clash and a breakdown of the working relationship. He might have declined to discuss the specifics of the Office of Legal Services for fear of exposing his agency to a public brawl, which would hurt the OEO program and budget. But instead of stoically absorbing the Lenzner-Jones attacks and passing them off as the emotional parting shots of derailed bureaucrats, Rumsfeld elected to meet them head-on and counterattack with the Panther-SDS-hippie buckshot. "Most people and many members of Congress won't remember the alleged guideline violations or who comes and goes as Director of Legal Services," said Senator Mondale. "All that will stick is the link between Legal Services and the unpopular."

In the New Orleans case, OEO spokesmen charged that Lenzner had mishandled the disciplining of the New Orleans Legal Assistance Committee (NOLAC) for its violations of OEO guidelines. NOLAC, it was said, had represented the Black Panthers in criminal cases, non-poor SDS members, and a pornographic underground newspaper called the *NOLA Express*. In early October, Lenzner found that NOLAC was representing indigent Panthers, but not in violation of the guidelines, except for one case in which a lawyer represented Panthers at a criminal arraignment (he was suspended from NOLAC the same day). He also found that one NOLAC attorney had in fact represented two SDS members the previous April, without filling out the proper indigency forms. Filling in for a friend, the NOLAC lawyer had appeared as the attorney of record in a one-day hearing. Lenzner ordered such representations to cease, but he could take no action against the guilty attorney since he had left NOLAC four months earlier. NOLAC had never represented the pornographic paper in any suit. Finally, Lenzner found that NOLAC was involved in eighteen criminal cases (of 1,825 active ones) other than those criminal categories explicitly approved by OEO. He ordered NOLAC to withdraw from them, even though OEO's General Counsel had approved the current NOLAC work program, which stated the intention to become involved in such cases because of special problems in New Orleans criminal representation.

Lenzner was also accused of mishandling a Dallas incident, involving the representation by attorney Ed Polk of Brett Stein, the twenty-seven-year-old publisher of an underground newspaper, *Dallas Notes.* Its June 3 issue had featured several photographs of a nude man in a Dallas municipal parade and a story about a Jack Anderson column that accused Congressman James Collins (R-Tex.) of accepting kickbacks from people he employed. Apparently, Collins found both the pictures and the story obscene, and he complained to OEO that Stein was ineligible for Legal Services representation because he is "voluntarily poor." Stein's only income is $100 a month from his paper, although he is a college graduate and the son of a wealthy businessman. Lenzner inquired into the case upon Collins's request (as well as requests from Senator John Tower and Congressman George Mahon, chairman of the House Appropriations Committee) and received from Polk the defense that the guidelines on voluntary poverty are hopelessly vague, prohibiting representation of people who are voluntarily poor "without good cause," and that the *Dallas Notes* was distributed free to poor people and carried poverty notices, services that no other Dallas paper would provide. Since the Stein case ended in early July, Lenzner took no action; but he requested a more specific definition of voluntary poverty from the General Counsel's office, and this revision is still being made.

In Los Angeles, the Western Center on Law and Poverty was accused by Senator George Murphy of representing a dozen financially ineligible employees of the California youth corrections department in a civil action against the department. The Western Center defended its action by arguing that its guidelines allowed such representation if financially ineligible clients were first turned down by three private attorneys from the local bar's referral service, a procedure which had been followed. The Center also said that the cases were directly related to poverty because they arose from disciplinary actions taken against the youth department employees for protesting the treatment of the youth wards, mainly poor, in California's correction centers. Lenzner found their case persuasive in view of the guidelines, which he said OEO should tighten up, but he later ordered Western Center to drop the cases anyway, which was done.

On October 12, Lenzner received a copy of three memos from the OEO General Counsel's office to Rumsfeld, recommending suspension of the Dallas and New Orleans programs and a strong "show cause" order to the Western Center. Each memo was accompanied by an implementing letter drafted for Lenzner's signature. Lenzner himself was surprised by the abruptness and indirection of this procedure, and he objected that each project should prepare a full written report before such stern measures would be justified.

The internal debate over these three cases, which Rumsfeld used to illustrate his impossible management problems, created an atmosphere in which the Office of Legal Services felt ulterior motives blossomed on the eighth floor. According to Lenzner, Rumsfeld summoned him shortly after the October 12 memos and outlined the plan of attack. Lenzner recalls that he wanted three things: a notice of suspension or at least a harsh reprimand to all three projects, a letter to every congressman and all 265 Legal Services grantees announcing the action as a "signal" about Legal Services, and a press release to be issued and attached to all the letttrs.

Lenzner won his argument against the blanket letters, and "interested" congressmen were merely informed of the actions. The press releases were compromised into press statements, not issued but made available to the press upon request. And the projects were not suspended, but sternly advised of the charges against them and ordered to produce explanations or else.

The New Orleans, Dallas, and Western Center cases, upon review, do not seem to be critical turning points in the relationship between Rumsfeld and the Office of Legal Services. The specific charges of regulations violations leveled at Lenzner and Jones are minor in the NOLAC instance, dubious in the Polk-Stein case, and ambiguous at the Western Center. The political content of the cases was the most important element of the public rationale for the firings anyway, and

Lenzner feels that the full array of targets was no political accident—the Panthers, SDS, pornography, and hippies. "Don knew there was an election coming," said Jones, "and he wanted to get the message out that OEO didn't like radicals either."

"I think he had already decided to fire us," Jones observed, "even though he never said flatly that he was dissatisfied with our work." "Things had been sour for some time," echoed a Rumsfeld aide. They had gone bad over the previous year, as a few case studies should indicate.

The Legal Aid Society of Mecklenburg County in Charlotte, North Carolina, was under criticism within the Office of Legal Services almost immediately after it opened its doors in September, 1967. The 1968 evaluation report was quite negative, chastising the program for a low caseload volume, which the evaluators felt grew out of the society's downtown office in the prestigious Law Building.

The October, 1969, evaluation was almost equally harsh on the program's commitment to the poor and on its vigor in seeking to use suits to make inroads on Charlotte's poverty. The major exception was the performance of staff attorney Martin Miller, who had opened a separate office in the poor section of Charlotte, and who was developing a large caseload from the surrounding neighborhood, including some test cases. In *Tucker v. North Carolina National Bank as Trustee*, for example, he established a defense for tenants against eviction, on the grounds that, according to state statutes, the housing was "unfit for human habitation." The evaluators found the board policy and the downtown office negative, the Miller office and Miller involvement positive, and called for more of the latter.

On January 7 and 16, 1970, Miller filed two lengthy complaints in United States District Court against the Charlotte Police Department on behalf of several clients, all poor and black. The complaints alleged repeated instances of forced entry, destruction of property, harassment, and midnight searches by policemen without warrants or reasonable cause. Miller sought injunctive relief against the practice and $100,-000 in punitive damages.

These complaints caused an uproar in the city of Charlotte and a sharp reaction from Legal Aid Society board president Alvin A. London. Miller, who now lives in Washington, recalls that "Mr. London was damn mad about the suits against the police. He said, 'In Charlotte, you don't sue the police department.' Then he told me to withdraw from the suits. I think he has about as much feeling for the poor community as one could expect to have from the ninth floor of the Law Building."

The Office of Legal Services in Washington investigated the Charlotte situation after Miller's cases received wide press coverage and found that London was not only applying political restrictions to the staff attorneys but also running the board of directors improperly. On February 27, OLS forwarded its evaluation report to London with an accompanying letter advising him that his grant would be cut off unless the board agreed by March 15 to cease interference with staff attorneys beyond the maintenance of eligibility requirements and professional standards. That same day, London convened the personnel committee of the board, which he had appointed a week earlier, and fired Miller. Then the politics began.

After London wrote Lenzner's office on March 12 that he could not comply with the February 27 conditions pending review by the North Carolina State Bar, Lenzner recommended to Rumsfeld on April 1 that the program not be re-funded and that other "vehicles" be explored for the provision of legal services to the poor in Mecklenburg County.

Lenzner's recommendation did not sell, partly because of intercession on London's behalf by Congressman Charles Jonas (R-N.C.), who apparently took enough interest in the dispute to become identified with the grant. On May 15, Rumsfeld, who still denies charges of political interference in the Charlotte case, wrote, "Where do we stand on the Jonas Legal Aid Program?" Dick Cheney, Rumsfeld's special assistant, wrote Lenzner on June 2, in the midst of stalled negotiations: "Terry, you and I need to sit down and chat about Charlotte Legal Services at your convenience. Congressman Jonas called the Director again and we need to get squared away on what our position is so we can tell him the same story."

In between these two memos, Rumsfeld and Cheney met on May 25 with Legal Aid Society president London and Robert G. Sanders, president of the North Carolina State

Bar, upon Congressman Jonas's request. London and Sanders are law partners, which is indicative of the close cooperation between the state bar and poverty law. According to a letter from Sanders to Rumsfeld dated July 7, the Charlotte lawyers were assured that the restrictions imposed on their grant by the February 27 letter would be "rescinded or withdrawn."

Lenzner, who obtained a copy of the Sanders letter on July 17, sent an angry memo to Rumsfeld protesting the whole procedure by which the Charlotte grant had been handled. It is clear from the memo that Lenzner knew he had been overruled on terminating the grant but thought that Charlotte's money had been released with instructions that the noninterference conditions be "negotiated" between the Legal Aid Society and the regional OLS in Atlanta. The Sanders letter indicated that Lenzner had, without his knowledge, also been overruled on the special conditions for the Charlotte grant.

In many other areas of the country—Chicago, Boulder, Albuquerque, Baton Rouge, Gary, Berkeley, Saint Louis—the same kind of detail can be marshaled. In Volusia County (Daytona Beach), Florida, for example, the county bar association became extremely disturbed when a staff attorney named Tom Goldsmith filed suit against the local justice of the peace system, alleging that it existed mainly to help merchants and landlords collect from poor people without due process. When Goldsmith *won* the suit, the bar turned a scrutinous eye to the Legal Services program. "Before that suit, Legal Services had 90 per cent support among the bar members," observed one Daytona attorney. "But it changed everything. Lawyers have to look to their clients."

Legal Services board chairman Bernard Strasser agreed that talk of allowing lawyers to "ferment turmoil," as he put it, sounded good. But, he said, "you can't do it locally."

The local board proceeded to fire Goldsmith three times—failing on the first two tries because of sympathies for Goldsmith at an appeal hearing and because of intercession from the Atlanta Legal Services office requiring due process. When the severance was finally executed, OLS sent a telegram on September 2 requiring restructuring of the board by September 30 as a condition for re-funding (the bar had almost twice the board representation required by Legal Services guidelines at the expense of poor representatives). Congressman William Chappell (D-Fla.) thereupon arranged for a Volusia County delegation to meet with Rumsfeld on November 6, without an OLS representative present. The delegation obtained a $25,000 interim grant to last until January 30, 1971. At that time, the bar association and the local Community Action Agency must present a proposal for a new board structure. Volusia County officials continue to bargain with the Community Action Agency, which is controlled by stubborn poor people, but they are taking no chances. A delegation of county commissioners has visited Washington to check up on the proper procedures for county authorities to take over a CAA. Led by Commissioner Dean Smith (brother-in-law of the Legal Services director who originally fired Goldsmith), the commission has already begun the take-over process, which will make the CAA more agreeable one way or another.

Instances like those described reduced the Rumsfeld-OLS relationship to one of bureaucratic guerrilla warfare long before the public debate over the dismissals. There were a few side issues to add to the friction, such as the Administration's political clearance system for all of Lenzner's appointive positions in Washington and the ten regional headquarters. Politics has always oozed forth in government employment, but the current system requires all nominees, down to the level of GS-9 (which begins at a $9,500 salary and is about the bottom level with any policy responsibilities), to survive a formal process of both local and White House clearance, often lasting for months. Anyone browsing in OEO files can come across passages like the following:

> . . . looks pretty good at this point. They have received okays from Ralph Smith and Charles Percy, have gotten a letter from Ogilvie, and other support letters from the Director of the Bureau of the Budget, etc. . . .
>
> This one may hang on forever. . . .
>
> As he is a registered Republican, there appears to be no problem other than the normal delays involved in springing these clearances loose. . . .
>
> Senator Tower's office has given "thumbs down" on this appointment . . . has made statements about the Senator in the past which he did not like.

But the major battle—which cut across almost all the disputes between OLS and Rumsfeld—involved "regionalization," or whether authority over Legal Services would filter out to the OEO regional offices. This fight has not yet been resolved and is a much larger issue than the Lenzner-Jones firing. The outcome, according to most knowledgeable sources, will determine the future usefulness of Legal Services programs, and the main new actor in the dispute is the American Bar Association.

The American Bar Association has always been heavily involved in the Legal Services program, pushing to insure that professional controls over the operation were very tight. ABA officials made sure from the beginning that attorneys would constitute a majority of the governing boards for all local projects and that the organized bar would be consulted about all high matters of policy regarding the national program.

When the Nixon Administration came into office, the bar's remaining anxiety about Legal Services was that the grants were still being funded through local Community Action Agencies, the OEO "vessel" for all its programs. The bar didn't like that because laymen were often scratching around in the attorney-client relationship and interposing nonprofessional judgments about how much money the poverty lawyers should receive and what kinds of cases they should bring to trial. In Chicago, for example, Mayor Richard J. Daley is chairman of the board of the Community Action Agency (CAA), which sponsored Chicago Legal Services but placed it under intense political pressure not to bring suits against the city or otherwise irritate the mayor.

The ABA also resented the fact that the ten regional directors of Legal Services were the employees of the over-all OEO regional directors. Thus, at both the local and regional levels, lawyers and a legal program were being subordinated to a general political program controlled mainly by lay administrators. It was clearly an affront to the dignity of barristers everywhere, and President Nixon himself was sympathetic to the worries of the organized bar.

Upon taking office, Lenzner began centralizing the Legal Services operation and, in effect, reducing the amount of administrative paperwork between his program and the other OEO offices. Generally, he was more successful at the regional level than at loosening the local CAA–Legal Services tie. The struggle there was a classic bureaucratic one, for the Community Action Agency administrator reports directly to the OEO regional director, who reports directly to Frank Carlucci, the Assistant Director for Operations in Washington and Lenzner's rival.

Local squabbles between CAA's and Legal Services programs were quickly translated into Lenzner-Carlucci battles in Washington, which were sometimes not successfully worked out.

In Chicago, the issue turned on political control; and Lenzner, after unsuccessfully trying to loosen Daley's hold on the program, proposed that Chicago's Legal Services be funded directly—bypassing Daley's CAA entirely. Carlucci thereupon produced fierce memos to Rumsfeld and Hjornevik opposing the move on the grounds that it would "defuse the Office of Economic Opportunity's management capabilities."

Lenzner won, at least temporarily, on the egregiously politicized Chicago program, but he and OEO were clearly on a collision path. OLS was moving to separate and invigorate its programs, stimulating more of the kind of poverty representation that would wound politicians—and OEO was simultaneously moving to increase state and local control over antipoverty programs and to "return the power to the states." Carlucci's chain of command was the most heavily politicized. His OEO regional director for the Western Region, for example, owes his job to Senator Hiram Fong (R-Hawaii), the deputy to Governor Reagan, and so on.

The poverty lawyers ran headlong into a phalanx of politicians and the established interests upon which they float. These forces produced the Murphy Amendment and its House counterpart (Quie-Green) to nestle Legal Services under the wings of state governors. When these efforts failed in late 1969, pressures began building to accomplish the same goals administratively by reversing the course that Lenzner had just launched with joint Nixon Rumsfeld blessing. Ironically, plans arose to decentralize Legal Services in early 1970—even as Lenzner's office was putting the last administrative touches on his independent OLS structure, trying to get out from under the restrictive Community Action Agencies, eliminating bureaucratic snarls with the OEO regional directors, and otherwise irritating Frank Carlucci. In February, 1970, while Lenzner was making speeches about the need to slap more poverty lawsuits on unresponsive government agencies, Hjornevik wrote Carlucci that "the Legal Services program will be decentralized again in fiscal year 1971." That same day, Carlucci reiterated to Rumsfeld his "strong opinion" that OLS projects should be direct-funded only, in essence, when local CAA's are nonexistent or when the CAA itself "does not want to be the grantee."

Long before his position decomposed to this point, Lenzner had appealed to his principal source of outside clout, the American Bar Association.

There are many aspects of the $61-million Legal Services program that draw the admiration of the legal profession, and high among them ranks the fact that most of the money goes to lawyers. "Also, every time a poverty lawyer files a suit," observed one member of the Florida bar, "another lawyer gets paid by the government or a company to represent the other side. A shrewd lawyer will vilify the ideology of the program but defend its independence on professional principles." Since Legal Services also siphons off much court-appointed attorney time, which was formerly donated, it adds up to a sizable net gain for the collective legal pocket, especially for a young federal program with high growth potential.

Beyond these gritty financial details, intelligent lawyers recognize the growing pressure in each new graduating class for *pro bono,* public interest work—often concentrated among the highly talented but socially committed lawyers whose sense of purpose receives no throb from real estate dealings or the prestigious corporate firm. There is an obstinacy about these views which teaches prudent bar members that to some extent the government must pay for these demands, or the firm will have to.

But the time-worn principle upon which the ABA relies to unite its membership in protection of independence for Legal Services is the proposition that the attorney-client relationship shall not be violated. This means that no layman should interfere in decisions grounded in the law and properly made by lawyers, period. This principle is in accordance with the prime maxim of all occupational guilds—enlightened self-interest requires sealing the portals so that renegades will not commonize the profession and thereby make it cheap. The bar has established its proscriptions primarily by statute, but the fringes must be left to the Canons of Ethics and vigilant watch over the attorney-client relationship. This task is far above politics. It is the lifeblood of the attorney's distinction. It has been said that law schools merely teach their wards to "think like a lawyer," and that few graduates emerge from this process without a pulverized imagination—as if their zest for mental wondering had been strained through a cyclone fence to produce the iron latticework of interconnected syllogisms that lead methodically from the precedent to the possible. It may also be said that far fewer lawyers finish their training without an impregnable reverence for the attorney-client relationship.

Therefore, when Lenzner sent out the word that Rumsfeld, Hjornevik, and Carlucci were planning to decentralize Legal Services into the hands of politicians and lay administrators, the organized bar responded. Not all the members responded solely on the basis of professional protection, of course. In fact, many ABA leaders seemed motivated primarily by the desire to have the most vigorous possible representation of the poor and to preserve that representation from any threat, including those by lawyers, politicians, or budget-cutters. For them, the choice of professionalism as the rallying cry was tactical, for professional integrity or sanctity from lay competition can stir even conservative attorneys who are philosophically opposed to the whole idea of poverty law.

The use of legal professionalism by the supporters of a strong Legal Services program is similar to the strategy that liberals once used to sell foreign aid as Gardol against communism. Those concerned about international poverty consciously determined that it was worth it to crow a little about stemming the tide and put up with large amounts of military aid in order to protect their development programs. Now Lenzner and the poverty lawyers, concerned about domestic poverty, are committing themselves to a kind of professional xenophobia and to the high principles of the legal guild in order to protect a crucial program. There is no question that the goal—protecting Legal Services from political control—is worth while, or that professionalism may be the only way to rally the crusty ABA around such an electric idea. But it is also true that more professionalism is precisely what the public interest does not need from the organized bar. The legal profession is already overprotected, inflated, and puffy

—harboring for degreeholders many specialized functions that should be separated out, and claiming too much for the degree.

But most poverty lawyers apparently believe in their professional shield, and it is definitely useful in the current struggle over Legal Services.

On October 5, John D. Robb, chairman of the ABA Standing Committee on Legal Aid to the Indigent, wrote ABA President Edward L. Wright as follows, zeroing in on the professional issue:

> I regard regionalization as an extremely serious threat to the Legal Services program. Essentially, it will transfer the administration of the program and the enforcement of its professional standards from Terry Lenzner, the director of the OEO Legal Services Program in Washington, to ten regional OEO directors, eight of whom are laymen.

The National Advisory Committee to Legal Services, a bar group whose consultation with OEO is required by statute, met in Washington on September 11. A special subcommittee on regionalization was created to study the question, and the group produced a legally passionate attack on decentralization.

Rumsfeld's aides assert that the advisory committee is unrepresentative of the national bar, and they are probably right. In fact, they might well have a case for the proposition that the average American lawyer would like to see poverty law confined to the guild absurdity syndrome—in which nonlawyers would be totally banned from any position of control or authority over Legal Services in the name of professional integrity, and then the poverty lawyers restricted by the bar itself to those standardized service cases which any H & R Block trainee could handle expeditiously and to which professional standards are largely irrelevant. Certainly, many local bar associations have trampled all over the attorney-client relationship to hold Martin Millers and Tom Goldsmiths and other controversial upstarts in line.

But there is an alternative to this sort of disreputable opposition to Legal Services programs—Judicare. Having watched their medical brethren wash away fears of socialized medicine with Medicare and Medicaid money, many wise lawyers feel that they can copy the plan and have the government pay for private legal services delivered to the poor from the Law Building. Some lawyers have become enthralled with the analogy, and bar committees are currently studying systems of "legal check-ups," "comprehensive legal care," and "preventive law" for presentation to Uncle Sam. When the Legal Services program in Albuquerque announced under questioning that it would accept poor peoples' reasonable cases against the police department, the Albuquerque Bar Association persuaded the local united charities fund to withdraw its $25,000 contribution to Legal Services and set up a Judicare program—run, of course, by the local bar.

"John Robb is chairman of the ABA committee on legal aid and he unfortunately comes from Albuquerque," said attorney Charles Glass, who helped engineer the Judicare program. "He has never spoken for our bar association, which has repeatedly spoken against the Legal Services program. Our state bar is also in favor of Judicare overwhelmingly, and has sent resolutions to all New Mexico public officials. In fact, elections to the state bar often turn on that question." ("Yes, Judicare is a very live issue within the bar," sighed Robb.)

In the face of such internal schism, it took considerable courage for people like Robb to continue fighting for Legal Services. It was no longer like the good old days, or even the Murphy amendment days, when the ABA could work up nearly unanimous hoopla in favor of its program—feeling positively liberal and unthreatened by it. Judicare and the increasingly controversial nature of Legal Services put the national ABA leadership in danger of losing its decidedly unradical constituency.

But after Rumsfeld testified before a Senate hearing chaired by Senator Walter Mondale on October 7 and 9, things looked so bad that ABA President Wright got heavily into the fight. Rumsfeld told the senators that he had always intended the centralization of Legal Services to be "temporary," that decentralization was crucially different from regionalization, that he felt compelled to act not by Congress nor by the ABA nor by the President but by his own sincere belief in sending power back to the states, and that some sort of administrative change was in the wind but no decision had yet been made. The senators seemed puzzled by all this but definitely dissatisfied. Wright wrote Rumsfeld on October 16:

> On behalf of the American Bar Association and its Board of Governors, I urge you to reaffirm the independent status of

the Legal Services program at all levels of administration within the agency.

Pressures continued to build on regionalization across the election period—until Rumsfeld announced, on November 14, "I have decided not to regionalize the Legal Services program." This startling reversal of trend was trumpeted in a press release for the November 15 Sunday papers. While the press speculated about the reasons for the reversal in Rumsfeld's thinking, OLS employees analyzed the memorandum he sent out on the same day as his announcement, stating, "While I am not regionalizing Legal Services, I am instituting new administrative procedures." These guidelines were spelled out in six single-spaced pages of solid bureaucratese—whose significance lay in the repeated provision that if one of Carlucci's regional directors objected to anything about a Legal Services project in his region, he could now appeal the issue to Carlucci and Lenzner. These two would have to agree, or the decision would be made in the Director's office.

The OLS people calculated that they had been regionalized even as Rumsfeld was announcing that they were not. (Rumsfeld announced that the changes were merely administrative minutiae handed down in the constant search for "more effective coordination." Most reorganizations are announced with great fanfare in an attempt to convince the public that the government is making great strides toward the solution of a problem, when in fact the government has no idea what to do and reorganizes solely to appear vigorously on the move and to get more money. A few other reorganizations are announced as barely even news, simple coordinative adjustments—and that is usually when the heads roll and power shifts. This change was definitely one of the latter.)

Everybody concerned with Legal Services, of course, was up in arms about the November 14 guidelines. ABA President Wright came to Washington on Thursday, November 19, for an emergency conference with Rumsfeld about them, a meeting from which Rumsfeld excluded Lenzner and Frank Jones. (Apparently, Wright was unsuccessful, for Rumsfeld fired them the next day.)

So Terry Lenzner and Frank Jones have left the Office of Legal Services and are now lobbying and pleading and pressuring on the outside to save their program from regionalization. It seems fair to say that Lenzner inherited a relatively complacent Legal Services operation from "the previous Administration," full of projects that were little more than patronage plans for local bar associations. He took a program that was naturally improving and, with Rumsfeld's approval, pushed it—hard, very hard.

Legal Services will no longer be pushed like that, although Lenzner, the ABA, and Senator Mondale did engineer a repeal of the formal regionalization guidelines on December 14. There is no zeal in the program any more. It is no longer in favor at OEO, and it has too many bureaucratic vulnerabilities. "There are many ways to gut a program," said a staff member. And the Administration has determined to find one for Legal Services.

Arthur J. Reid, a forty-one-year-old black Republican from Cincinnati, came down from the General Counsel's office to take over Lenzner's job and absorb the repercussions of the "terminations." "God knows it's been hell," he lamented. "I'm right on the hotseat, and everybody thinks I had a hole in my head for coming down here." Reid's problems are complicated by the fact that Lenzner's staff considers him a kindly lightweight and an unassailable black figurehead who will preside over the demise of Legal Services or move on, depending on his orders.

Most people in the program foresee the regionalization of Legal Services—or some other form of its emasculation—and believe that such political control of the poverty lawyers would quickly restrict them to routine matters like divorce cases and garnishments and evictions and other nasty things that the right people have always expected happen to the poor. Rather than attacking poverty, these cases would remain its symbolic by-products, which must be tended efficiently like everything else. You have to feel pretty guilty about controlling the poverty lawyers like that—if you are afraid that the poor might zap you in the halls of justice. But most politicians would have it that way. They would, in short, administer poverty for a slight government subsidy, and simultaneously enjoy the budgetary fruits of administration.

The poverty lawyers were not just helping the poor. They were forcing responses from that great enveloping blanket known as administrative government, which warms all our problems. They were beginning to act almost like a fourth branch of power, kicking those huge agencies that murder equity and then bury the responsibility in a corridor somewhere while the PR men explain. Perhaps the thought of a single independent lawyer—totally unprogramed and uncoordinated—standing there and causing change on the basis of principle was too much for the politicans, who are lost in the blanket, too. They have a place there woven together, along with the old differences between liberal and Republican and Democrat and conservative. Everyone has a spot to protect. There is little support for the idea of that independent lawyer any more, for he is out of style. And if the powers keep the poverty lawyer from suing city hall or HUD or HEW or the police department, Legal Services will itself be incorporated into the blanket and become another program with problems to protect and jobs to keep by not gouging its neighbors. If the control of Legal Services is mailed out to the politicians and bureaucrats and special interests, one of the last best hopes and the best idea in the war on poverty will be absorbed into the great woolly fabric and wetted down. That is how it is.

The outcome of the scuffle is important to the poor and those who care about poverty or are paid to care about poverty, for the work of the poverty lawyers has been a rare, multifaceted success in the war on poverty. Legal aid is a profoundly conservative program, since the lawyers can do nothing for the poor without first convincing a judge of their case. They are impotent without written sanction from the robed men who have passed so many societal screenings for undignified quirks that the establishment itself must seem a little offbeat to them. And the lawyers in Legal Services have to accept these ground rules and the loftly courtroom atmosphere before they even begin. At the same time, Legal Services employees pontificate about professional standards, guard the attorney-client relationship from besmirchment at the hands of "lay" people, and call other law school graduates "Esquire" in all their letters.

Despite all these neutralities and the firm legal gaze back toward precedent, the poverty lawyers have been winning an extraordinary number of cases. Their successes have placed the squawking defendants—typically, landlords, government agencies, and corporations—in an awkward position. They must either accept the justice of the courtroom outcome produced by two well-represented adversaries contending before the law, or they must argue that the courts are biased in favor of the poor when the poor are represented and that justice is better served without poverty lawyers. Feeling a simultaneous need to uphold society's legal pillars and to avoid being hurt by them, most defendants sidestep the dilemma by charging the poverty lawyers with fomentation, character deformity, and grandstanding—in other words, by politicizing the legal question.

There is an additional element of the fight over Legal Services that makes the outcome important—the poverty lawyers have not only been the most effective of all the efforts in the war against poverty but they have also offered new hope in the general struggle against unresponsive, unaccountable bureaucracy. Faced with an inert government agency sitting expansively on a real problem that touches people's lives, a poverty lawyer could simply file suit for court-ordered relief from such illegal inaction—complete with heavy contempt sanctions for defendants who still failed to act. Thus, he could begin to control the bureaucracy—something that neither Congress nor the White House has been able to accomplish. He could independently make waves and cause change without going through mounds of red tape, establishing a new program, or building an unwieldy organization. He could make the bureaucracy abide by its own rules without having to become a bureaucrat himself, with the attendant risk of being absorbed. In this sense, Legal Services provides the freshest idea yet in the critical task of bludgeoning governmental institutions into responsiveness. Poverty lawyers have brought more than 100 suits against federal agencies and countless more against state and local governments. They are, therefore, controversial, but they are indeed potent weapons against both poverty and sleepy entanglements in government.

But what of Rumsfeld? Why did he, after earning wide respect for not dismantling OEO, part so unceremoniously with the Legal Services chief who accomplished precisely what Rumsfeld and President Nixon called upon him to do? Why did he, after building the Legal Services budget and repeatedly overriding gubernatorial vetoes of the program, move to gut the program so deviously?

Part of Rumsfeld's problem in dealing with the OLS staff flowed from the imperial flavor of his internal management. He seldom cultivated the feeling that *we've* got to sell our program to *those* people out there, and thus violated one of the first rules of bureaucracy. "What really made us angry was that he almost never acknowledged political pressures but tried to sell his plan on some twisted version of its merits," said Jones. "Rather than saying, 'Look, there is a political problem here and how can we solve it,' he would try to rationalize things on substance. Things got so bad that I would just sit in meetings and stare at Don when he started orating about poverty and why it urgently required that we re-fund Charlotte or reprimand Dallas or decentralize. He never had anyone around him who knew poverty. And I would just stare, knowing that his plan was plastered politics and that his oration was a fraud. And he knew that I knew. We never got along, actually."

One reason Rumsfeld gave less than a full boosting to OEO against its adversaries was that he concurrently held the positions of special assistant to the President with Cabinet rank, complete with a second-floor office in the West Wing of the White House. His allegiance was obviously divided—his programs were run out of OEO, but his *future* would be determined in the White House. There was a time when his function was to build a demonstrably good track record for his agency in order to dispel politically dangerous notions that the Administration would summarily dissolve antipoverty efforts. It was then that his sincerity and positive attitude about doing a good job for the poor was put to good use, and then that scores of prominent liberals could genuinely praise his efforts at OEO. (Among them, his wrestling friend Allard Lowenstein said in May, 1969, "I know he is interested, deeply interested, in doing something about poverty in this country. . . . He is intelligent, he has integrity, he is committed.") But then there came a time when OEO was no longer a real image problem and could be run as a holding operation, freeing Rumsfeld for more important affairs.

He has been on the move this year, securing a position in the 8:00 A.M. breakfast group with five of the President's closest White House advisers—Haldeman, Shultz, Ehrlichman, Finch, and Kissinger. For about two weeks this fall, Rumsfeld was designated Republican political coordinator for the 1970 elections. (He was, perhaps fortunately for him, replaced by Finch when objections were raised that it might be unseemly for the antipoverty director to manage a political campaign, especially the one planned by the Administration in 1970.) He even obtained one of the coveted White House videophones, which allowed him to gaze at the other lucky owners while consulting.

Things looked good for Donald Rumsfeld—young, bright, loyal, successful at OEO, and a Nixon supporter long before the nomination in 1968. It was highly unlikely that he would sacrifice his prospects at the White House for a measly Legal Services program. It was perhaps painful to make the opposite choice, but there were compensations.

This decision does not make Rumsfeld unusual in the slightest, for most people spend their whole lives working for smiles, grades, offices, certificates, awards, cheers, gifts, words, and votes of approval. And the fact is that all Rumsfeld's power and status and success depended on his receiving the approval of the President. Everything hangs on the chief's nod and his favor. As if driven by some neurotic cocklebur, most of official Washington locks its internal organs in place and positively drives for that high ground of the blessed, where the compliments are dispensed and people have so much attention paid to them.

In the political battles over the Legal Services program, Rumsfeld was obviously not going to adopt Lenzner's position and battle it out with the White House on behalf of his OEO subordinates. Nor could he even explain painfully that the nasty old White House politics must prevail over the clear justice of the OEO–Legal Services team. Rumsfeld became incapable of making these distinctions, for he had *absorbed* the Administration's politics to be more like them. In a sense, he had become Nixon to make sure he retained the chief's approval, and this made it much easier to fire Lenzner and Jones. It was required to retain voter approval. And it made sense for a Rumsfeld aide to say, "I don't know what Don will do now. He'll do what the President wants him to do."

On December 11, Nixon wanted Rumsfeld to move closer to him as a full-time Counselor to the President. (He is now head of the new Cost of Living Council.) And Frank Carlucci—Princeton, Harvard Business School, career Foreign Service Officer on leave from the State Department, arch-foe of Legal Services, and architect of re-regionalization—would also be rewarded. The President wanted him to be the new director of OEO. As the President said, he "has done an outstanding job in that particular position and I believe in promoting a man who has done such a job to the top spot."

Of course, there is no such thing as the top spot. Even the President is still pushing upward, seeking broader and more lasting approval.

Rumsfeld, for his part, made a prophet of Senator George McGovern, who had spoken on November 23 of the Lenzner-Jones firing:

> I would imagine that now that he has performed the Nixon Administration's dirty work, Mr. Rumsfeld will be rewarded with a chair closer to the President, as was Robert Finch after he performed the *coup de grâce* on James E. Allen, the then Commissioner of the Office of Education.

The timing of Rumsfeld's move was handy, as it removed him from OEO and out of congressional range for probings of his *coup de grâce* and regionalization. These current politics require delicate footwork and eager soul-selling, but you may get a videophone when you really arrive.

Since the firing of Lenzner and Jones, the Legal Services program has limped on—with support from the organized bar and senators like Mondale and Cranston saving it from near-extinction. As of late 1971, the transfer of the program from OEO to a public-private corporation is almost a certainty. The remaining issue is how much control the President will have over the corporation's board members. It is clear that he will have a great deal of control, although civil rights leaders are fighting a rear guard action to preserve as much independence as possible. The upshot of the whole struggle appears to be that Legal Services, like much of the civil rights movement, has been wound down—from a crusade to a commitment of some excitement to, finally, a holding action for embattled residual forces.

6 Terror in Bac Lieu

Jeffrey Record is a graduate student at the Johns Hopkins School of Advanced International Studies in Washington. His article describing the use of Cobra helicopter gunships in the Phantom Mission program, based on his experiences in Vietnam, was published in the *Washington Monthly* in April, 1971. It provoked an Army inquiry into the program and much comment.

"Bac Lieu," Record began his story, "is a small, out-of-the-way province at the southern end of the Mekong Delta. It rarely makes the 6:30 news."

Under the title "Maximizing Cobra Utilization," he continued:

> When I was there in 1968–69 with the American advisory team serving as the Assistant Province Adviser for Psychological Operations, there were no North Vietnamese troops in the province. What Viet Cong strength there was consisted largely of part-time village and hamlet guerrillas armed mostly with single-shot vintage German Mausers. They concentrated primarily on blowing up bridges with uncanny accuracy and mining the few passable roads. They were experts at placing booby traps, and the South Vietnamese soldiers obliged them by returning again and again to the same place, tripping the same wires with deadly consistency.
>
> Americans believed there were about 3,000 full-time, hard-core Viet Cong in Bac Lieu, or 1 per cent of the total population. Arrayed against this scanty enemy presence were over 20,000 well-armed men: elements of the 21st Division of the

Army of the Republic of Vietnam (ARVN), Regional Force companies, Popular Force companies, and the ubiquitous People's Self-Defense Force, a kind of local home guard. This vast military structure was supplemented by numerous Revolutionary Development Teams, the Provincial Police, the paramilitary Police Field Force, and the Provincial Reconnaissance Unit—an extortion and assassination team run directly by the CIA and composed mostly of criminals, deserters, and former Viet Cong.

On top of this overwhelming numerical superiority, the Vietnamese government possessed, as in every province in South Vietnam, complete control of the air through its American ally.

I arrived in Bac Lieu in August, 1968, and my first impressions were favorable. Both the Province Senior Adviser (the head of the American advisory team) and the Province Chief (the Vietnamese "governor" of the province) seemed acutely aware of the military and political dangers inherent in the indiscriminate use of firepower, particularly in a heavily populated province like Bac Lieu. The Province Chief had refused to permit B-52 strikes, and the Province Senior Adviser had repeatedly denied U.S. Navy requests to shell the province from offshore. He had also forbidden the use of .50 caliber machine guns, because their range and velocity made them too destructive.

Airpower in Bac Lieu was confined mainly to logistical support: the helicoptering of troops and ammunition to various outposts and the airlifting of critical supplies to hamlets inaccessible by road or canal. The only aircraft permanently stationed at Bac Lieu's small dirt airstrip were five or six light single-engine planes used for aerial observation. Airstrikes could be had, but only on request. Within thirty minutes of first contact with the enemy, American helicopter gunships and jet fighter-bombers would fly in from the large airbase at IV Corps military headquarters in Can Tho, several provinces away. They would bomb and strafe whatever targets were given them by the Bac Lieu Tactical Operations Center. Outside of actual support for ground combat operations, the only airstrikes ever called in were occasional sorties over the province's three small, and virtually unpopulated, free-fire zones.

This atmosphere of modest restraint soon changed, however. There had always, of course, been considerable resistance within the advisory team to any restrictions on the use of airpower. Although civilians and military men could be found on either side of the airpower debate, most of the opposition to restrictions came from the older officers, many close to retirement, for whom Vietnam provided their first and last chance to see real combat. Some found the idea of restraint incompatible with war. Others appeared troubled by the suggestion that military effectiveness was not commensurate with simply the amount of firepower at one's disposal. All the opponents of restraint seemed oblivious even to friendly argument. The moral argument, that unrestricted use of airpower would result in the unnecessary killing of many innocent civilians, ran into the simple reply that "war is hell." The political argument, that such indiscriminate destruction would serve only to generate more recruits for the Viet Cong, confronted the firm conviction that aerial terror would drive the rural population into government-controlled areas, thus denying the enemy his source of manpower. The military argument, that there were no targets in Bac Lieu of a size warranting massive airstrikes, was dismissed out of hand.

The supporters of unfettered airpower were understandably overjoyed when IV Corps headquarters announced in October that every province in the Delta would begin receiving helicopter gunships on a regular basis. Twice a week, each province (for Bac Lieu, Mondays and Thursdays) would get a "Phantom Mission" composed of two to three Cobra assault helicopters accompanied by an older Huey helicopter, which, as the "command-and-control" ship, would coordinate and direct the strikes. Since the missions were scheduled independently of any military operations in Bac Lieu, their aim was clearly not that of supporting troops on the ground. According to the operational memorandum, the purpose of the Phantom program was (1) to destroy enemy personnel and installations, (2) to interdict known and suspected enemy lines of communications, and, in general, (3) to harass and terrorize the Viet Cong.

Even more ominous than the open-ended language of the program's guidelines were the weapons themselves. The high-speed Cobra assault gunship is a "killer" helicopter—it carries only a gunner and a pilot. Its sole cargo is ammunition for its guns. Each Cobra is equipped with two rocket pods capable of handling fifty-two rockets and an electrically operated turret machine gun that spews out lead at a rate of 100 rounds per second. Many have built-in automatic grenade launchers that fire grenades as a machine gun fires bullets.

I have never been able to discover the origins of the Phantom program. Like many such programs in Vietnam, this one may have been dreamed up by a colonel at corps headquarters, far removed from Bac Lieu. The Cobras were late-model helicopters and were making their first appearance in large numbers in Vietnam. Apparently those assigned to the Delta were not being fully utilized. This made the helicopter program bureaucratically vulnerable, because "underutilized" capacity may be taken as a sign that the Phantom operation was either inefficient, unnecessary, or too large. To avoid program cuts, Phantom-supporters needed to cultivate allies and get the helicopters fully engaged—piling up what could be called indispensable achievements. The solution was simple: divide the use of the new gunships equally among all the provinces in the Delta. There was no evidence of an awareness at the corps level that some provinces might have greater need of Phantom missions than others, or that still others (in my opinion, Bac Lieu) could get along quite well without them. Nor, apparently, had any of the provincial advisory teams been asked for their opinions.

In spite of strong opposition from most of the civilians and some of the younger officers on the advisory team, the Province Senior Adviser accepted the program. Evidently he felt he could restrain the employment of the Cobras as he had the employment of other weapons. He failed to grasp that the the problem lay not in their *indiscriminate* use but in the very nature of the gunships themselves. *Any* use of Cobras in a densely populated province having only a small enemy presence would be indiscriminate. He had also learned from years of experience in Vietnam to take whatever was offered from on high—someday there might be a real need for Cobras in Bac Lieu. Perhaps more important was the heavy military pressure within the team for acceptance. By making a major concession on the Cobras, the Province Senior Adviser could extract concessions from the military on other divisive issues.

The results of the Phantom program were, at least in my mind, never in serious doubt. Having no real targets to shoot at, the Cobras would, immediately upon arrival in Bac Lieu, head for the free-fire zones, hoping to find what few Viet Cong there were in the province. The enemy quickly learned that Phantom strikes occurred only on Mondays and Thursdays and remained well hidden on those days. The Viet Cong appeared to have advance warning of even the few unscheduled missions.

Soon there were indications that the missions were no longer confining their destruction to the free-fire zones. Airstrikes had always been permitted outside the zones, but, until the advent of the Phantom program, they were severely restricted and closely monitored. In November, 1968, five people were blown to pieces in Vinh Chau district. One turned out to be a government agent; the others were identified as "friendlies." Although the incident was written off as one of those inevitable misfortunes of war, all five were carried on the enemy body count.

Shortly afterward, I began receiving disturbing reports from Viet Cong defectors and Americans who worked at the provincial hospital. Part of my job involved interviewing defectors. An increasing number of them recounted stories of rocket attacks on villages, strafings of farmers and water buffalo working the rice paddies, and machine-gunnings of sampans along the countless canals that interlace Bac Lieu. The attacks had three things in common: All occurred without warning, all took place outside the free-fire zones, and all were conducted by helicopter gunships. Americans at the hospital reported a growing number of peasants coming in from the rural areas wounded by rocket and grenade fragments. Most were women and children. Yet there had been a decrease in the level of ground combat during this same period.

I brought these facts to the attention of those at the Tactical Operations Center (TOC) who were most involved in the planning and coordination of the strikes. Their response was not unexpected: Other than the "accident" in Vinh Chau, there were no "reported" civilian casualties. The TOC was firmly convinced that the Cobras were killing only Viet Cong. When I asked the American Operations Officer how, several hundred feet above the ground and traveling at a speed of well over 100 miles an hour, anyone could be so certain of a target's identity, he replied: "We don't shoot individuals on the ground unless they run away when the Cobras approach. People that run must be Viet Cong. Why would they run unless they had something to hide?"

My worst suspicions were borne out when I began accompanying Phantom missions in December. I rode along in the command-and-control ship—ostensibly to drop leaflets—and observed the terror first hand. Returning from my first mission I witnessed the machine-gunning of an entire herd of water buffalo along with the six or seven buffalo boys who were tending the herd. No command had been given. The Cobras simply broke formation and began their deadly dives. Within seconds the still waters of the rice paddy in which the buffalo and their little friends had been resting was transformed into a bloody ooze littered with bits of mangled flesh. The dead boys, and the water buffalo, were added to the official body count of the Viet Cong. I was stunned. By the time I got back to the TOC, I was shaking uncontrollably in anger. I demanded—both as a human being and as Psychological Operations Adviser—severe punishment of the pilots. "But they're not under our command. Only Can Tho has jurisdiction" was the reply. What had started out as a program designed to hamper Viet Cong military operations had become an unmanageable and monstrous terror directed against the entire rural population.

There is not much left to tell. Incidents similar to the butchery of the buffalo boys and their buffalo continued unabated in the months that followed. On one occasion the Cobras, evidently not content with attacks on civilians, rocketed a government outpost (the pilots claimed the soldiers were shooting at them), wounding several soldiers but killing two women and three children. In April, a group of younger civilians on the team (myself included), supported by a young American major who was the senior officer assigned to the largest district in the province, submitted a lengthy memorandum to the Province Senior Adviser calling for the complete termination of the Phantom program in Bac Lieu. The memorandum was detailed, based on painstaking surveys of hospital patients and Viet Cong defectors. Their stories were cross-checked with the official logbook of Phantom strikes in Bac Lieu to make sure that the details of the horror were congruent with the dates and locations of the strikes.

The memorandum came too late. By April, the Province Senior Adviser and most of the officers on the team had become convinced that the Phantom program was indispensable to the defeat of the Viet Cong in Bac Lieu. They had become mesmerized by the familiar litany of aerial warfare in Vietnam: "Kills by air, sampans sunk, enemy structures destroyed." The Phantom program had increased by twofold the enemy body count demanded every month by the insatiable computers in Saigon.

I have been told the program is still being executed in Bac Lieu. I have also been told by the very same officers who supported the program—a program designed to destroy what few Viet Cong there were in the province—that enemy activity is now more intense than ever before. What happened in Bac Lieu has been repeated countless times throughout South Vietnam.

"Maximizing Cobra Utilization" elicited no great public clamor, but after its publication, Jeffrey Record was visited by officers of the Army's Criminal Division at Fort Meyer, Virginia. The officers were interested in evidence of specific incidents that might lead to the prosecution of helicopter pilots for killing noncombatants. Record supplied the information, but he did not—and still does not—expect any action. Moreover, he feels that the incidents were so widespread and common in Bac Lieu that it is difficult to distinguish between Cobra gunship policy and deviant behavior on the part of individual pilots. Record believes that the Phantom program itself should be the focus of any effort to stop the indiscriminate killing.

Of readers who reacted to the article, those who generally favored the war often contended that Record had overestimated the number of unwarranted deaths caused by the helicopters and that, in any case, the program could be "cleaned up" to make sure that Cobra victims were positively identified as enemy supporters. Some antiwar readers found the Record piece suspect, since it seemed to accept the basic objectives of the war; they disliked the implication that the Phantom program was bad primarily because it seemed "counterproductive" in the effort to pacify Bac Lieu for the Thieu-Ky regime in Saigon. These disagreements, on a matter of policy, indicate one difficulty that awaits a whistle-blower who singles out for criticism a specific situation or circumstance in a context that is itself a matter of controversy.

On a simpler, human level, however, judging from the letters the *Washington Monthly* received, readers who have been searching for clues as to how Americans can so casually kill innocent people found Record's bitter recollections of Bac Lieu very powerful.

7 Countering Intelligence

Patrick J. McGarvey was an intelligence officer with the Central Intelligence Agency and the Defense Intelligence Agency for a number of years. After leaving the latter, he wrote an alumnus whistle-blower's article for the *Washington Monthly*. Headed "DIA: Intelligence to Please," it appeared in July, 1970. Slightly condensed for reasons of space, it appears below:

> Among a multitude of examples of the Pentagon's proclivity for laboring mountainously and bringing forth mice, an instructive one is the Defense Intelligence Agency. DIA is responsible for providing the Secretary of Defense, and ultimately the President, with up-to-date facts about military matters of all kinds and with dispassionate assessments of what those facts portend. Presumably, it is because statesmen possess this crucial secret information that they can resolve so much more wisely than an uninformed man in the street such issues as, say, whether or not to send American soldiers into Cambodia. However, the assiduous cultivation by the diplomatic and military establishment of the presumption that it is on the basis of "having all the facts" that a President acts does not mean that this presumption has much basis in reality. Leaving aside the fascinating question of the extent to which any secret intelligence, as compared with political calculation or predilection or dogma, influences decisions, the secret intelligence dispensed by DIA is all too often of a quality that makes it more of a hindrance than a help to rational decision-making.

Two kinds of defects are pervasive in DIA—an outfit commonly referred to in the intelligence community as "the taxi squad" or "the country club" or "the old people's home." One, probably the less injurious of the two because it is so common a Washington phenomenon that most officials are bound to suspect it and try to compensate for it, is the tendency of any operating agency's evaluation arm to justify the agency's operations. Thus, DIA's reports about, for example, the amount of damage bombing the Ho Chi Minh trail inflicts and how much that damage limits Hanoi's capability to fight, are almost certain to be the highest possible guesses, not so much through slovenliness or mendacity as in accordance with natural bureaucratic law. Or, to cite another example, in determining whether or not the F-105 that the Chinese shot down in May, 1966, had really strayed into Chinese air space as the Chinese claimed, there were two basic sources of data: radar plots and the accounts of the pilots of the other planes in the mission. The radar plots, which had an impressive record of previous accuracy and no personal ax to grind, showed that the flight had flown well into Chinese territory. The returned pilots, who if they were human had some inclination to exonerate themselves, said the flight had done no such thing. DIA resolved this conflict in accordance with the natural law: It took the word of the pilots.

This kind of self-justification, which is by no means an exclusively military vice, may be absurd; but a good deal of the time its sheer blatancy insures that it won't be taken very seriously. Much harder to detect and guard against are the workings of DIA's policy of compromise and of blandness, of pleasing everybody and therefore of informing or edifying nobody. For example, during the early days of the bombing of North Vietnam, the Army, which was pushing for a big buildup of ground forces, wanted to show that North Vietnamese forces were pouring into the South at unprecedented rates. However, the Air Force's interest was to show that very few northern troops were getting through its barrage. In theory, DIA was set up to choose among such conflicting claims; in practice, it generally refuses to admit that a conflict exists and comes up with something like "Enemy infiltration continued at a rate higher than last month. However, the cumulative effect of U.S. bombing has seriously degraded his ability to mount a large-scale offensive"—never mind whether mounting a large-scale offensive was what the enemy had in mind. It is hard to imagine how such an evaluation could help produce anything but an intellectual miasma.

Figures are used to support any imaginable position, and often they are the same figures. I was treated to a fine example of number shuffling in early 1970. A knowledgeable source in DIA informed me that the personnel office was concerned about the attrition rate among the agency's college trainees and had called a conference of young men who had gone through the year-long training program to find out what was on their minds. At this session the personnel staffers disclosed that better than 60 per cent of college trainees in the past two years had quit. A confidential survey among those remaining indicated that 55 per cent were actively seeking employment elsewhere. When I published an article containing these figures, DIA quickly denied it. It stated that the figure was approximately 27 per cent, normal attrition rate in government and industry. Further digging revealed that in the "refining" of the original 60 per cent figure DIA had:

- diluted the issue by "broadening the data base" to take into account all hirings and resignations during the period, including clerks, messengers, and secretaries;
- included in the total only those who quit within twelve months of completion of training; resignations after twelve months were deemed immaterial to the question at hand;
- omitted from its new figures men who had resigned to return to school for graduate work;
- dropped from the total all men who had been drafted and failed to return to DIA after discharge;
- included in its new figures only those men who had resigned while in grades GS-7 and GS-9; higher-grade resignations were not included.

Perhaps one reason DIA is so proficient at compromise is that it is a product of compromise itself. It was formed in October, 1961, by former Secretary of Defense Robert S. McNamara in the hope that he would receive intelligence appraisals without service bias and to eliminate some of the duplication of intelligence activities in the Department of Defense (DOD). Pitched battles took place as the agency was formed. The Army was totally against it. It fought every suggestion, preferring to hang onto the responsibility of producing its own intelligence. The Navy, too, was against the formation of DIA but fought less vehemently. The Air Force seized the ball and ran with it. As a result, most of the top management jobs at the beginning went to blue-suiters. This brawling forced a crucial compromise between McNamara and the service intelligence staffs. To quiet the opposition, McNamara finally allowed the DIA to be placed under the supervision of the Joint Chiefs of Staff. In short, it was agreed that DIA would serve the civilians through the military rather than report to the Secretary through a (civilian) Assistant Secretary of Defense for Intelligence.

By charter, then, the DIA serves two masters—the JCS and the Secretary of Defense. What this entails with respect to the JCS is providing intelligence background and assessments for just about every decision paper that is put out by the chiefs, briefing the JCS daily on overnight developments and keeping them abreast whenever necessary of longer-range developments worldwide, and working closely with every component of the Joint Staff, the working arm of the JCS. If, for example, the J-5 Plans Staff is drafting a contingency planning paper on Africa, DIA must provide as much detail as is necessary, which could include data on coast and landing beaches; urban maps that show key installations; political, sociological, and economic studies of the countries involved; and, of course, in-depth assessments of the countries' military capabilities. In other areas, such as science and technology, DIA must keep the JCS informed on such technical breakthroughs as are achieved by any and all potential enemies around the world. If the J-3 Operations Staff wants to plan a bombing campaign, the DIA must come up with suitable lists of targets, pinpointing them on maps and assessing the likely effect the destruction of the targets would have on the target country—a service that reached new heights of absurdity, which will be touched on later, during the bombing of North Vietnam.

DIA's performance with respect to Vietnam should have proved the futility of a joint service approach to intelligence, and in fact Secretaries McNamara and Clark Clifford finally stopped paying any attention to DIA and went to the CIA for answers. From 1964–65, when U.S. involvement in Vietnam began to be considerable, until late 1966 or early 1967, the generals in Saigon worked to build up U.S. troop strength.

Therefore, they wanted every bit of evidence brought to the fore that could show that infiltration was increasing. DIA obliged and also emphasized in all reports the enemy's capability to recruit forces from the South Vietnamese population. In 1967, a second period began. The high priests of Saigon decided that we were "winning." Then the paramount interest became to show the enemy's reduced capability to recruit and a slowdown in infiltration due to our bombing. The tone and emphasis of reports from the field changed radically, and so did those put out by DIA.

It should not be concluded that anyone suppressed evidence. No one did. The military in Saigon sent all the facts back to Washington eventually. During the buildup period, infiltration data and recruitment data came in via General William C. Westmoreland's daily cablegram. Data from field contact with enemy units came amid the more mundane cables or by courier up to five weeks later. Cables from Westmoreland, of course, were given higher priority in Washington. When we started "winning," detailed reports highlighting "body counts" and statistics on how many villages were pacified were cabled with Westmoreland's signature; recruitment studies were pouched or cabled with the reports on the fluctuating price of rice. It was all a matter of emphasis.

During all this time, DIA was thoroughly enmeshed in the numbers game. It paid little or no attention to what Hanoi was saying on the radio, discounting it as propaganda. It made little effort to perceive the enemy's view of the war. It made little effort to reason out what the enemy's strategy was, why he believed he was winning, what he was saying publicly about how he was going to fight the war, or how the bombing was affecting his morale. It was too busy keeping up with the flow of numbers from Saigon.

As the air campaign crept northward, the Operations people on the Joint Staff wanted bigger and better targets. They didn't ask the intelligence people what was worth hitting or what a rational plan of attack might be. On the contrary, they demanded targets that a certain weapons system could attack. They had a TV-guided missile, and they wanted to use it. "Pick out a building for us to hit," they'd say. DIA could have told the JCS this was the wrong approach, but it played the game. It sent photo-interpreters scurrying to their scanners to find, say, a two- or three-story building in an area open to U.S. raids. If they saw no signs of military activity around the building they would dub it a "possible military storage area," a description that gave J-3 the right to go hunting.

The Operations staff's biggest hangup was over the prohibition on bombing the port of Haiphong. It refused to accept the judgment of the CIA that bombing the port wouldn't stop the flow of goods into North Vietnam. It refused to believe that the North Vietnamese man-packed arms across the Chinese border and imported little by sea. DIA, bowing to J-3's insistence, came up with a list of several hundred small, insignificant targets in and near Haiphong, listing them as crucial and suggesting that the cumulative effect of hitting all 200 or more barge and ferry landings, rail spurs, bridges, and road intersections would be the same as flattening Haiphong—again a triumph for the art of compromise and no doubt small comfort to the pilots shot down in that heavily defended area.

When the enemy buildup at Khe Sanh first became obvious, well before the Tet offensive of January, 1968, two DIA analysts who had been studying enemy tactics and strategy for four years sat down and wrote a paper that concluded that the enemy was planning a feint at Khe Sanh. They based this judgment on their interpretation of General Giap's fighting methods over the previous two years. They outlined a likely enemy course of action designed to draw American forces to the Khe Sanh area so that the populous coastal plains would be left thinly defended and concluded that perhaps it would be unwise to react to the Khe Sanh buildup. They presented the findings of their paper at a briefing, much to the amusement of all present. They suggested that the paper be cabled to Saigon as a DIA assessment of the situation and that the JCS be given the benefit of their thoughts. This, too, caused merriment among the assembled. "How could you possibly know more than General Westmoreland?" they were asked. Their boss, an Army colonel, finally got angry at their persistence and taped the paper to the wall beside his desk, claiming that the analysts had just stuck their professional reputations on the line, and adding he hoped they were wrong. The paper hung there until late in March, 1968, after the Tet offensive, which occurred largely on the coastal plain, and after the enemy ended the siege of Khe Sanh without ever assaulting it. Then it was taken down quietly. The colonel never mentioned the subject again. The JCS was never given a copy, and it was never cabled to Saigon.

The pressures on DIA to conform to the views of the military are hard to resist. Take a mechanism known as the National Intelligence Estimate (NIE), which is supposed to represent the best judgment of the intelligence community on a particular issue and is used by the President and his Cabinet in formulating policy. Everyone in the intelligence business has a chance to assert his point of view in these estimates, and it is here that DIA's role is crucial. DIA is well aware that many service judgments are biased and don't reflect reality. Its obligation, in those cases, is to assume its responsibility as arbiter among the services and establish a Defense position on the issue, and it works hard at doing just that. But strong pressures usually come in through the back door.

For one thing, there is something called the "Eyes Only" cable that is sent "back channel" and is severely restricted in dissemination. Usually no more than five people see it. I have seen "Eyes Only" cables come in from the U.S. Commanders in Honolulu and Saigon to the Director of DIA requesting that he give more than a passing consideration to the command viewpoint about this or that. The language is always moving. Such a cable is likely to start off complimenting the recipient for the fine job he is doing and then work in high-sounding phrases on the importance of the uniform. It then implies that the sender would like to see a particular judgment or set of figures changed to conform to the command view. It rarely offers any evidence to support this request. It is sure to close with a veiled threat that the recipient's career is in jeopardy if he doesn't play the game and "get on the team." Many estimates have been changed or reworded because of an "Eyes Only" cable from a field commander. In one instance the Air Force Chief of Intelligence called my boss at DIA about a nearly completed estimate on U.S. bombing in Laos. He told him that he was sending a team down to change the wording of the estimate and that my boss had better remember what color his uniform was. Of course it was the same as the general's blue. The team arrived, and, over the protests of the DIA analysts, a compromise was reached.

The classic example of command influence on intelligence matters occurred just after the Tet Offensive in January, 1968. In the early weeks of February the JCS insisted that the offensive was a total military defeat for the enemy—General Westmoreland told them so in his daily cables. DIA didn't agree with this interpretation, but it watered down every paper it wrote on this subject so that its position was impossible to determine. Then General Earle G. Wheeler went to Saigon and came back with Westmoreland's request for 206,000 troops to "clean up" the "defeated" enemy. Suddenly it was legitimate to say that the Tet offensive had really "set us back." Everybody on the service staffs, with DIA leading the pack, started writing gloomy estimates with uncustomary forthrightness and clarity.

Everyone connected with DIA is partially at fault for the agency's shortcomings. This includes the military who run it, the civilians who staff it, the Secretary of Defense, the JCS, and the individual service staffs. As far as the military men who manage the agency are concerned, their guilt or incompetence results simply from the fact that they are uniformed men with a parent service. Imagine, if you will, what the prospect of a tour with DIA looks like to a military officer. He knows or soon learns that he will be thrust into a position in which, on occasion, his professional judgment will diverge markedly from that of his parent service. He will be expected to defend a position that could enrage his Chief of Staff—but officers who do so more than once get to be known fast and are accorded an appropriate "reward" at a later date in terms of promotion and assignment. Consider also that a tour at DIA—normally two to three years—is very short when compared to a twenty- to thirty-year military career. And so most officers assigned to DIA go through a predictable pattern. They come on board as "hard-chargers," ready to set the world on fire. They stick to their principles through one or two scrapes. Then they become a little more circumspect, letting individual issues slide by and rationalizing that it wasn't a crunch question anyway. Finally, they resign themselves to "sweating out" their tours and playing every situation by ear. They avoid committing themselves or making decisions. They refuse to tackle the agency's long-term organizational ills because doing so would make too many waves.

The shortness of the tours of duty of the military managers of the agency (about nine-tenths of management jobs are filled by military officers) causes some long-term problems. These officers are interested largely in getting good performance out of staff while they are there, not in building up long-run staff or agency capabilities. They want to impress the general, let him know that he's running a "crackerjack" outfit. The general, of course, is largely occupied with current problems, so his subordinates gear up to service his needs. This has resulted over the years in the reduction of DIA's long-term research capability to near zero. More than 95 per cent of the effort expended in DIA on Vietnam, for example, is on current problems. Long-term study groups have been disbanded and the staff reassigned to the current problem area. Basic intelligence for detailed studies is simply not getting done or is whipped out with a weekend's furious overtime. The managers who choose to cut the long-term staff don't worry about the ultimate effect, because by the time it becomes evident they'll be off on other assignments.

Another problem is the "can do" attitude that prevails among the officer corps. It is unthinkable for an officer to tell his superior that he cannot complete a task. It is a form of heresy. Officers accept a requirement for four or six extra hours work a day when they know their staff already puts in twelve- or fourteen-hour days. Rarely, if ever, does anyone say no, or point out that certain jobs take time, "Yes, Sir, can do!" is all that is heard. The result is an attitude among DIA staff members that is captured in their motto, "If you want it real bad, you're gonna get it real bad."

There is the age-old military problem of "time in grade"—the tradition that confers genius-like powers on the man who's been around the longest. The impact that this practice has on the efficient functioning of DIA can be illustrated by the fact that I had nine bosses within two years and that each of the first eight was unseated because someone with more time in grade came along. The game of musical chairs goes on constantly. One Army colonel had been the Commander of the Special Forces in South Vietnam before he was assigned to DIA. He came into the Vietnam division and was contributing tremendously until another colonel with more time in grade came along. So they transferred the Special Forces colonel to the Soviet division and assigned the new colonel to the Vietnam division. The new colonel was a graduate of the Army's Foreign Area Specialist Training program in Czech affairs.

Then there is the civilian staff. It is second rate, particularly at the middle and upper levels. The military who run the place have made it that way. They have consistently shown over the years that there's no room in DIA for truly capable civilians. They have discouraged original thought, drained the civilian staff of initiative, and inculcated them with the "don't make waves" approach to everything. Very few civilians hold down management slots in DIA, but that doesn't mean they are without influence. Throughout the agency there are civilian deputies at most levels of command. They form an infrastructure that wields a great deal of influence in the day-to-day operation of the organization. The problem is that the ones who have survived that long in the bureaucracy are thoroughly bureaucratized. They are the ones who advise a brash lieutenant colonel to "soften his judgment," "temper his language," and "play the game." Their strength, in many cases, comes from their detailed familiarity with the inner workings of the complicated JCS paper mill. They know when to delay a paper, when to react quickly to one, how to insure that it gets through, and, most importantly, how and where to find out exactly what the general wants the paper to say. They then set out to insure that the general's wishes are translated verbatim into the final product, even if those wishes conflict with the evidence on hand or the views of knowledgeable analysts.

Finally, there are half-breed civilians at DIA—retired military officers. These men are generally capable in their areas of job experience, but two factors virtually negate their experience and job skill. The first, and more important, is the fact that they are retired and looking for an easy deal. Their fighting days are over, and they want to take it easy. They never make waves. They simply do what is asked of them. The other factor is simply that they are heavily biased in favor of the military, and they color all of their judgments with this bias. Their attitudes and actions also have a definite influence on the civilians in the agency. For one thing they are hired at the middle grades and clog up the promotion cycle for the younger men. They also have an "in" with the military managers and can frequently be seen on the fairways and greens of the Army-Navy Country Club. Somehow they are always the ones to get the trips abroad.

As far as I can see, the only way to extricate DIA from this morass is to take it altogether out of military hands. There should be an Assistant Secretary of Defense for Intelligence, a civilian. The line of command within the agency should be staffed by civilians—though not those now present, who are too far down the bureaucratic path for salvation. In the think-tanks around the country, in the universities, and in other areas of government, there is a pool of very capable men who could enable DIA to meet its enormous responsibilities. With civilians in the management positions, the chances that service bias would overwhelm, distort, or avoid intelligence judgments would be considerably less. Military men can play an important role in DIA, but not in the management of the agency. In substantive areas dealing with foreign military capabilities, the expertise of U.S. infantrymen or armor specialists, for example, can be put to good use.

Any prediction for the future of DIA has to be grim. One recent glimmer of hope (now fading) came when Secretary Laird directed his assistant for administration, Robert L. Froehlke, to take a hard look at Defense intelligence activities. However, it seems that Froehlke has fallen prey to the military briefings that he was given at DIA. He has set up an office to "coordinate" all DOD intelligence activities—and if there is one thing the DOD can do without, it is another office to coordinate things. DIA probably will grow larger, less productive, and more expensive as time goes on, coordination to the contrary notwithstanding. It will probably continue to drop the ball in emergencies like the Tet offensive. DIA will doubtless continue to supply the nation's decision-makers with evaluations that do them little good and potentially much harm. One can only hope that the decision-makers pay little attention to what DIA tells them.

McGarvey's article steered much too close to the inner workings of the Defense Department and the culture of its bureaucracy to be of great interest to the public. His observations about the way DIA produces self-serving intelligence for the parent military services were hardly likely to propel the antiwar movement in new directions. Neither would they be of comfort to the victims of the bombing strikes around Haiphong he mentions—strikes that were justified by DIA intelligence, which was in turn tailored to the wishes of the Air Force and the Joint Chiefs of Staff.

Although there has not been great pressure from outside the Pentagon to reform DIA, Secretary of Defense Melvin G. Laird has continued to push for a reorganization that would make the agency a civilian operation reporting directly to him through a civilian, not a military, director. According to the McGarvey analysis, such a move would be in the Defense Secretary's self-interest, since he has to take political responsibility for decisions made partly on the basis of DIA intelligence, and he has been stung by the little twists that the services manage to add to the reports. In the fall of 1971, the *Washington Post* reported that Secretary Laird was still trying to take advantage of President Nixon's "Second American Revolution" government reorganization plans to install a civilian Assistant Secretary of Defense to head DIA. Such an effort is far from guaranteed to succeed, because the services will continue to fight for their "input" to intelligence estimates—to add a military filter to the lens before the Secretary of Defense squints through the glass. Thus far, the services have been effective in opposing the "demilitarization" of DIA.

Nevertheless, Laird's ongoing attempt to wrest control of DIA from the services shows that, on rare occasions, a whistle-blower's position can have powerful supporters within the government—especially from insiders who are rivals of those who are the whistle-blower's target.

8 Flim-Flam, Double-Talk, and Hustle

James A. Kalish, a Peace Corps official, was a Washington-based adviser to the federal and various local governments on urban planning, management, and poverty programs. He made a lot of people in his line of business mad in November, 1969, when the *Washington Monthly* published his revelations about "The Urban-Problems Industry."

"In 1830," Kalish wrote, "the Secretary of the Treasury contracted with the Franklin Institute in Philadelphia for a study of boiler explosions. The government has been buying studies ever since. In fiscal 1969, it bought $13.5 billion worth. As in every year for a generation, the subject of most of these studies was either making war or exploring space—two activities about which, if expenditure of public funds is a reliable indicator of intensity of public interest, the American people have a curiosity that is not only insatiable but almost exclusive."

However, he continued:

> there is a field, if such soggy terrain can be called a field, that for ten years or thereabouts has been making small but steady gains on defense and space as a suitable seed-bed for governmental research and development money: urban problems, which means, to cite the titles of a handful of recent studies American taxpayers have bought: *Delivery and Financing of Health Services to the Poor; Economic Analysis*

of the Northeast Corridor Transportation Alternative; The Economy of Harlem; Cost of Negative Income Tax Plans in Vermont; Ideological Foundations for Negro Action: A Comparative Analysis of Militant and Non-Militant Views of the Los Angeles Riot; and *Cooperative Trusting Behavior as a Function of Ethnic Group Similarity, Dissimilarity, and Delayed Reward in a Two-Person Game.*

In short, an urban problem is anything that has happened, is happening, could happen, or should happen in a city, a suburb, or a metropolitan area. In addition, it is sometimes something that hasn't happened, isn't happening, couldn't happen, and shouldn't happen in a city, a suburb, a metropolitan area, or anywhere else, like, say, *Cooperative Behavior as a Function of Group Similarity in a Two-Person Game.* Compared with studying military problems, studying urban problems is a small industry and doubtless always will be. (Everybody knows how much less pressing they are than military problems, and how much easier to solve.) There is no way of calculating precisely how big, in dollar terms, the urban-problems industry is, but it is safe to guess that it receives something like half a billion dollars of federal money a year—$2.25 per citizen. This would be a small price to pay for the solution of even one urban problem. But it is a big price for the performance the urban-problems industry actually delivers.

What the industry is supposed to deliver, according to the claims it makes to the world and the contractual promises it makes to the government, is expert advice about the policies the government should pursue in dealing with urban problems, the resources it should allocate to guarantee that it is able to pursue those policies, and the technical measures it should take to make sure that those resources are used effectively and economically. Clearly the government needs such advice. Urban problems are complicated, and many of the top-level bureaucrats charged with dealing with them, including some of the most competent, owe their positions to their administrative, not their technical, skill. Moreover, problems of the size and scope of crime and traffic and education and pollution and housing cannot be solved by the government alone; solving any one requires the participation of the public. An urban-problems industry could be—indeed should be—the public's technical arm in this endeavor. When such an industry takes advantage of the government's need for it by double-talking, by flim-flamming, by feathering its own nest —which is what the urban-problems industry does fairly consistently today—it does more than fail to solve urban problems; it actively impedes their solution.

It is reasonable to speak of the urban-problems industry and the military-problems industry in one breath because, intellectually and spiritually—and to a large degree physically as well—the former is, in the characteristically pseudoscientific trade metaphor, a "spinoff" from the latter. If a career systems analyst, which is what many of the most prestigious and prosperous urbanists are, is more than thirty-five years old, it is likely that he got his start in military research. Indeed, many of the officials who oversee the research and development programs of such departments as Housing and Urban Development and Health, Education, and Welfare spun into their jobs from the Pentagon. These men started emigrating from military work in the late Eisenhower, or maybe early Kennedy, years. Americans had stopped fighting in Korea and hadn't quite started in Vietnam, and, as a result, military research was in a temporary slump or, in the argot, had "unused capability"—and everyone knows how much nature abhors an unused capability. At the same time, there was the coming of age of the computer, which, with its ability to arrange, disarrange, and rearrange millions of pieces of information simultaneously, tends to give its operator a feeling that the solution to any problem in the world lurks somewhere in the circuitry and shouldn't be too hard to locate. With the announcement of Lyndon Johnson's Great Society, and especially with the attempt to create that Great Society by imposing the Pentagon's Planning, Programing, and Budgeting System on civilian departments, the urban-problems industry, already growing apace, experienced its finest hour. PPBS, with its "hierarchies of goals and values," its guesses about what will happen five years from now, its assumption that all phenomena can be reduced to numbers and all numbers can be arranged in systems, is something that flusters assistant secretaries and thereby makes consultants rich.

The fact that the urban-problems industry has such a strong and direct military heritage does much to explain why it deals with urban problems as it does. The mental set that successfully creates missile delivery systems is not suitable for creating livable cities. It is the mental set that, in deference to cost effectiveness, puts freeways through slums and parks. It produces, in a study of mass transportation, a sentence like "Comfort is a complexly distributed random variable," which, in the doubtful event that it means anything, means that since you can't quantify comfort, you might as well forget about it and leave the strap-hangers with their elbows in each other's ribs. And it is the mental set that produces study after study whose principal purpose is to lead to study after study or, for that matter, to create a market for the studier's management services or hardware.

A look at the personnel of the urban-problems industry will confirm the justice of this last assertion. The principal product of a major part of the industry is one or another thing that studying urban problems can help sell. Just about every large manufacturing corporation, insurance firm, utility, and transportation organization in the land has a division or a subsidiary active in the field. Philco-Ford has its Tech-Rep Division, Xerox has its Basic Systems Inc., Time-Life and General Electric have teamed up to form General Learning Corporation. Lockheed and North American Aviation operate consultant firms that sell advice to airport authorities and transportation agencies. Travelers Insurance developed so much computer and systems capability for its own use that it now has overcapacity and excess manpower to sell to villages and towns in New England. Peat, Marwick, Mitchell, and Company, one of the country's largest certified accountant firms, uses its many accounting offices across the country to help get work for its urban-problems entry, Peat, Marwick, and Livingston. Management firms like Booz, Allen, and Hamilton and McKinsey and Company work on urban problems. AVCO and Litton Industries operated Job Corps camps where they were able to test programed learning techniques they were planning to sell throughout the country later on. And perhaps the most profitable of all are the giant think tanks that study anything or everything—like General Gavin's Arthur D. Little, Inc., and Herman Kahn's Hudson Institute. There are even conglomerates. Planning Research Corporation, a "professional service organization engaged in total systems analysis," has acquired a string of specialized consulting firms so that, in the words of PRC's brochure, "Multidiscipline teams can be assembled . . . to attack and resolve complex urban problems." PRC is one of several giant consulting firms listed on the New York Stock Exchange. Its 1968 profits were $2.8 million on $57 million of sales.

On the "nonprofit" side of the industry, perhaps the best known outfit is the MIT-Harvard Joint Urban Studies Program, which used to be headed by Daniel Patrick Moynihan and now is headed by the former Under Secretary of the Department of Housing and Urban Development, Robert C. Wood. Big ex-government names are a staple of the industry: General Gavin at Arthur D. Little; Francis Keppel, erstwhile Commissioner of Education, at General Learning; and Stewart Udall, chairman of the board of The Overview Group, which specializes in environmental problems. There are several dozen research centers constructed on the Harvard-MIT model. And of course hundreds, perhaps thousands, of academics are free-lance urban specialists who work directly for the government or for firms carrying out government contracts for per-diem stipends ranging from $100 (the government maximum) to $300 a day. The academics are not necessarily inspired by motives different from those that make the profit-making firms run. One veteran campus urbanist has said, "You need the federal loot to do the research to do the book to get the loot."

Then there are over fifty "not-for-profit" corporations originally created by the Defense Department as independent institutions that could provide services for a government agency without depending on the annual authorization and appropriation cycle of that agency. By now most of them have moved far off their original turf and in many ways operate much like high-powered private consultant firms. The most famous, RAND, has a contract with New York City to study police and fire department problems, a contract that has been renewed or extended several times. The Institute for Defense Analyses is trying to establish a reputation for expertise about crime. The Stanford Research Institute, Battelle Memorial Institute, and the Mid-West Research Institute are other big not-for-profit corporations battling for urban contracts.

One last curious form of nonprofit urban consultant is the professional association that presumably exists solely for the purpose of serving its membership. The National Association of County Officials and the American Institute of Planners, among many others, have set up subsidiaries to bid for and undertake government contracts, sometimes at the urging of the government. The National Association of Public Administration calls its consultant arm the National Academy of Public Administration and has contracted for work with such agencies as HUD, the Port of New York Authority, HEW, the City of Cleveland, and the Council of Library Resources.

As the foregoing paragraphs suggest, competition for government contracts to study urban problems is fierce. For one thing, of course, it can be a lucrative business, either directly or indirectly. For another, in the intellectual community—on whose fringes, at least, most consultants hover—concern with urban problems is a way of showing how public-spirited you are. But perhaps the biggest reason is that studying urban problems is a wide-open game. Anybody can play. There literally are no standards of experience or expertise or performance or, especially, ethics. Since few urban problems ever have been solved, few of the people who let out contracts know what a solution looks like, much less how to arrive at one. Granted that it is in the nature of research that much of it leads nowhere, still it is hard to understand why the taxpayers should have paid for *Inter-Urban Residential Mobility in Seattle as It Relates to Poverty and OEO Programs*, at least if the summary its authors wrote is accurate:

> The analysis in the report demonstrates that the patterns of residency change of poverty families in the central area of Seattle differ vastly from all other segments of the Seattle population. . . . The key variable of difference appears to be Negro families versus white. Thus, based on the restrictive channels of movement, the high degree of rental property, and the apparent inability of Negroes in the ghetto to participate in the normal choice in housing, some new approach is required. 155 pages.

Some new approach surely is required when a team of professors gets paid for giving the government the astonishing news that Negroes in the ghetto have an "apparent inability . . . to participate in the normal choice of housing." No wonder almost anybody feels he has a decent chance to get a contract. No wonder hundreds of new firms and organizations are created every year to "solve" the urban crisis—and that many of them fold or sell out to one of the giants before the year is up. They use a gamut of tactics in their efforts to survive. A favorite one, for whatever good it does, is to devise a presumably catchy firm name, preferably by making a goulash of such words as "research," "system," "dynamics," "technical," and others of the ilk: Systemetrics, Information Dynamics Corporation, Opportunities Systems, Inc., Decision Research Corporation, Consultec, Techumanics.

A more effective business-getter than playing word games on the letterhead is finding a black partner or associate. In the last few years there has been a desperate search by the urban-problems industry for black employees, and, more recently, for Chicanos. The old-line defense and management firms have traditionally been all-white operations. However, in many urban situations a firm simply must have black employees even to be considered for a contract; sometimes just the presence of a black face during the bidding process will do, even though it is never seen again, there being other bidding sessions to attend.

The way contracts are obtained tells a lot about the urban-problems industry. In theory, the process works something like this: When a government agency thinks it needs technical assistance in dealing with some aspect of poverty, urban growth, housing, education, crime, or what have you, it calls for what is loosely termed a study (or, in the trade, a comprehensive plan, a cost-benefit analysis, a project design, a project evaluation, or an information and data system). No government agency has, or could have, on its permanent payroll all the different kinds of experts whose services it occasionally needs. What the agency does is insert a Request for Proposal (RFP) in the *Commerce Business Daily*, a journal whose principal function is to broadcast the government's request for bids. Those interested in a specific RFP attend a pre-bidders' conference at which agency officials describe their project and prospective bidders size up their prospective competition. Each firm then prepares and submits a proposal. The agency reviews the proposals, using either a panel of outside experts or a group of agency employees. Then, presumably, the best proposal from the best firm is chosen.

That, to say the least, is an oversimplification. The process is seldom as effective or as fair in practice as it is in theory. Leaving aside the occasional instances where officials are given kickbacks, or campaign contributions, or football season tickets, or promises of future employment, the competition still is not always competitive. The highest level of management in the urban-problems industry is usually responsible for sales, and its techniques are powerful. Friends, casual acquaintances, and former colleagues in government are systematically lunched and quizzed for the inside story on who needs what when. At the same time, a firm tries to develop a reputation as a "good guy," willing to help out this time without getting paid for it. Presentations ("dog and pony shows") are carefully prepared for prospective clients. Advertising as such is taboo in the industry, but you can buy part of a page in a professional journal or a "public message" ad in *Time* or *Fortune* or send out embossed cards announcing a new vice president of the firm. The industry is careful to watch for new legislation and for changes in department administrative procedures, as well as for the comings and goings of key government personnel who might turn out to be customers. Washington is a major focal point for all this marketing activity, and most of the large firms have either an office there or a paid representative.

Under these circumstances, agencies and individual government officials are bound to have favorites who are selected for contracts regardless of the quality of their proposals. Sometimes the total process is a sham. Firms are "wired in" to a contract before the competition even begins and go through the motions of competing only to meet regulations. The city planning firm of Candeub and Fleissig "owns" many of the small towns in New Jersey. Alan Voorhees and Wilber Smith, two of the country's largest transportation planning firms, are said to be "owned" by the U.S. Bureau of Public Roads, because they always follow its wishes when working for state and local highway departments. McKinsey and Company and Booz, Allen, and Hamilton have been known to act as organizational hatchet men for newly appointed administrators faced with a hostile second-level bureaucracy.

There are also ways of getting government contracts without even pretending to go through the competitive process. A firm or institution can be given a "sole source" contract on the grounds that no one else can possibly do the work under the circumstances. Grants, as distinct from contracts, can be awarded to nonprofit organizations without going through any bidding process. Grants also go through quite a different in-agency review process, which can avoid, if necessary, a bureaucratic bottleneck or a difference of opinion on the merits of the project. An agency can require potential bidders to submit a pre-proposal "capability" package and then go through a competitive process limited to the few firms adjudged capable. An agency sometimes solicits a consultant friend to submit an "unsolicited" proposal for funding, on the assumption that he will receive the contract on a "sole source" basis. Occasionally this is a risky procedure; unsolicited ideas have been stolen from the writers and handed over for execution to rival firms, favorites of this or that agency. It is not unusual for a federal employee to ask a consultant friend to prepare the Request for Proposal itself.

Even when the competition is legitimate, agencies find it difficult to distinguish between good proposals and bad. Few proposal-writers can say something intelligent about every subject they write about, and so most proposals talk in generalities, using jargon that can be, and sometimes is, used interchangeably among proposals. Consultants are masters at parroting back the RFP in only slightly different words, and they are fond of describing the obvious in elaborate detail. As one veteran put it, "Use lots of vague phrasing; you get caught later if you are too clear on what you mean."

In accordance with this sound advice, proposal-writers have developed an amazingly useless vocabulary. Etymologically, its roots trace to early McNamaran and to the nonsense words of virtually every discipline. Such terms as "delivery systems," "interface," "stochastic," "meaningful analysis," "empirical," "heuristic," "feasibility," "time frames," "indicators," "decision flows," and "alternative system models" roll onward through the proposals. A proposal to OEO for an automated data system to keep track of civil-rights progress indicated concern for blacks and Mexican Americans by using this language:

> The initial step in developing alternative system models will be to use the analysis of existing and proposed systems as the basis for constructing several different designs for each system component. These components include system objectives, data inputs, collection mechanisms, processing procedures, and utilization patterns.

The paragraph could just as well have been talking about missile systems, and indeed may have been when it was first written, for plagiarism is an everyday phenomenon in the industry. Whole sections of federal documents are blatantly reproduced and pawned off as original work. Many reports are simply rewritten versions of previously prepared materials, ideas, and recommendations, which may or may not fit the situation at hand. Parts of studies prepared by a consultant under contract to the Economic Development Administration have been used and paid for again recently under another contract with the Department of Housing and Urban Development. Consultants get paid in one community to design a shopping center or prepare a land-use zoning code and get paid again in another community for using essentially the same plan. It is not much of an exaggeration to say that all some consultants do is change a few numbers, insert the name of the client, and put in a different letter of introduction—and the report is finished. Several of the larger firms automate this process by using computerized memory typewriters to store up paragraphs, tables, and charts to be later spit out at the touch of a button and inserted into a new report.

A medium-size research or evaluation contract from HUD or HEW is worth something like $100,000. It is not unusual for seventy-five separate firms to take an active interest in such a contract, with fifty delivering formal proposals to the agency. A proposal takes from ten to twenty man-days to prepare and costs from $3,000 to $5,000; consequently, the total dollar cost of the proposals for a contract can easily exceed the value of the contract. This is really a taxpayer's expense, because the firms that incur it are sure to include it as part of overhead costs next time they are awarded contracts. In addition, much government staff time, and therefore money, is spent in reviewing proposals, deciding on the winner, and negotiating contract details.

What the government gets for this $100,000-plus is some manpower and presumably some know-how. One hundred thousand dollars will buy the time of perhaps three or four professional urbanists for the equivalent of one year. There are different ways of calculating this figure, but it generally comes out to be two and a half times the direct salary of the professionals the consultant says will work on the project. The time of a $10,000-a-year man, who is the most inexperienced and inexpert man a firm is likely to have, will cost the government $25,000 per year, if he works a full year. Project directors, who earn at least $20,000 and usually much more, cost the government at the rate of $50,000 per year and up. Charge rates of $30 and $40 per hour for supervisory and management-level personnel are common.

These last figures include a factor for overhead, or "burden" as it is called in the industry, to pay for secretarial services, rent, equipment, and printing and to provide profits for the firm. This income, applied to overhead, also pays the staff for the time it is not working on a contract, time usually spent in looking for more work and preparing new proposals. The objective of the company is to keep this "down-time," time spent not working on a contract, to a minimum. Progress is measured by the number of hours the staff has clocked in on a project, rather than by the quality of the work. When the hours of work originally assigned to a contract are used up, the consultant wants to be able to redirect his attention and his staff to other income-producing activities. The faster a study is submitted, the more profits there are. It is not a system that encourages quality: A conscientious firm can easily become a bankrupt one.

Government has the power to change the system, if for no other reason than that it pays the bills. The federal government has shown no interest in even modifying the system, although many individual employees who have been involved are personally concerned and disgusted. Nobody even knows for sure how much money the government gives the urban-problems industry, although the National Science Foundation keeps copious data on other kinds of government research. One clue, a very rough one, is the amount of money contracted out for research development by agencies concerned with the urban problems: HUD, $46 million; Office of Education, $131 million; Economic Development Agency, $17 million; OEO, $48 million; Department of Transportation, $411 million—much of which pays for demonstration projects. In addition, some small but unknown fraction of the $16.7 billion in grants-in-aid that the federal government gave state and local governments last year was reawarded to the urban-problems industry. This money never shows up in the federal budget as being contracted out to private industry. For example, HUD's 701 program, the major source of general planning money for cities and counties, had 45 per cent of its $45 million last year forwarded to private consultants, even though one of the program's objectives is to increase the in-house staff capability of local government. Moreover, the American Society of Consulting Planners, an organization representing a few of the country's planning firms, is currently lobbying strenuously to ensure by law that the objective of the 701 program is abolished. Senate Bill S. 2699 was introduced this fall by Senator Wallace F. Bennett (R-Utah) as a private bill prepared by this group of consulting planners. It amends sections 701 and 702 of the Housing Act of 1954 that prohibit an areawide planning agency from providing assistance to a local government. Instead, technical studies would have to be contracted to private firms. The passage of this bill would be a body blow to the current struggling effort by states and others to improve the internal capability of local governments to think and act on their own.

The government job of monitoring a contract during its life is seldom performed very diligently. Periodic written reports and an occasional review meeting in the offices of the agency are usually the extent of such monitoring. Site visits are discouraged, and often the inexperienced government project monitor has relatively little idea of what is going on except for what he reads in the final report. When the written materials do arrive, there are few readers who are equipped to understand the technical aspects of the work. Basic assumptions and technical computations are often left out of a report; thus even the few available, knowledgeable government reviewers have difficulty understanding how the conclusions were arrived at.

After final reports are submitted, many of the concerned parties never get a chance to look at them. The required twenty-five or fifty copies are quickly distributed to the files, and the 200-word precis are inserted into the computerized but little-used government research data banks. Only occasionally do such reports find themselves translated into a professional journal article or, under contract from the consultant firms, commercially distributed through "specialty" publishing houses such as Community Services, Inc., of Washington. Six months later, if you somehow find out about a $100,000 study and ask for a copy of it, you are told to come up and use the file copy, if it can be found.

From time to time and for various reasons, reports disappear and the public that paid for them never gets a chance to read them. This can happen when the agency gets an answer it does not like, or when a study has unearthed a situation that is politically threatening to the agency. Restrictions are written into most consultant contracts stating that the report and all that went into it are the property of the funding agency and that the consultant cannot release the documents without prior approval. There are good reasons for treating a report as "executive confidential" for a period of time. Reports can include highly controversial recommendations, or they can include inaccuracies and misstatements, which must be corrected before the government gives any public indication of accepting the validity of the recommendations. This confidentiality clause, however, sometimes is used simply to kill a report. The Public Disclosure Act, which isn't very helpful to begin with, cannot help at all when the public does not know that a document exists.

In 1968, HUD contracted with a consultant to work with an Indian reservation to develop a "model cities" type of program. The initial background report by the consultant described all sorts of irregularities and government program redundancies and made some imaginative suggestions about coping with the situation, including many that would have forced major changes in the operation of the Bureau of Indian Affairs. With BIA's help, a tribal election was held, the reservation administration was changed, and the consultant was kicked off the reservation. To avoid further interagency quarrels, HUD confiscated all the copies of the report, even though many HUD officials believed the accusations to be accurate. The public never has been allowed to read the report. Even the staff director of the Joint Economic Committee, who was interested in manpower training programs for Indians, found it difficult to get a copy.

The trouble is that a consultant must serve several masters at the same time, and in so doing he all too often serves none of them adequately. Beyond working to further his personal interests and the interests of his organization or institution, he must balance the demands of the contract funding agency against a professional responsibility to come to impartial conclusions, even though that agency gets hurt in the process. There comes a time in almost every contract when these demands come into conflict.

According to one viewpoint—the bureaucrat's—when a consultant firm signs a contract with a government agency, its loyalty should be totally committed to that agency. All data, insights, rumors, inside information, and opinions should be turned over to the agency, and, if the client chooses to alter the consultant's work or change his recommendations, that is his right. In return the consultant gets paid and gets another contract.

The alternative view is that the consultant is first and foremost responsible for the professional work laid out for him in the contract. He is charged with solving problems, with "telling it like it is." If the hand that feeds him is part of the problem, the consultant must not hesitate to bite it. If the program is inadequate or corrupt and the planning requirements ludicrous, then the consultant should say so. Whether he should even take on work that he believes is worthless is a problem with which he and his conscience must struggle.

These conflicting pressures on the consultant's loyalties have impaled the industry on a dilemma from which it has not been able to lift itself on its own power. Somebody outside the industry must do the job. So far, "concerned" foundations and organizations—The Urban Institute, Urban America, the Ford Foundation, the General Accounting Office, the Senate Governmental Operations Committee, the Department of Housing and Urban Development—have all backed away from funding any inquiry into the industry. They have said that it is not within their mandate or that they cannot knock their competition or that they have on their board of trustees a consultant who would not permit it or that they are afraid of being blacklisted from every government and foundation grant source in the country. But the fact is that the government and the people are not getting the information they need to make sound urban program and policy decisions. Huge amounts of time and money are being wasted: the wrong questions are often asked, the wrong people do the work, and the research is often of questionable quality or usefulness. It would be nice if someone found the time and the courage to study the studiers, to analyze the analysts, to measure the measurers, and to make some strong recommendations about the recommenders.

The Kalish article was itself an act of pure whistle-blowing, for Kalish was employed in the same urban-problems industry that he characterized as a sophisticated but useless wart on the public. These whistle-blowing credentials gave him credibility problems, however, leaving him open to the charge that he was merely exposing inefficiencies in other consulting firms to create opportunities for himself. Although such charges were probably false in their implications of opportunism—Kalish hardly enhanced his future in the consulting world with the article—they are indicative of the questioning (often snide) of his motives that every whistle-blower must face.

The best way around the motives problem is for the whistle-blower to be visited with some signs of martyrdom—that is, to be seen clearly to lose rather than gain personally by his act. The public has come a long way in its ability to detect such a loss. No longer is the dramatic execution of the hero needed as proof that he is selfless. But some minimal outward signs of personal strife are still considered wise as insurance that the whistle-blower will be taken seriously. In modern, enlightened times, he may be allowed to go on living—perhaps even fairly well—after his scrape with the authorities. But to be able to expire quietly on the lecture circuit forty years later, he must show that he is too sincere to be in the whistle-blowing game for the headlines or the loot.

The motives problem is particularly vexing for the whistle-blower when he puts forth an interpretation or an opinion rather than an indictment based on facts that can be objectively checked out. The average citizen may buy *evidence* submitted by someone he regards as an opportunist, just as he buys the products of the self-interested manufacturer, but he will not as readily accept the presumed opportunist's opinions.

The tongue-in-cheek tone of "Flim-Flam, Double-Talk, and Hustle" is characteristic of articles that, like the Hochschild piece on the Reserves and National Guard (Chapter 3), attack an institution as useless. Apparently, the boldness of such a proposition stimulates in the whistle-blower-as-writer a half-humorous approach, perhaps unconsciously taken to soften his blasphemy against all the executives and secretaries and pension plans and pockets of self-esteem that are built on contrary assumptions. The fact is that, although his tone diffuses that sting a bit, Kalish does in effect argue that poverty studies provide money to be carried off to the suburbs by consultants, money obtained in the name of the poor but only very indirectly in their behalf. It seems that the huge quantities of mushy money around modern government agencies, from which people get paid without being quite answerable to the supplier or the consumer for the product, makes it easy for the contract middleman to get by handsomely on the appearances of respectable activity. This, Kalish had the temerity to suggest, should not be. (Some thinkers have applied the Kalish wisdom to the poverty problem to suggest a new approach: Let the government hire every poor person in the country as a poverty consultant.)

Kalish concluded by recommending that someone "study the studiers" and "analyze the analysts." Since whoever undertakes such a complicated task would have to have considerable expertise in all the relevant policy areas, the contracts probably would be scattered throughout the urban-problems industry itself. Thus, Kalish's haymaker to the craw of the consultants would be transformed by subtle jujitsu into a bright new field for McKinsey and RAND and all the versatile college graduates pouring into the job market. This reversal illustrates the danger that a whistle-blower's criticism may actually strengthen his target. Just as an inadequate bureaucracy responds to charges of inefficiency by successfully demanding more money, the consultants in Kalish's government fringe may wind up taking advantage of their own failure by getting paid to study themselves.

9 A Cost Manager's Arithmetic

Robert S. Benson served in the office of the Assistant Secretary of Defense (Comptroller) as a cost manager and budget examiner during the last two years of the Johnson Administration. His "How the Pentagon Can Save $9,000,000,000," which appeared in the March, 1969, *Washington Monthly*, has often been considered the effective beginning of a slowly building campaign against excessive defense spending. A few others, most notably James Phillips in *Congressional Quarterly*, had been making similar points, but Benson made them with the authority of an insider. His article inspired many subsequent ones on the same theme and was itself the subject of an editorial in the *New York Times* and long features in *Fortune* and *Look*. Within six months, his number one target, the Air Force's Manned Orbiting Laboratory (MOL), which Benson called "a carbon copy of the National Aeronautics and Space Administration's spacecraft operation," was canceled at a saving of $576 million.

Benson's article was more than an attack on specific programs like the MOL—for it had a general educational impact on a problem that most citizens assumed was beyond their critical faculties and better left to the national security experts. His recommendation that $2.7 billion be saved on military procurement contracts by "wiping out inefficiency" may be fairly criticized for its imprecision about how to go about it, but at least

Benson made people aware of the huge sums of sheer fat being burned by the Pentagon each year. An alumnus whistle-blower who had planned his next step before the publication of his article, Benson went on to coedit the National Urban Coalition's *Counterbudget: A Blueprint for Changing National Priorities, 1971–1976* (New York: Praeger, 1971), a detailed study of how the federal budget could be revised to put new spending priorities into effect. He is now working for a firm in Chicago that designs and manages day-care centers. Benson's *Washington Monthly* article, here slightly condensed, began:

> I have a modest proposal.
>
> I should like to demonstrate, in as brief and as simple a way as the complexities permit, how $9 billion can be cut from the Pentagon budget without reducing our national security or touching those funds earmarked for the war in Vietnam.
>
> Let me emphasize at the outset that this is truly a modest proposal, offered from an earnest belief in its practicality and with the conviction that savings from its adoption could be applied to our fiscally undernourished concerns for human opportunity.
>
> The process by which the Pentagon budget—as well as the rest of the federal budget—is shaped and reviewed is a strange and not always wonderful thing. Any new program is usually given thorough scrutiny in Congress: debate rages over the program's purposes and over the level of funding required. Once it is accepted, however, only the funding level is certain to receive continuing congressional attention. A nation's needs change, but rarely is a program's reason for existence ever challenged again, either in the executive branch or on Capitol Hill. On the contrary, its administering agency and its congressional advocates, cheered on by its beneficiaries, strive to perpetuate or expand it, seldom pausing to ponder whether it is still worthwhile or whether something else is needed more.
>
> Because a mystique of secrecy and complexity surrounds the Pentagon, most Americans feel uncomfortable, or even vaguely unpatriotic, if they question any part of the military budget. But the fact is that the federal budget's provisions for defense far exceed our national security requirements.

Although not many Americans realize it, a great deal of information about the threats to our security (and the forces we procure to meet them) can be gleaned from unclassified papers: budget statements of the President every January, annual posture statements by the Secretary of Defense, transcripts of congressional hearings, and articles in the newspapers. Any serious student will soon discover that items in the defense budget, as in any other, range from fundamental to marginal. The difference is that in the Pentagon budget (a) vastly larger sums are involved, and (b) far less congressional scrutiny is applied to them.

(Benson then proceeded to explain the rules of his cost-cutting exercise and added up, with startling subtotals, what could be subtracted.)

Using the sources above, my two years of experience in the Comptroller's office of the Department of Defense, and my own judgment of the issues, I hope first to outline how the budget can be trimmed by $9 billion and then proceed to a discussion of the weaknesses in the system which allowed this fat to survive even in the cost-conscious regime of Robert S. McNamara.

In our budget-cutting exercise these ground rules will apply:

- None of the cuts is related to the war in Vietnam.
- None of the cuts would impair our national security requirements.
- All of the cuts are in what the Pentagon calls ongoing core programs.
- All of the cuts could be effected within the next twenty-four months, which would allow the savings to be applied rather quickly to unfilled domestic needs.
- The focus is on areas where forces or weapons systems are either duplicated or outmoded, where an enemy threat is no longer credible in today's political and technological environment, or where money is being lost through grossly inefficient performance.

Perhaps the best place to begin is with the Manned Orbiting Laboratory, which receives half a billion dollars a year and ought to rank dead last on any rational scale of national priorities. The MOL, a carbon copy of the National Aeronautics and Space Administration's spacecraft operation, is in the budget because the Air Force wants a piece of the extraterrestrial action, with its glamour and glory, and Congress has been only too happy to oblige.

Although there have been valiant attempts to make the MOL seem different, Pentagon space research is alarmingly similar to that of NASA. Listen as Dr. Alexander H. Flax, Assistant Secretary of the Air Force for Research and Development, tries to draw the distinction for members of the House Appropriations Committee:

> If you view the objectives of these programs as being simply to get data on humans exposed for some period of time, I think you have to conclude that there is a great deal of duplication, but I tried to make the point that our objective is primarily to test equipment, not humans. The humans interact with the equipment, of course.

True, there are potential military uses for space vehicles. But little thought appears to have been given to whether a separate program was required or whether the same results could have been achieved through slight adjustments in the parallel NASA activities. The MOL program is duplicative and wasteful. Of the $600 million requested for it last year, Congress approved all but $85 million. This year's budget calls for $576 million. I would strike all of it—**saving $576,000,000.**

As for grossly inefficient Pentagon performance, the most obvious example is manpower management and utilization. Manpower is the single largest commodity the Defense Department buys; this year, the Pentagon will directly purchase the services of nearly 5 million Americans. Assuming an average of $7,000 each in pay, allowances, and supplementary benefits, the department payroll is about $34 billion, of which about $22 billion goes to military personnel and $12 billion to civilians.

The Pentagon has little direct control over the costs of its civilian personnel, who are recruited mainly through a government-wide civil-service pool. But its control over military personnel is complete, covering not only the $22 billion payroll but also about $7 billion annually in training costs and nearly $2 billion in moving expenses for men changing assignments.

Most men enter the armed forces either because they are drafted or because they enlist in preference to being drafted. All enlisted men entering the service receive basic training, which in the Army takes eight weeks and costs about $1,000 per head. After advanced training in a specialty, these short-term new servicemen generally spend the rest of their hitches on assignments requiring that specialty.

A more flexible training policy would not employ such a lockstep approach. Some basic training is needed for everyone, and combat infantrymen certainly need the full eight weeks. But not all of the Army's 535,000 new soldiers this year will serve in combat, and four weeks would suffice for the others. The Navy and Air Force have already abbreviated their basic training; the Army could also do so—**saving $50,000,000.**

Although the pattern of training and assignments for officers is far different, even greater economies are possible—and with a clear gain in individual job performance. After initial training, which is more diverse than it is for enlisted men, almost every officer is shuttled around through an amazing variety of assignments and further training designed to give him enough breadth of experience to become Chief of Staff some day, often at the sacrifice of obtaining no deep experience in any one field. The expectation is that every seasoned officer can lead an infantry battalion through a swamp on one assignment, promulgate personnel promotion policies behind a Pentagon desk on the next, and discuss black separatism with Ethiopians as a military attaché in Addis Ababa a year later.

In this age of specialization, such a philosophy is anachronistic and expensive. No efficient business would move its men around in so illogical a pattern. By perpetuating the illusion that every officer can aspire to the top organizational position, rather than screening the candidates earlier in their careers, the services suffer from having an excessive number of men struggling to learn totally unfamiliar jobs. Moreover, today's technological and analytical complexities demand the development of specialists whose entire experience is focused on performing one particular function well. In the attempt to fill the growing number of specialist slots with generalists, job performance diminishes for all.

Reducing by a modest one-fourth the present number of assignment changes (whereby servicemen move almost once a year), would mean **saving $500,000,000.**

A further saving can be accomplished by changing the way the military calculates individual manpower requirements. Unlike business, which requires work units to absorb the impact of absences, the Pentagon includes a cushion to compensate for men absent on leave, in the hospital, in school, and en route to new assignments. And the military's thirty days of annual leave—which all servicemen get—is far more than the norm for civilian work forces of comparable age and experience, even acknowledging that the thirty days includes weekends. The military argues that this amount of leave time is compensation for being on duty twenty-four hours a day, seven days a week—but this is a myth long in need of explosion. Except for those at sea and in Vietnam, most military men work evenings or weekends no more and no less than civilians do. Cutting leave time to twenty days a year—with the exception of men on hardship duty overseas—would at the same time reduce the annual total armed forces manpower requirements, **saving $450,000,000.**

Thanks to Beetle Bailey, *Catch 22,* and the fact that so many Americans are veterans, the supernumerary theory of military staffing has had great visibility. But an area of far greater inefficiency—supplier performance on large weapons system contracts—draws almost no attention at all. This is especially serious because the same contractor who can be extremely efficient under the conditions imposed by the private competitive market place can waste millions when working under a government contract. Few Americans are aware that about 90 per cent of the major weapons systems that the Defense Department procures end up costing at least twice as much as was originally estimated. Some of this cost growth comes from Pentagon-ordered changes in design or configuration, but much of it results from the contractor's inefficient practices or from his knowledge that the government will underwrite his excessive overhead.

It is up to the government, therefore, to impose on a non-competitive defense contractor the same cost discipline that the contractor would be forced to impose on himself in a competitive situation. Instead, the present procurement system is geared almost exclusively to securing timely delivery and good technical performance. Cost comes last.

The engine contract for the controversial F-111 fighter-bomber offers a classic illustration of what happens to costs after a decision is reached to proceed with procurement.

An aircraft of this kind has three major components: airframe (wings and fuselage), avionics (electronic navigation and weapons-guiding gear), and engines. For a technologically advanced fighter-bomber, the airframe will account for about 55 per cent of total cost, avionics 25 per cent, and engines 20 per cent. The initial F-111 contract for 2,053 engines was awarded to Pratt & Whitney on the basis of an estimated cost of $270,000 per engine. Today the engines are expected to cost more than $700,000 each.

In the F-111 case, and in general, four major factors account for such cost escalation:

1 *The Buy-In.* Our procurement system encourages contractors to play the game called "buy-in." The rules are simple. Contracts are awarded to the company which offers the lowest bid with a straight face. Later cost overruns may bring a mild reproach or a stern reprimand, but they will not prevent the contractor from getting enough money to cover all his costs and pocket a profit. A contractor rarely takes these reprimands seriously; he knows that his competitors have similar experiences. Besides, the procurement officials have told him to worry about performance and prompt delivery, not about cost. So the buy-in game produces initial cost estimates that everyone knows are unrealistically low.

2 *Design Changes.* From the time bids are requested on a new weapons system until final delivery, a great many changes in design specification develop. These changes are often initiated by the Defense Department, although some reflect contractor production problems. In either case, the costs change—usually justifiably, but almost always upward.

3 *Volume.* Changes in volume are even farther beyond the contractor's control. In large contracts, economies of scale are often achievable; if a weapons system is found highly useful, as was the F-4 fighter, and more units are ordered

than were initially planned, the later unit costs are lower. In the case of the Air Force F-111, however, cancellation of British orders and the Congressional decision to kill the Navy version reduced the number of aircraft to be purchased, thereby raising the unit cost.

4 *Sheer Inefficiency.* These costs arise because a contractor has slipshod purchasing procedures, poor scheduling of men and machines, ineffective work standards, or other managerial deficiencies. Such extra costs would be a threat to a company's survival in the competitive private market place; they should not be tolerated in defense procurement.

In calculating how much of the F-111 engine's cost growth was due to this intolerable fourth factor, we need to begin by figuring how much the first three factors cost.

We know that the original $270,000 estimate was artificially low. Allowing for buy-in fibbing and for some early required changes in design, an initial figure of $450,000 would have been more realistic. Later design changes may have raised the allowable price to $500,000. But the contractor's final estimate of $700,000-plus, made after the British action but before the Congressional cutback, probably should not be adjusted for volume changes, because the British buy was to have been proportionately very small and there are good indications that this actually enabled Pratt & Whitney to disengage itself from some expensive subcontracts. So unjustifiable contractor inefficiency amounted to around $200,000 per engine.

It could have been worse. Past practice in such cases, where the government is dealing with a single supplier rather than with several competitors, has been to accept whatever price is commensurate with the costs the supplier has incurred, regardless of how efficient or inefficient he is. But, in an unprecedented action, the Defense Department ordered an investigation of Pratt & Whitney operations to determine how much such an engine ought to cost if produced under efficient manufacturing procedures. After that, the Navy—which had contract responsibility for all F-111 engines—took the further unprecedented step of unilaterally setting the price it intended to pay. Indications are that the Navy compromised its position somewhat after some hard bargaining, but the final contract did reduce by about 15 per cent the price proposed by the company, which under customary procedure would have been accepted outright. This saved the government roughly $200 million.

Conservatively assuming that aerospace and shipbuilding contractors harbor an inefficiency of 15 per cent, and figuring that the average annual amount provided for research and procurement of such systems over the past three years is about $17.9 billion, then wiping out the inefficiency would mean annually **saving $2,700,000,000.**

This is no pipe dream. It requires no dramatic breakthrough in management techniques. Such savings could be achieved quickly if the Secretary of Defense and the secretaries of the individual services resolved to focus the energies of their top financial and engineering men on procurement of these major weapons systems. What is needed is some truly independent cost-sleuthing into contractors' operations, with firm backing from top Defense management for appropriate follow-up efforts.

The most fruitful way of all for saving defense dollars is to eliminate forces that no longer pack a credible punch or were designed to meet a threat that is no longer credible.

The Navy's Polaris/Poseidon fleet ballistic missile program is vital to our national security. But the Navy's three primary and independent conventional warfare missions—tactical air, amphibious operations, and shipping protection—are overequipped, as are their associated support units. Current force levels cannot be justified by any potential threats. In my view, President Nixon was misguided when he decried America's loss of sea power during the campaign last fall. He made the mistake of applying the same argument the admirals use when they attempt to eternalize and expand their favorite programs: that the United States must have superiority in numbers, ship-type by ship-type, over the Soviet Navy. This is a legacy of late-1940's thinking, when it was assumed that we must always be ready to fight and win an extended war at sea. In the nuclear age, such thinking is highly unrealistic.

Fifteen aircraft carriers are at present assigned to the Navy's tactical air mission. Since the wallop they pack is purely the firepower of their aircraft, they should be compared with the alternative means of delivering that firepower

—Air Force tactical aircraft. Carriers can deploy quickly to areas where we have no airfields, and they are safe from insurgent attacks (though they now appear to be vulnerable to Russian Styx missiles). But this flexibility comes at a high price. Independent studies place the cost of carrier-based tactical missions at three to four times that of similar missions flown from ground fields. Because of the many air bases we have built all over the world, we can rapidly deploy land-based aircraft to most areas. Carriers still play a necessary role in providing the potential to fight in a handful of otherwise inaccessible places and in meeting initial "surge" requirements for a nonnuclear war. But there is no justifiable reason to use them on extended deployments in major wars as we do now in Vietnam. Although the Defense Department will never admit it, the only reason we continue to employ carrier-based air strikes there is that the jealous Navy doesn't want to be shut out of some role in the war.

Tactical aircraft carriers could be cut from fifteen to ten without risk to the country's security. The average annual peacetime operating and modernization/replacement cost per carrier appears to be about $120 million. Assuming that the costs of expanding Air Force tactical missions to take up the slack were one-third as much, eliminating five carriers would mean **saving $400,000,000.**

Marine Corps amphibious assault tactics have been used in minor contingencies such as Lebanon and the Dominican Republic, but against a major power they would be highly vulnerable to a tactical nuclear weapon. Nor are Marine forces now structured logistically for sustained combat, the type of war that Vietnam would suggest is most probable. Without eliminating any Marine troops, we could restrict their amphibious training and equipment and phase out a proportionate share of assault ships—thereby annually **saving $100,000,000.**

A classic example of continued spending for protection against a no longer important threat is the third major area of Navy tactical forces—protection for shipping. The structuring of our antisubmarine and supporting anti-aircraft and fleet escort forces harks back to the post–World War II prospect of a sea war with Russia. If we ever do begin destroying each other's ships, there seems to be little prospect of avoiding escalation to nuclear war, which would make shipping protection irrelevant. Further, as various jumbo aircraft near production, the cost gap between a ton-mile of plane transportation and a ton-mile of ship transportation is narrowing. Yet instead of scaling down our protective forces, we are keeping them up and even expanding them, through 1968's implausible decision to begin procuring VSX antisubmarine aircraft. Killing this program and reducing over-all shipping defenses to a sensible level—four antisubmarine carriers and three air groups rather than the present eight carriers—would mean annually **saving $600,000,000.**

Another major area in which our involvement is unreasonably large is our troop commitment in Europe. We have about 310,000 soldiers there now, accompanied by more than 200,000 dependents. Such a staggering share of the NATO burden was appropriate while our World War II allies struggled to get back on their feet, but they can now afford a larger load. Part of the thesis behind U.S. deployments is to make certain that any substantial attack by Warsaw Pact forces would engage American forces, thereby creating potential consequences that the Soviet Union would find untenable. But this could be assured with far fewer than 310,000 U.S. troops. Says Senator Stuart Symington (D-Mo.), a former Air Force Secretary recently assigned as chairman of a Foreign Relations subcommittee that will investigate the involvement of U.S. forces abroad: "Surely 50,000 American troops would be sufficient to make sure that no Soviet probe could succeed in Berlin or elsewhere in Europe without a direct confrontation with the United States."

Realistically, we could cut back to a total of 125,000 troops in Europe plus 50,000 at home earmarked for NATO contingencies, and cut by one-fourth the air power assigned to the European theater (a McNamara comparison shows that NATO air forces can deliver a payload more than three times greater than that of their Warsaw Pact counterparts), annually **saving $1,500,000,000.**

The final two programs of questionable value—the SAGE Air Defense Command system and the Sentinel antiballistic missile system—share some common characteristics. Both are defensive, in an age when the balance of terror rests on offensive missile strength. Both encompass a detection function and an intercept guidance function. And numerous technical experts express serious doubts about the potential operational effectiveness of either.

SAGE represents yesteryear's attempt to defend against the Soviet version of our Strategic Air Command. It is widely conceded that the Soviets have grounded their bomber development efforts and no longer pose their primary strategic threat in this area. Nonetheless we persist in trying to further refine our bomber defenses, when in fact we have already achieved a satisfactory capability in the detection sphere. Moreover, SAGE's role as a guide to interceptor pilots is rather superfluous, given its imperfections and our primary reliance on a strong offensive deterrent. Some reductions have already been effected in the Air Defense Command, but conversion from a full defensive system to purely a warning system ought to add up to annually **saving $600,000,000.**

If SAGE is intended to sustain a mostly futile yesteryear system, the Sentinel ABM represents a misguided attempt to provide protection tomorrow. Against the destructive power of the missile, our best defense is a good offense. Particularly tragic is the staggering cost of a full-blown "thin" Sentinel system. Because it is so expensive, and the work is therefore parceled out to many congressional districts, many politicians have favored it. It therefore may be difficult to stop before we have spent $40 billion. However, the Sentinel program faces increasingly fervent opposition in the Senate this year—partly because residents in four cities where ABM sites are being developed have objected so loudly. Halting the Sentinel now, before it acquires irreversible momentum, could mean this year alone **saving $1,800,000,000.**

The items above do not exhaust the list of things to cut—there are other savings to be made in such areas as mapping operations, the reserve forces, logistics—but the total here will serve as a start. It amounts to:

Total Savings, $9,276,000,000.

If all these Pentagon budget cuts are so obvious, why didn't the cost-conscious McNamara regime push them through? Did the Whiz Kids fail? Were they really trying? I think a fair assessment would have to conclude that they were trying hard but were only partly successful, for five basic reasons.

First, McNamara's Band was greatly outnumbered by experienced adversaries bound together by a shared goal—more and bigger military programs. All the elements in this military-industrial-congressional complex are served by an enlarged defense budget, though their motivations are different. Industry wants greater sales and profits. The military wants expanded power, plus the assurance that it will be on the forefront of technology. Congressmen respond to pressure from contractors and military employees in their districts, and those on the military committees yearn for the prestige and power that comes from presiding over a bigger slice of the federal pie. The combination made life difficult even for a man as strong and courageous as Robert McNamara.

Second, in selecting systems to analyze for effectiveness, the Whiz Kids chose to concentrate on the relatively uncluttered strategic programs instead of digging into such fat and messy activities as we have catalogued here. Within their selected framework, they generally performed technically sound, objective initial analyses. Once they arrived at a position, however, they too often "overdefended" their conclusions; that is, they were unwilling to reassess them against subsequent cost experience, technological advances, or a changing international political environment. For example, the current structuring of our programed airlift/sealift needs emanates from a carefully developed linear programing model. This model attaches a high value to rapid deployment, stemming from an early 1960's Europe-oriented study that showed high benefits in terms of political bargaining power and casualty minimization. This analysis still makes good sense in Europe, but now appears grossly misapplied in Asia. Yet nothing has been done to revise the high value placed on rapid deployment. Such a change would point to a different desired mix of airlift and sealift.

Third, the Defense Department's budget review process concedes too much at the beginning. Last year's budgeted amounts are generally taken by everyone as this year's starting points. This practice ignores the possibility that fat crept into preceding budgets or that some of last year's activities are now outmoded. Consider, for example, the subject of training, in which the armed services have been pioneering for years by applying new technology to education. This area should be a prime candidate for frequent review from the ground up (what the managers call "zero-base" budgeting). Rather, the Defense Department budgeting process virtually concedes last year's amount and focuses on whatever incremental changes have been requested. The result, of course, is higher budgets, with past errors compounded year after year.

Finally, the President and the Budget Bureau have shied from making public any meaningful comparisons between military and domestic programs. Systems analysis, the technique that aims to measure the relative national worth of results obtained from alternative programs, cannot precisely compare the benefits to be gained from highly diverse activities. Yet inexact as such comparisons may be, the Budget Bureau does make them and present them to the President from time to time. If the President, for his part, were to discuss national priorities more frequently and candidly with the public, then congressmen might be less likely to base their judgments on the only other available view—that the present balance of activities is about right.

The present balance of activities is anything but right. Unmet national concerns for human opportunity and the quality of life require an investment even larger than the amount that would be freed if all of the Pentagon reforms outlined in this report were carried out.

Perhaps the clearest, most thorough delineation of these high-priority social needs is found in the report of the National Advisory Commission on Civil Disorders. To redress root causes of despair and frustration, the commission recommended a long series of measures that, if enacted in full, would cost between $13 billion and $18 billion a year over their first several years.

The only way to begin addressing these unfilled needs is to take money away from Pentagon programs that must rank lower on any rational national-priority scale. Examples provide compelling support for this argument. We have such choices as:

• Funding the Manned Orbiting Laboratory—or providing Upward Bound summer courses for the 600,000 additional ghetto students who have the potential to go to college;

- Spending this year's Sentinel funds—or training 510,000 more hard-core unemployed;
- Continuing to operate one of the marginal tactical aircraft carriers—or training and supporting 20,000 more Teacher Corps members;
- Maintaining our full troop complement in Europe—or diverting an additional $10 million to each of 150 Model Cities;
- Permitting excessive contractor costs to flourish unchecked —or providing Head Start education for 2,250,000 more children, plus enough school lunches to feed 20 million children for a whole year.

These alternatives are real and immediate. They do not represent wishful dreaming. The choices are up to Mr. Nixon, to the Congress, and ultimately to ourselves.

10 Grounds for Protest

Gary J. Greenberg practices law with the New York firm of Strook, Strook, and Lavan. From September, 1967, until October, 1969, he was a trial attorney with the Civil Rights Division of the Department of Justice. In the summer of 1969, he was a leader of the attorneys' fight against the legal positions of their department regarding civil rights, which he described in the pages of the *Washington Monthly* for December, 1969. The article, dealing with one of the first battles over the civil-rights policies of the Nixon Administration, appeared one month after Greenberg, a pure whistle-blower, was forced to resign.

Revolt at Justice

August 19, 1969, was an historic date in the field of civil rights. It was on that day that Robert H. Finch, the Secretary of Health, Education, and Welfare, in letters to the United States District Judges for the Southern District of Mississippi and to the Chief Judge of the United States Fifth Circuit Court of Appeals, sought to withdraw school desegregation plans that his department had filed in the district court a week earlier.

Less than a week later—on August 25—Attorney General John N. Mitchell placed the Department of Justice imprimatur on Finch's actions when Jerris Leonard, the Assistant Attorney General in charge of the Civil Rights Division, joined local officials in a Mississippi district court to argue for a delay.

The same day, in Washington, some of my colleagues in the Civil Rights Division and I prepared and distributed a memorandum inviting the Division's attorneys to a meeting the next evening to discuss these and other recent events, which had, in the words of the memo, cast ominous shadows over "the future course of law enforcement in civil rights." The meeting's purpose was "to determine whether we have a common position and what action, if any, would be appropriate to take."

When a lawyer is admitted to the bar, he takes an oath to support the Constitution of the United States. When a lawyer joins the Department of Justice, he takes another oath—the same one that is taken by the Attorney General and, in fact, by all federal employees.

That oath reads:

> I solemnly swear (or affirm) that I will support and defend the Constitution of the United States against all enemies, foreign and domestic; that I will bear true faith and allegiance to the same; that I take this obligation freely, and without any mental reservation or purpose of evasion; and that I will well and faithfully discharge the duties of the office on which I am about to enter. So help me God.

It was largely because of this oath—and the pressures we were under to violate it—that a majority of the attorneys from the Civil Rights Division of the Department of Justice gathered in a Washington apartment the evening of August 26. We wanted to ascertain whether, under the Constitution, there was any legal argument which might conceivably support the Nixon Administration's request, in a Mississippi courtroom, for a delay in implementing desegregation in thirty-three of that state's school districts. The assembled lawyers concluded that there was not. Thus was born the reluctant movement which the press was to call "the revolt" in the Civil Rights Division.

The forty who attended the meeting that night first heard detailed factual accounts from those lawyers with firsthand knowledge of the government's actions in school desegregation cases in Mississippi, Louisiana, and South Carolina. We discussed the legal principles at length. We could find, as lawyers, no grounds for these actions that did not run crossgrain to the Constitution. We concluded that the request for delay in Mississippi was not only politically motivated but unsupportable under the law we were sworn to uphold. I then asked whether the attorneys in the Civil Rights Division should protest the actions of Messrs. Mitchell, Finch, and Leonard. Much to my astonishment, the answer was an unhesitating, unequivocal, and unanimous call for action.

But how? The group's immediate, though probably unattainable, goal was a reversal of the Justice Department's actions in Mississippi. Beyond that, however, we wanted to insure that future Mississippi-type decisions would not be made; we wanted guarantees that the Administration would, in the future, take the actions that were compelled by law, without reference to the political exigencies. We hoped that the protest could serve as a deterrent to future political accommodation. We agreed to write a dignified and reasonable statement of protest by which we could make our views known and demonstrate our unity and resolve. We chose a committee of six to draft the document.

Two evenings later, on August 28, we held another meeting to review the draft submitted by the committee. The fifty attorneys in attendance discussed the draft, modified it somewhat, and then adopted it unanimously. (It was later signed by sixty-five of the seventy-four nonsupervisory attorneys in the Civil Rights Division, some of whom had missed one or both of the meetings because they were out of town.)

The four-paragraph, 400-word document expressed, in painstaking language, the continuing concerns, motivations, and goals of the signatories. The last two paragraphs said:

> It is our fear that a policy which dictates that clear legal mandates are to be sacrificed to other considerations will seriously impair the ability of the Civil Rights Division, and ultimately the Judiciary, to attend to the faithful execution of the federal civil-rights statutes. Such an impairment, by eroding public faith in our constitutional institutions, is likely to damage the capacity of those institutions to accommodate conflicting interests and insure the full enjoyment of fundamental rights for all.
>
> We recognize that, as members of the Department of Justice, we have an obligation to follow the directives of our departmental superiors. However, we are compelled, in conscience, to urge that henceforth the enforcement policies of this Division be predicated solely upon relevant legal principles. We further request that this Department vigorously

enforce those laws protecting human dignity and equal rights for all persons and by its actions promptly assure concerned citizens that the objectives of those laws will be pursued.

Why did the consciences of sixty-five federal employees compel them to protest a government law-enforcement decision? Why did sixty-five members of a profession which generally attracts the conservative and circumspect to its ranks —and reinforces these characteristics in three years of academic training—launch the first "revolt" within the federal bureaucracy?

Part of the answer lies in the fact that the new Administration was elected largely by voters who expected—and, from the rhetoric of the campaign, had every reason to expect—a slowdown in federal civil-rights enforcement efforts. Those political debts ran counter to the devotion and commitment of the attorneys in the Civil Rights Division. They had labored long and hard in civil-rights law enforcement and had come to realize by experience that only unremitting pressure could bring about compliance with the civil-rights statutes and the Fourteenth Amendment. Yet this conflict of commitments did not of itself lead to the revolt. There was no inevitability in the situation.

Certain other irritants played a part in creating an attitude among the attorneys which made "revolt" possible. There was Mr. Leonard himself, a politician from Wisconsin with no background in civil rights, and, indeed, very little as a lawyer. He was insensitive to the problems of black citizens and other minority-group victims of discrimination. Almost from the beginning, he distrusted the attorneys he found in the Division. He demonstrated that distrust by isolating himself from the line attorneys. Still another element was the shock of his ineptitude as a lawyer. In marked contrast to the distinguished lawyers who preceded him in his job, Mr. Leonard lacks the intellectual equipment to deal with the legal problems that come across his desk.

His handling of the Mississippi case enlarged this mood of irritation and frustration. Secretary Finch's letter—drafted in part, and approved in full, by Mr. Leonard—said that the HEW plans were certain to produce "a catastrophic educational setback" for the school children involved. Yet the Office of Education personnel who prepared the plans, and

Dr. Gregory Anrig, who supervised their work, and the Civil Rights Division attorneys who were preparing to defend them in court had found no major flaws. Indeed, Dr. Anrig, in transmitting the plans to the district court on August 11, wrote that in his judgment "each of the enclosed plans is educationally and administratively sound, both in terms of substance and in terms of timing." It was not until the afternoon of August 20, only hours before the attorneys were to defend the plans in court, that Mr. Leonard called them in Mississippi to inform them of the Administration's decision. Finally, in justifying the government's actions to his own supervisory attorneys—and in arranging that they, and not he, would inform the line attorneys of the reasons for the requested delay—Mr. Leonard could be no more candid than to say that the chief educator in the country had made an educational decision and that the Department of Justice had to back him up.

But, again, these superficial signs of malaise were not what led to the lawyers' widespread revolt. Discontent only created the atmosphere for it.

The revolt occurred for one paramount reason: The sixty-five attorneys had obligations to their profession and to the public interest. As lawyers, we are bound by the Canons of Professional Ethics and by our oaths upon admission to the bar; as officers of the United States, we were bound by our oaths of office.

Membership in the bar entails much more than a license to practice law. One becomes an officer of the courts, duty-bound to support the judiciary and to aid in every way in the administration of justice.

The Canons of Ethics command that an attorney "obey his own conscience" (Canon 15) and strive to improve the administration of justice (Canon 29). The Canons also state that

> no . . . cause, civil or political, however important, is entitled to receive, nor should any lawyer render, any service or advice involving disloyalty to the law whose ministers we are, or disrespect of the judicial office, which we are bound to uphold. . . . When rendering any such improper service . . . the lawyer invites and merits stern and just condemnation. . . . Above all a lawyer will find his highest honor in a deserved reputation for fidelity to . . . public duty, as an honest man and as a patriotic and loyal citizen. (Canon 32.)

Bearing these obligations in mind, examine for a moment the situation which confronted the attorneys as a result of the decision to seek delay in Mississippi.

In May, 1954, the Supreme Court declared that "in the field of public education the doctrine of 'separate but equal' has no place. Separate educational facilities are inherently unequal." One year later, the Court decreed that school officials would be required to make a "prompt and reasonable start" toward achieving the constitutional goal with "all deliberate speed." Tragically, a decade went by and little was accomplished; that was the era of "massive resistance." In 1964, the Supreme Court ruled that "the time for mere 'deliberate speed' has run out." In 1968, the Court held that school officials were under a constitutional obligation to come forward with desegregation plans that worked, and to do so "now." The Fifth Circuit Court of Appeals interpreted that edict, in the summer of 1968, to mean that the dual school system, with its racially identifiable schools, had to be eliminated in all of the states within its jurisdiction by September, 1969. (Mississippi is one of those states.)

Secretary Finch's letter, besides suggesting the possibility of a catastrophic educational setback if desegregation were effected at once, spoke of the certainty of chaos and confusion in the school districts if delay were not allowed. That allegation was based upon the uncontestable existence of hostility to desegregation within the local communities. While there was, and continues to be, a danger that chaos and confusion will accompany the desegregation of public schools in Mississippi, the Supreme Court had ruled again and again that neither opposition to constitutional rights nor the likelihood of a confrontation with those opposed to the constitutional imperative may legally stand as a bar to the immediate vindication of those rights.*

Thus, while pledged by our oaths to support and defend the Constitution and bound by duty to follow our conscience and adhere to the law, we faced a situation in which the Administration had proposed to act in violation of the law.

* On October 29, of course, the Supreme Court unanimously rejected the Administration's efforts at delay by enunciating the rule that the Constitution requires desegregation "at once." That ruling is not a part of this narrative except as it demonstrated anew that the position we had taken on the law was unassailable.

We knew that we could not remain silent, for silence, particularly in this Administration, is interpreted as support or acquiescence. Only through some form of protest could we live up to our obligations as lawyers and as officers of the United States. The form that this protest should take emerged so clearly that it then became a matter of inevitability, rather than a "choice" made from among several alternatives.

For the duty to serve the law, to promote the administration of justice, to support and defend the Constitution is more than a negative command. It is an affirmative duty to act in a manner which would best serve and promote those interests. Thus, at the first group meeting, we immediately and unanimously rejected the notion of mass resignation because it would have served no positive purpose. It would only have removed us from association with the supporters of delay; it would not have fulfilled our obligation to act affirmatively to insure that constitutional rights would be protected and that the civil-rights laws would be vigorously enforced.

Many of the attorneys thought that our obligation could not be met by merely drafting, signing, and delivering a protest statement. If delay for the purpose of mollifying a hostile community did not comport with the Constitution—thus impelling us to raise our voices in protest—then we were likewise duty-bound not to support the Mitchell-Finch-Leonard position through any of our official actions. The bureaucratic concept of "loyalty" notwithstanding, some of us concluded that we could not, for example, defend the government's position in court.

The question arises as to whether the action taken by the group met the burden imposed upon us by our obligations to the law and the public interest. Did our fidelity to these obligations demand more than the soft and lofty importunings of the protest statement? Should all of the attorneys have explicitly refused to defend in court the action taken in the Mississippi case? Should the attorneys have embarked on a more direct course of action to block the government's efforts to win a year's delay for school desegregation in Mississippi?

To begin with, we were hard pressed to come up with some appropriate alternative to the protest statement as a vehicle to make the views of sixty-five people known. But beyond that, it was vitally important to preserve the appearance of dignity and professionalism if our protest were not to be dismissed as the puerile rantings of a group of unresurrected idealists who, except for their attire, bore a close resemblance to the Weathermen and the Crazies. To generate the public support we thought vital to the success of the protest, we had to act in a responsible and statesmanlike manner. Furthermore, it seemed to us that the presentation of any statement signed by nearly all of the attorneys in the Division would be a remarkable feat and that the demonstration of commitment was more important than the words actually used. In our view, the soft language implied everything that a blunter statement might have said. It also had the virtue of not putting the Administration up against a wall, which would have forced them to respond with a hard-line position of their own.

Though duty and conscience compelled a protest, reason dictated the nature of the protest. We did not merely seek an opportunity for catharsis; we sought to devise a course of action which had a chance to reap a harvest of practical results. That being the overriding consideration, the attorneys chose the course of a mildly worded group statement. Other overt manifestations of disagreement were left open for individuals to pursue as they saw fit.

The group action we took—that is, the drafting and signing of the statement—was a "protest," if by that we mean a dissent from the actions of one's administrative superiors. The language of the statement did not move into the area of "revolt," if by that we mean an explicit refusal to obey the orders of one's superiors—although the statement was intended to imply that "revolt" was in the air.

Compelled by what they felt to be their obligations to the law, individual attorneys took a number of actions on their own, most of them in that murky area where there is a confluence between "protest" and "revolt."

Even before the first group meeting, the Division lawyers in Mississippi expressed their disinclination to present the government's case for delay in the district court. As a consequence, Mr. Leonard made his first appearance in a federal district court as Assistant Attorney General and argued the motion for delay himself. In mid-September, two Division attorneys (the author being one) appeared in federal courts in other school desegregation cases. When pressed by those courts to reconcile the government's "desegregate now" position in those cases with Mr. Leonard's position in Mississippi, both attorneys said they could not defend the government's action in Mississippi.* Some of the Division's attorneys went a step further: They passed information along to lawyers for the NAACP Legal Defense Fund in order to aid their Mississippi court battle against the delay requested by the Administration. Others spoke with the press to insure that the public was fully aware of the role that political pressures had played in the decision to seek delay.

These actions, while neither authorized nor approved by the group as a whole, were individual responses to the same crisis of conscience that led to the protest statement itself. One may have reservations as to the propriety of some or all of these acts of defiance. (Indeed, I have doubts as to whether it was proper for a Division attorney to furnish information to the NAACP after the government's action transformed it into an opposing party.) But it is important to recognize that the demands of conscience compelled more than just the signing of a piece of paper, and, in this sense, the protest was, realistically, a "revolt."

When the storm clouds first began to gather within the Civil Rights Division, the hierarchy of the Department of Justice, including the Attorney General and Mr. Leonard, reacted with a professed sense of surprise, and even shock. Despite this, however, the Administration's actions were, at the outset, nothing short of accommodating.

* In my situation, I was in Saint Louis before the Eighth Circuit Court of Appeals sitting *en banc* (i.e., the full seven judges of the court were present), arguing that a delay granted by the district court to an Arkansas school district for the desegregation of its high schools should be reserved. One of the judges asked whether I could assure the court that the Attorney General would not "come along and pull the rug out from under" them if they ordered instant integration. I was pressed to reconcile my request for immediate integration in Arkansas with the position taken in the Mississippi case. After the court listened to my attempts to distinguish between the two cases, one judge said it appeared to the court that the practical effect of the government's posture was that Mississippi was being given special treatment. At this point, a number of judges called upon me to state my personal views on the contradictory positions taken by the government. I responded by saying I assumed that the court knew from the press accounts of the "revolt" what the feelings were in the Division. I indicated that, as a signatory of the protest statement, I could not be expected to defend the government's action in Mississippi.

The supervisory attorneys in the Division took the position that we had a perfect right, under the First Amendment, to meet and discuss matters of mutual concern. Prior to our second meeting, Leonard Garment, President Nixon's special consultant for youth and minority problems, let it be known through an intermediary that the Administration was likely to respond favorably to a reasonable and responsible protest. Indeed, Mr. Garment and the Deputy Attorney General, Richard G. Kleindienst, facilitated the protest by allowing us to hold our second meeting behind closed doors in the Department of Justice.

But later, when the Administration came to a fuller appreciation of the depth and unanimity of the protest, this attitude began to change.

On September 18, Mr. Leonard responded to the attorneys' statement for the Administration. We were informed that the reply was a final articulation of policy and that if we did not like what we read we should resign. The reply was curiously unresponsive. Whereas the attorneys' statement was carefully limited to questions concerning the intrusion of political influences into areas of law enforcement where only considerations of law belong, Mr. Leonard's reply outlined how the Administration would go about desegregating public schools. To this extent the reply completely missed, or avoided, the point of the protest. We had never challenged the discretionary authority of the Attorney General and the President to determine by what method the constitutional objective would be achieved. In matters where discretion was vested in the Attorney General to choose between policy alternatives, the attorneys did not challenge his right to make the choice. But in the matter of enforcing constitutionally required school desegregation in Mississippi, the Attorney General had no discretion. He was bound to uphold the dictates of the law, an obligation that could not be squared with the decision to seek delay.

Aside from its nonresponsiveness to the questions we had raised, Mr. Leonard's reply was disturbing on two other counts. First, it conceded, with delayed candor, that political pressures had played a role in the Mississippi decision. Second, it announced a new touchstone for civil-rights law-enforcement policies: Future actions would be taken not on the basis of the law but, rather, on the basis of "soundness."

Thus, when ABM and other defense appropriations are thrown into the balance, a decision to seek delay of school desegregation in Mississippi in return for the continued support of Senator John Stennis (D-Miss.) in defense matters can presumably be certified as a "sound" decision, notwithstanding its inconsistency with clear legal mandates.

The attorneys decided that we would neither accept the response nor resign. But that situation demanded further action, and we chose to reiterate our commitment to the law. On September 25, we delivered to the Attorney General and Mr. Leonard a new statement. It expressed our view that Mr. Leonard's reply "indicates an intention to continue with the policy of civil-rights law enforcement toward which our August 29 statement was directed, a policy which, in our view, is inconsistent with clearly defined legal mandates."

The Attorney General's patience was wearing thin. The next day he told the press that "policy is going to be made by the Justice Department, not by a group of lawyers in the Civil Rights Division." At a news conference three days later, Mr. Leonard said that he thought the position taken by the attorneys was wrong. He warned that the revolt would have to end as of that date.

On October 1, Mr. Leonard called me to his office. He told me that he considered it to be the obligation of all of his attorneys to defend the government's Mississippi action in court. He asked whether I would be able to do so in the future. I said that I could not and would not. Our obligation was to represent the Attorney General, he said, and John Mitchell had decided that delay was the appropriate course to follow in Mississippi. I countered by explaining that my position dictated that I represent the public interest in court, and my responsibility was to enforce the law. Mr. Leonard then made his attitude on the meaning of law enforcement very clear. "Around here the Attorney General is the law," he said. The difference of opinion was irreconcilable, and I was told to resign or be fired. I said I would forthwith submit a letter of resignation, and did—effective immediately.

Later that day, Mr. Leonard issued a memorandum which banned any "further unauthorized statement . . . regarding our work and our policies." He directed the attorneys to keep all "discussions of our work and policies within this Department."

Thus, the Administration's official attitude boils down to an absolute ban on any further protest activity. The public is to be kept in the dark. Law-enforcement decisions are to be made by John Mitchell, and the test for those decisions is soundness, including the relevant political considerations. The attorney's job is to articulate and defend the Attorney General's decisions in court, and that obligation applies without reference to one's individual oath of office and the dictates of conscience.

As attorneys, I and my former colleagues who remain in the Civil Rights Division cannot accept this point of view. The Justice Department lawyer's primary obligation must be to the Constitution. That should hold true whether the attorney is John Mitchell, Jerris Leonard, or Gary Greenberg. In his role as an officer of the United States, the Justice Department lawyer represents the public interest. While Jerris Leonard equates that obligation with obedience to the President and the Attorney General, I and my former colleagues could not. The Justice Department lawyer is not hired to represent John Mitchell in court. He is hired to represent the United States.

Whether or not the revolt achieved its long-range objectives one cannot yet judge. There are indications that in the area of civil rights, as in other matters, the Attorney General is either unaware or contemptuous of the forces which conflict with the politics of the Southern Strategy. The attorneys in the Civil Rights Division continue to take a hard line in individual cases. They assume this posture every day in the pleadings and briefs they present to the Attorney General and Mr. Leonard for approval. So long as the Administration is kept in the position of having to say no—an attitude adopted so far in only those few cases in which the political pressures were intense—it is not likely that they can effect the wholesale retreat on enforcement of the civil rights laws which the Administration seems ready to permit in return for political support. But while it is vital that the revolutionaries remain within the Division, and while their presence within the system may deter future Mississippi-type decisions, there is some question whether their determination will sustain them for the next three and a half years. If not, the prospects for even the grudging enforcement of civil-rights laws are bleak indeed.

It is clear from the Greenberg account that he and his colleagues made their case to Mr. Leonard and Mr. Mitchell like lawyers, staking out a position and then adorning that stance with all sorts of solemn oaths, canons, and Achesonian language. In this case, the attorneys argued that they would abide by the Attorney General's decisions "in matters where discretion is vested in the Attorney General to choose between policy alternatives," but that they would protest when the Attorney General swerved from the "dictates of the law." This statement of the issue left little room for choice or disagreement, for the attorneys said they would dissent only when the Attorney General violated his oath to uphold the law. In that case, conscience and the law left them no choice other than dissent. The lawyers thus gave the Attorney General a great deal of maneuvering room but drew the line when he deviated from the school desegregation mandates of the Supreme Court.

Shorn of its embellishments, the Greenberg argument boils down to the heart of the case for whistle-blowing: that an employee's loyalty to the boss should be overridden by his loyalty to the public when the boss crosses a distinct line into behavior that is contrary to the public interest. The employee has to be able to prove himself *right* in his charges that his superiors are injuring the public by lying, stealing, or, in the case of the civil rights lawyers, acting contrary to the law. These charges are strong ones, and when made they understandably cut the whistle-blower off from the employer he accuses. Whistle-blowing is therefore a sign that the employee has ceased efforts to persuade his superior to change, relying on the force of his public charges to create enough pressure to force the superior to adopt a different course.

Greenberg and his colleagues were addressing themselves to the Attorney General rather than to the public, as evident in the statement that press contacts during the protest were "neither authorized nor approved by the group as a whole." Greenberg later said that one attorney in the group had leaked word of the protest letter to a *New York Times* reporter. This made public what was intended to be an internal protest. The lawyers, in short, had not intended to make the sharp break with their superiors that whistle-blowing requires, and they became whistle-blowers by accident. "Everyone was disappointed with the publicity," Greenberg remembered. "It really hampered what we could do."

It may be that a whistle-blower cannot afford to pull punches as the civil rights lawyers did in describing the actions of their superiors. While the lawyers said it would be unconscionable and contrary to oath, canons, and law for them to enforce Mitchell's policy, they did not say that it would be a violation of oaths and canons on *Mitchell's* part if he persisted in the policies, or that the Attorney General would demonstrate a lack of conscience by doing so. Their emphasis was on justifying their own actions and on writing a "dignified and reasonable statement of protest," rather than on assembling the strongest case against the policies of the Attorney General.

The civil rights lawyers selected a strategy different from one of pure whistle-blowing, because they calculated that their collective opinion within the Department of Justice would carry more weight toward changing the policy than public charges through the press. Their actions were consequently designed to place maximum *internal* pressure on the Attorney General, but in a manner of such boardroom dignity that their jobs and continued effectiveness within the Department would not be jeopardized. A tougher stance than the one taken would have weakened group support, as some people would have dropped out on principle and more would have left out of fear for their jobs. "The way we went about things there was little fear of reprisal," said Greenberg, "but eight of the nine lawyers who refused to sign the protest letter did so because they did not want to risk losing the jobs they had lined up outside. They figured that a law firm might be hesitant to hire a potential malcontent or an enemy of the Attorney General."

The strategy was not necessarily wrong because of its deviations from the whistle-blower's path. It was merely different. One reason for their approach was that the lawyers really had no new evidence to lay before the public. A whistle-blower usually stands or falls on the validity of the objective evidence he offers, which, if verified, should convince most people that the boss is a descendant of Albert Fall or at least incompetent in a way that injures the public. Notwithstanding the attorneys' legal and professional arguments that their position was based on facts and cold canons, the protest letter was essentially a statement of collective opinion. It was reported in the newspapers as such, as a political disagreement and break with the Attorney General. Like participants in sit-ins and demonstrations, the lawyers sought to persuade by virtue of the strength and intensity of their convictions, professionally phrased. Theirs was not a textbook whistle-blower's case. It was a mixture of whistle-blowing and on-the-job dissent—a remarkable development for staid pipe-smokers in the Department of Justice. Such an expression of stinging dissent in that part of the federal government indicates either something sour in the times or something new in the lawyers, or both.

11 Group Dissent

Peter Gall resigned as a press relations officer with the Office of Civil Rights (OCR) of the Department of Health, Education, and Welfare (HEW) in February, 1970, shortly after his superior, Leon Panetta, was fired from his position as head of the OCR. Gall, a Republican and former newspaperman, teamed with Panetta to write *Bring Us Together* (Philadelphia: Lippincott, 1971), a book about civil rights in the Nixon Administration. He is now a staff reporter for *Business Week*.

More than 2,000 employees in HEW protested the dismissal of Leon Panetta. This group protest, with the responsibility spread among a great many people, was closer to philosophical dissent than to real whistle-blowing, according to the subtle distinctions of the art. Gall and his fellow employees were expressing disagreement with HEW Secretary Robert H. Finch and the Nixon Administration over policies with which the public was generally familiar. They were not exposing new evidence that they felt incriminated Secretary Finch on its face. Although the employees' feelings on the civil rights issue were very deep, their protest was mannerly enough for almost all of them to keep their jobs without reprisal.

Still, this group of 2,000 did go public with open criticism of the Nixon Administration's desegregation policies, in what was clearly an effort from inside the bureaucracy to call attention to the retreat from civil rights momentum that they had seen in its beginning stages. And they did this while still employed by the agency whose changing policy they disliked. Such a sizable protest by government employees was unprecedented and caused quite a stir in the press, albeit not a very long-lasting one.

The fact that the dissenters were still employees of HEW when they criticized Finch publicly was crucial to the atmosphere of tension that surrounded group strategy discussions. This tension is symbolic, in many ways, of the difference between pure and alumnus whistle-blowing—the fears that inhibit even the mildest pure whistle-blowers. Apprehension permeates Gall's account, published in the *Washington Monthly* of June, 1970.

Mores of Protest

The actions of nearly 2,000 employees of the Department of Health, Education, and Welfare to protest the dismissal of Leon Panetta, Director of HEW's Office for Civil Rights, were, as protest actions go these days, pretty mild. No protester called the Secretary a pig, or broke a window, or poured ox blood on an official document, or, for that matter, stayed away from work sick a day or even an hour. No policeman, much less a National Guardsman, got called in or needed to be.

No banner headlines reported what we 2,000 did. Indeed it made few front pages, which is scarcely astonishing in view of what we did: Five members of the OCR staff (including me) resigned; 125 members of the OCR staff wrote a letter of remonstrance to the President and made the text of it public; 1,800 members of the staffs of various of the Department's offices signed a memorandum to Secretary Finch ("Subject: Bring Us Together") asking for a full departmental staff meeting at which the Secretary would explain his view of HEW's civil-rights policy in the light of Panetta's removal. Yet, tame as it was, our protest may have been more significant than many a far more sensational event. For one thing, we were professional and clerical employees of a government department, traditionally the most "loyal," not to say timid and docile, class of employees in America. For another thing, we were not protesting our wages or our working conditions or anything that even remotely touched the daily lives of more than a handful of us, but an action that gave us moral offense, that we believed compromised an important program to which we were dedicated. In short, hundreds of government employees publicly expressed dissatisfaction with their employer's policy in a conspicuous and controversial field: school desegregation. It was not a kind of thing that had been done many times before, nor was it done without considerable agonizing by most of us who did it.

Of course, Panetta's "resignation"—which was announced simultaneously to the public and to him on February 17, 1970—could not of itself have set off the protest. As seen by us in OCR, the dismissal was simply the climax of a series of attacks by the Administration on "the program," a phrase we used to characterize school desegregation, one part of the general goal of desegregation authorized by Title VI of the Civil Rights Act of 1964. The gist of Title VI is that the federal government may not subsidize discrimination on grounds of race, color, or national origin; under this prohibition, HEW's responsibility, exercised by OCR, is to see to it that schools, hospitals, nursing homes, welfare agencies, and universities that receive subsidies from the Department or enter into contracts with it do not discriminate, under penalty of not receiving federal funds. Only 106 of the 278 members of OCR's staff deal with the schools, and only 48 of those with the Southern schools. However, the Southern school program is the one that has caught the attention and whipped up the emotions of both the public and the politicians. It has been moderately successful. In 1964, before the act went into effect, about 2 per cent of the black children in the eleven Southern states went to desegregated schools. In 1968, almost entirely because of the threat of withholding funds, that percentage had risen to 20; by mid-1969, to 29.

From almost its first month, the Nixon Administration began to nibble away at the program. First, the desegregation guidelines were weakened in a joint HEW-Justice statement drafted primarily at the White House. Then several school districts got favored treatment that violated all the standards that had been maintained until then. Then Secretary Finch sent a letter to the Fifth Circuit Court of Appeals, asking for a delay for thirty Mississippi school districts, in what then appeared to be (and was later held to be) direct conflict with rulings of the Supreme Court. Finally, the Administration adopted the code words "busing" and "neighborhood schools" as the definition of what school desegregation was all about, abandoning the contention of the Supreme Court, Congress, and the previous Administration that the issue was equal educational opportunity under a very explicit law. It was no wonder that Panetta's removal precipitated a crisis in OCR.

Leon Panetta is an old friend and colleague of mine. We served together on the staff of California's moderate Republican Senator, Thomas H. Kuchel, himself a civil-rights advocate, who was defeated in the 1968 primary by conservative Max Rafferty. Leon asked me to come to OCR as one of his special assistants to handle, among other things, press relations. I arrived, somewhat uncomfortably, as a Republican appointee in the middle of a holdover Democratic staff, devoted to a holdover Democratic program. Nine months later I found myself comfortably joining voices with those Democrats to protest politically motivated attacks on that Democratic program.

My own involvement in the protest began on Thursday, February 20, three days after Leon was fired, when Paul Rilling, OCR's regional director in Atlanta, walked into my office, sat down, and demanded, "Well, what are we going to do about it?" I suddenly realized that I had taken little time in the last three days to think of the consequences of Leon's dismissal or how I would react to it. At the close of the Tuesday press conference, at which Panetta's firing was announced, I had told Bob Gruenberg of the *Chicago Daily News* that I saw "no way" that I could stay as a spokesman for the Office for Civil Rights in the light of what had happened. I had been towed away by a well-meaning office friend who whispered that "nobody needs to fire himself in the press like that—think it over." So, I had deferred hard thinking for forty-eight hours.

Rilling was one of eight regional civil-rights directors, a man holding, but not enjoying, a job as GS-15, making $26,000 a year. He had more cause than most to brood about it all. An adoptive Southerner who had been a teacher, a newspaper man, and a civil-rights worker before former Secretary John Gardner appointed him to OCR, he had opened the Atlanta office in 1967, and since then it had been a stronghold of the drive to eliminate dual school systems. Several political attempts to remove him as "overeager" had been made, but with Panetta's help he had survived them. However, he had been thinking a lot about quitting since the previous summer, when he had confided to me in his office that, while Leon was fighting enough, "I'm just worried he isn't winning enough." Now Paul sat there employed, while Leon was out.

I told Paul that I was likely to quit, but had not planned how I would do it or when. He said he was definitely going to go and thought he would make an issue of it. He asked if we might consider coordinating our efforts. I said we certainly might.

But Paul, along with some of those who would be left behind, wanted to see something more done. Consequently, six like-minded OCR people had lunch the next day, Friday. They were hardly grass-roots types—four GS-15's ($22,000 a year and up), a GS-14, and a GS-12. They were all white, but most had close ties to the black staff. All were totally committed to the goals of the office, and they shared a feeling that an injustice had been done. They considered, and rejected, a number of styles of protest, including an outright strike. "Frankly, we knew the fear of getting fired would reduce participation to almost nothing, since so many just aren't young any more and have mortgages and children," said one of the group. She added that mass resignation also was "out of the question." Two gestures finally were found acceptable: a letter to the President expressing strong feelings over Panetta's ouster and the lack of civil-rights policy generally, and the selection of a common day of leave without pay "for personal reasons." Without being a strike, that would still convey sacrifice (no pay) and rebellion. Someone in the group had even thought ahead to news photographers' recording the empty offices and halls.

I did not participate in the luncheon, nor, except in the most passive and counseling way, in any of the protest planning by the civil-service staff. As a political appointee, I thought that it was better for me to follow my own course and resign with a shout, and not be in the position to risk taking anyone else down with me. On the other hand, Paul had few qualms about exerting such leadership among professionals in Washington, partly because he felt he had invested enough of himself in the program to be able to rally others, and partly because he felt, as a civil-service, nonpolitical career man in government, that he had a right to call on others to make a gesture.

The next step on Friday after the lunch was to test out the sentiment among headquarters staff and among the regional directors assembling for a meeting with Panetta (who was serving out a two-week pay period). The employees who would be approached had been doing some thinking of their own along these lines, naturally. The staff was one of the most racially integrated in the federal government, with 147 minority-group employees, mostly black, and 131 white employees. The word that came back that Friday afternoon from the OCR rank and file was that some would sign a letter and make other signs of displeasure. They felt so strongly that—although others did not want to sign—it was clear that the project should go on. Leon outlined to them, as he had outlined to the full headquarters staff on Wednesday, what he saw as the limits of civil-rights enforcement in the immediate future—grim in the schools, better in other programs—and he observed that "you are all grown men and women and know what is best for you; I'm not going to try to tell you." He made no suggestion that anyone resign or take any action other than to perform well in his job. Then he took seven of the eight regional directors to meet with Under Secretary John Veneman, whose message was that the direction in which the office was moving when Leon was there would be continued in his absence, and that the Secretary wanted to get a good man quickly to replace Panetta. The regional directors listened with only one or two sharp questions directed at Veneman. When Panetta left, the regional directors stayed behind and quickly agreed after listening to Paul Rilling that they would participate in some sort of protest. Again, no political appointees like me were at that meeting, although I knew of it.

The regional directors left Washington with the understanding that they would go back to their home offices and relay not only Veneman's message but the general thrust of the proposed actions over Leon's firing. Before three of them left that weekend, though, they called me at home to express concern that the "day-off" routine might be too negative in tone and could hurt not only the cause but also some employees. I promised to relay their concern and added that in any case it probably would be fair to specifically rule out participation by secretaries in such an act.

Beginning the following Monday, February 23, the eight days until the letter to the President was sent went by like a blur. Monday a letter was drafted and shown around the office for comments. A regional director called and suggested that, instead of the day-off activity, there should be a weekend work-in. "We'll just be doing our thing, man. It will be better public relations and they won't dare to keep us out," he said. This drew a generally favorable response, although some saw it as a cop-out from a stronger confrontation with the Administration.

Tuesday the letter draft was dictated on the phone to regional offices. The letter, which began by telling the President of "our profound dismay" over the circumstances leading to Panetta's dismissal, concluded with two strong paragraphs:

> But the question strikes further than this. It is our conviction that developments in the nation have progressed to the stage when issues affecting race relations can no longer be subverted in deference to expediency, and that to do so now is to risk everything in terms of bringing Americans together. The recent flow of White House statements, as well as a certain untimely and critical reserve, have served to becloud the school desegregation issue and thus to lend credence to the supposition that the national government has grown insensitive to the importance of keeping this cause alive. In this context, the forced resignation of Mr. Panetta only underscores the bitter disappointment of those who have worked hard to achieve an end under law to prejudice and discrimination in this country.
>
> We earnestly hope that you may be prevailed upon to exercise the strong moral leadership that we feel is now essential to avoid a reversal of the nation's long-standing commitment to equal opportunity.

This was too strong for some to sign, too weak for others, like the black secretary who wanted to say, "Why don't we just remove you as President?" One regional director offered a counterdraft of his own. But the consensus was to keep this draft and see how many signed it.

Wednesday and Thursday signatures were collected, and there was general agreement that, instead of staying out of work a day, those who wished would come in on Saturday, March 14, and put in a full day's work for no pay, as a sign that there should be more done in civil rights, not, as the Administration had signaled, less. This would happen at each regional office and headquarters and would be made known to the press.

All this time there had not really been a leader of the effort. There was, instead, Paul Rilling as the moving force behind the regional directors, and four or five activists in Washington who tried deliberately to keep anyone from being identified as a leader. Bertram Carp, twenty-five, a lawyer from the civil rights division of the Office of General Counsel, explained, "We felt it would not only protect some whom we did not want to see fired, but it would also make the whole thing a more broad-based gesture." Two of Carp's responsibilities were to check out the legal ramifications of sending a letter and to contact other lawyers in the office to see if they wanted to sign. Seven lawyers signed the letter with him.

On Friday the price to be paid for lack of leadership became apparent. A representative of the San Francisco office who had come to Washington on official business brought thirteen signatures with him; he found so much confusion in Washington over the final form and timing of the gesture that he took the signatures back to San Francisco. They never were attached to the letter, although it had been intended that they would be. Also on Friday, other crises broke. I got a phone call from an HEW official who had heard about the letter, asking me to bring a copy over. I declined, explaining that it was not my letter, and although I could obtain a copy, it would be a breach of faith with the employees for me to share it. Later in the day, I was told that the Dallas HEW regional director, Charles Green—a former business executive who was put in charge of southwestern regional HEW affairs because of his Republican political connections—had obtained a copy of the letter from one of our employees in Dallas, had telephoned its contents to Secretary Finch's office, and had fingered a high-ranking career man at OCR as the ringleader. Finally, one more high-ranking caller from HEW's front office told me that the letter or any other action "might hurt the office and could hurt Leon, which none of us want." There was nothing specific, no threat, just a plea for reconsideration. I promised to relay the message.

There was near panic among some of the organizers. The man who had been wrongly identified as the ringleader thought briefly of removing his name, but left it on, "because it is important to the meaning of the letter." I said I did not think that anyone was trying to intimidate us. But meanwhile, back in Dallas, the regional chief was proving me wrong. He not only had received the letter, but had talked threateningly to a senior OCR staff member with a government lawyer present in the room. "It was definitely intimidation, let's just leave it at that," said one of the regional staff. In the end, the Dallas office was the only regional office that intentionally did not have one signature on the letter.

There were numerous worried telephone calls over that last weekend. Monday morning, I decided someone had to tell all the Washington staff what was happening, so I asked them to meet with me that afternoon. About sixty showed up. I told them about the calls on Friday and some of the organizers' concerns. We had a count of the number of signatures, the proportion of professional to clerical (60-40), and the racial breakdown (about even). I said I had no role in the plan because I would have a letter of my own the next day, and that I was not trying to influence decisions one way or the other. It was just important to know all of the factors, so everyone could withdraw or add his name as he saw fit. (One activist complained that I had made "everything sound pretty scary.") Six others signed the letter after the meeting. Even in the face of possible strong reaction from the top, some staff were determined to go on record.

At the meeting, it was also agreed that those who wished would come in to work on March 14, a Saturday, and that the $125 left over from the collection for Leon's farewell gift would be given to the NAACP Legal and Educational Defense Fund. The money would be more symbolic than materially helpful, but it would show where a lot of the staff were pinning their hopes for the future—it was the Legal Defense Fund that in November had won a Supreme

Court reversal of the Administration's request for a delay for thirty Mississippi school districts.

Tuesday, March 3, turned out to be the day that everything happened: Paul and I issued statements of resignation around noon; the front office at HEW said it would announce later in the day a new director to succeed Panetta, and in consternation the letter group decided they had better get that document down to the White House immediately, with copies to the press, so it would not appear a deliberate slap at the new boss. The result was that the new director's appointment was buried by the protest story in some papers. However, in other papers, the protests were overshadowed by the appointment, a result not altogether unforeseen by the HEW high brass.

Earlier, Paul Rilling and I had exchanged copies of our statements, so that I could distribute his to the press with mine in Washington, and he could return the favor in Atlanta. It was not a step taken lightly by either of us. A month later, we would still be unemployed. But we both had strong reasons for quitting, and we felt those reasons should be stated publicly, in an effort to focus public attention on what we thought were tragic civil rights policies of the Administration.

I made public a letter of resignation to Secretary Finch in which I noted the "impossible position of one who believes in the Office for Civil Rights, its deeply committed staff and its legal goals, but who knows he owes his appointment as a Republican spokesman here to an Administration which has steadily and increasingly undermined that office and its director." I added that "I cannot any longer try to justify to the public the actions of this Administration regarding either the subject of civil rights generally, or its treatment of your Office for Civil Rights in particular."

I had alerted several people in the Secretary's office whom I respected that this letter would be made public. The reaction varied, from one official who understood why some of us wanted to do this but warned of burning bridges and saying things that would hurt our cause, to another who started by saying that no one would want to hire a man who said nasty things about his employer when he left ("It isn't professional"), and ended by trying to point out the difference between peddling my letter to news media and waiting for them to come to me ("There is a question of ethics if you are using government facilities"). I thanked both of them, but said I had thought it out carefully, and it was all I could do.

Several weeks before Leon was ousted, Carl Flaxman, the regional civil rights director in Dallas, had quit, citing interference in civil rights matters on the part of the Administration's new HEW boss in the Southwest. After March 3, Bertram Carp resigned, mentioning disagreement with Administration civil-rights policies on his resignation form. Gordon Rubin, twenty-nine, the education branch chief in San Francisco and a veteran of OCR struggles in the South, left in May. "I was ready to leave because of some of the recent events, anyway, but the topper was Leon being fired," Rubin told me. He had drafted a letter to Leon on February 25, signed by every available member of the San Francisco office, saying Panetta would be remembered warmly "as one who was not afraid to speak the truth."

That makes five resignations as of this date over policy; others are actively seeking other jobs in a market which at present can only be called squishy soft for civil-rights workers.

As for the 1,800-signature petition to Secretary Finch, I know little about its genesis. We in OCR became aware that it was being drafted in the Department at the time we were planning the letter to the President. We stayed away from planning and drafting sessions in order to make sure that the petition's grass-roots origin in the Department could not be questioned, that it could not be dismissed as a put-up job by members of OCR's staff. We first saw it only when it was being circulated for signatures, several days after our own protest had been made. About forty members of OCR's staff signed it, most—but not all—of them people who had signed the letter too. The most prominent signatories of the petition were Mary E. Switzer, head of the Social and Rehabilitation Service, and Jule M. Sugarman, Director of the Head Start program. Miss Switzer has since retired and Sugarman has left HEW to become the head of the New York City Human Resources Administration.

So there was the big gesture: a letter, a petition, a few resignations. The weekend work-in never materialized, because of a general feeling that the new director, Stanley Pottinger, should not be hurt before he had a chance to prove himself. The check for $125 was presented in Leon's name to the Legal Defense Fund a week and a half later by Mrs. Verbena Crowley, a black OCR secretary with a child in a Maryland school district that Panetta had said must desegregate or lose federal funds. The letter has not been answered, or for that matter acknowledged, by the President or any member of his staff, although we have learned that Leonard Garment, the White House assistant for minority affairs, drafted an acknowledgment some time before March 24, when the President issued his big statement on school desegregation. None of us who signed the letter is especially surprised at this silence from 1600 Pennsylvania Avenue. Indeed, a chief reason we decided to flout protocol and make the text of the letter public was that we felt that the only way the President would even become aware of the existence of the letter was through publicity. We had answered too many letters—including those bitterly attacking the retreat on segregation—referred unread by the White House mail room to have any illusion about what the fate of our letter would be. In fact, our standing joke while we were drafting it was that we would probably be asked to answer it ourselves. The petition has done somewhat better. Secretary Finch has promised to meet with all HEW employees to discuss the Department's position on civil rights and school desegregation, though at this writing he has not yet done so.

The protests in HEW raise a crucially important—although perhaps ultimately unanswerable—question: What is the correct balance between a bureaucrat's right under the First Amendment to express his views as a citizen and his obligation to follow the policies of his seniors, especially that senior of seniors, the President? Not long ago HEW's Deputy Under Secretary, Frederick V. Malek, a thirty-three-year-old top management expert and a powerful voice in upper-level personnel affairs, framed the orthodox answer to this question in a telephone interview:

> The employee, whether he is civil service or a political appointee, has not only the right but the obligation to make his views known in the most strenuous way possible to his

> superiors, and through them, to their superiors. He should try like hell to get his view across and adopted within the organization—but *not* publicly, and only until a decision is reached by those superiors. Once the decision is made, he must do the best he can to live with it and put it into practice. If he finds he cannot do it, then he ought not to stay with the organization.

To stay within these guidelines, Malek says, the OCR staff should have presented their protest to Secretary Finch (as the 1,800 non-OCR petitioners did) and should have done it quietly, avoiding the press (unlike the non-OCR petitioners). Malek says "flatly"—his own word—that because the OCR protest was "spontaneous, philosophical, and was not meant as a damaging act of disloyalty," there will be no reprisals against signers of the letter with respect to promotions or any other sort of personnel action. But he adds that under "other circumstances" such a public protest might well affect the protesters' future. Malek's view is of central importance to the HEW staff, of course, but as far as I am concerned, his recommended line of action would have been a waste of everyone's time. To begin with, the OCR staff members probably would have made their protest to Secretary Finch if they had felt that Finch's views were being listened to, or acted upon, at the White House. They didn't. They saw the Secretary, rightly or wrongly, as a man who on the whole subscribed to the arguments of Leon Panetta, their representative, but who could not make those arguments heard in turn. Therefore, they cut out both middlemen when one was fired. As for the publicity, there was every reason to believe that the letter would not even have come to the attention of the President if it had been dropped off quietly at the White House mail room.

Beyond that, there are myriad problems over the manner in which a protest is hatched. The most important of these is the question of pressure, one way or another, on the lower-level employees. In my view, to hurt, or expose to injury, a secretary, messenger, or even an $11,000-a-year professional, is a bigger sin for a bureaucrat by far than to insult the President. Extraordinary pains must be taken to be sure that participation is not forced from above, even indirectly. In our office some secretaries most emphatically volunteered to participate. And supervisors all say they were as neutral as possible, assuring no reprisal if subordinates did or did not sign. But ideally, supervisors would not have laid the matter out at all. Secretaries would have talked to secretaries, and only lower-grade professionals would have presented the case for action.

Then there is the matter of the use of the taxpayer's time and facilities. One regional OCR staffer felt so strongly against meetings about the protest on government time that he drafted a letter to the President protesting the protesters. His zeal in this matter was so selectively aimed, however, that his line of argument seems suspect, because there is scarcely an office in government where high-level officials do not use the Xerox machine or the telephone for personal business or have their secretaries type personal letters. So, while a protester must bear the penalty for improper use of government resources if his superiors wish to make an issue of it, the fact is, in this variety of wrongdoing, good and bad examples most often are set at the top.

Whatever the tactics employed or niceties observed, it would not surprise me or many of my friends who work for the government to see more expressions of displeasure, dismay, or outrage over principles issuing from the mouths and government typewriters of the bureaucracy. Partly it is the influence of the young people who have shunned the cop-out of hippiedom, or the corporate goals of financial enrichment, to enter government. Partly, it is the pattern of protest engendered in reaction to the war in Vietnam. But mostly it is that President Nixon appears to many committed workers who entered the government during the reform years of the 1960's to be intent upon retarding, if not completely undoing, some of the progress that had been accepted as a minimum in American life.

That seems to stir an uncommon, nonbureaucratic reaction.

The meeting of all HEW employees with Secretary Finch, to which Gall refers near the end of the article, never came off. Secretary Finch postponed it several times, and, while the government workers were assembling for the meeting at the final rescheduled time, Finch fell ill with a paralysis and numbing of his arm. The authenticity of this illness was widely, and sometimes comically, disputed in the press, but most sources within HEW say that the disorder was genuine. Finch showed physical signs of enormous strain, demonstrating that the pressure felt by the employees was also affecting some persons in the top management.

Gall leaves the impression of a slow exodus of workers from HEW over the new civil rights policies of the Nixon Administration, but he has said since the publication of his article that such a flock of resignations did not in fact occur. "Most of them have stayed at their posts and chafed," he said. "They made their decision to stay on—unhappy—last year. A lot of those people have families and mortgages, and there aren't a whole lot of places for them to go, especially in current job market conditions."

The absence of reprisals against the petition-signers indicated that HEW does not regard protest as automatic grounds for disciplinary action. However, there has been little or no follow-up resistance to the civil rights slowdown from department employees. "Most of the ones I know," says Gall, "feel that they pushed their luck last year and can't expect to get away with things like that any more."

The chief significance of the Panetta firing and the subsequent whistle-blowing was not the immediate impact on public opinion and certainly not the impact on the policies of the government. The positive effect of these events was more indirect—the stamping of February, 1970, as a landmark in the twisting course of the civil rights issue, a shift that was noticeable enough for 2,000 government bureaucrats to issue an historic dissent. The events were noteworthy enough to be recorded, and that record might be used in the campaign arsenal of any candidate who wants to push civil rights again. Also, the protest over the Panetta firing made a small dent in the great psychic wall among government employees against criticizing the policies of their own organization, even when they regard those policies as unconscionable.

12 Three Who Paid

The atmosphere of hesitancy and caution in the preceding Greenberg and Gall accounts of civil rights protests during the Nixon Administration gives some hint of the job fear that so often paralyzes potential whistle-blowers. Inhibitions of the purse have an especially crushing effect on those with families and widespread financial obligations, and giving in to these inhibitions has a demoralizing impact on employees who would like to believe that they are in their jobs for more than the money. Economic vulnerability is so critical a concern in whistle-blowing that a whole specialty in the art centers on the means of sidestepping reprisals and otherwise hanging on to a paycheck.

Unfortunately, survival is not always as easy as it was for most of the Justice Department and HEW employees—whose group actions produced no fresh disclosures of departmental decay but rather criticized policies that were already known to the public (and believed by the Administration to have wide support). When a pure whistle-blower comes forward with fresh evidence of unmistakable corruption, the reaction is certain to be more vigorous, more on the order of Senator Dodd's response to the Boyd charges. Whistle-blowing follows Newtonian principles, as the reaction against an employee varies according to how intensely his actions gore the employer agency. If his charges strike home, he can expect tribulations like Jim Boyd's—and some of Boyd's successors.

Charles Pettis

About the time Drew Pearson was cranking out his first attack on Senator Dodd in early 1966, Charles Pettis was heading for Lima, Peru, to his new job as resident engineer on a project to build Peru's long-standing dream—a highway across the Andes. A forty-four-year-old geological engineer, Pettis was to play a crucial role in the 146-mile, $46 million construction effort that was designed to open up trade for the first time between Peru's coastal cities on one side of the mountains and the isolated interior regions on the other.

The highway would not only bolster the hopes and incomes of most Peruvians, it would also refurbish the image of American foreign assistance. It was an aid project through and through, with $12 million from the Agency for International Development and $23 million from the Export-Import Bank, and the balance from Peru. Although there were the usual minor irritants for the recipient country, such as AID contracting regulations that eliminated all but American firms from the bidding, such things were overlooked in general enthusiasm for the road.

Pettis was under contract to Brown & Root Overseas, Inc.—an international engineering firm based in Houston, whose foreign aid business had prospered mightily since Lyndon Johnson entered the White House. Brown & Root was hired to protect the interests of the Peruvian Government by overseeing the construction efforts of the main contractor, Morrison-Knudsen of Boise, Idaho. There was a substantial conflict of interest involved here, because B & R had also been paid several million dollars for the original survey and design work on the road—whose quality would be in question during any dispute with Morrison-Knudsen. These things were overlooked, perhaps out of AID habit. Charles Pettis went to work for his client, the Peruvian Government; and his signature was required on the payroll to signify that Peru's interests were protected and that the contract specifications were being enforced.

Pettis's misgivings about the project began when he surveyed the design and found that it called for cutting channels up to 300 feet deep through the notoriously unstable Andes mountains—with sheer cliffs to be left on either side of the road. He was further disturbed by the fact that the design team had taken few geological borings in the earth to determine its susceptibility to slides, which is considerable. (Pettis charges that the Brown & Root employee in charge of the design made a favorable impression within the organization by spending so little on the project that a substantial profit was reaped.) These faults and many others led him to conclude: (1) that the road could not be built as designed, and (2) that large cost overruns would result. Nevertheless, Morrison-Knudsen commenced work.

Open conflict set in at the construction site when Morrison-Knudsen demanded that the monthly payroll be padded to include extra charges for slide removal (thirty-one men were killed on the road, many because of slides). Pettis refused on the grounds that such payments were not called for by the contract and that the Peruvian Government would lose a great deal of money by such laxity. "At first, Brown & Root supported me," says Pettis, "but they had a big meeting in February of 1968, and the tables began to turn. Bert Perkins, the executive vice president of Morrison-Knudsen, said he bid the job low because of prior association with Brown & Root all over the world—and because they expected to get a break. I'm sort of hot-tempered and old-fashioned in things like that, and I said I wouldn't be a party to collusion."

Brown & Root soon ordered Pettis to begin padding the payroll—out of fear that Morrison-Knudsen might otherwise attack the flimsy design, or perhaps out of corporate understanding. When Pettis would not go along, he was replaced by a more pliable man named B. W. Donelson—who promptly began authorizing supplementary payments to the contractor. Donelson brought an element of the old Yankee *bandido* to the plot by obtaining a subcontract from Morrison-Knudsen to feed the construction workers. By cutting food costs, he was able to harvest a profit of some $250,000 from the very contract that he was overseeing. He also managed to divert about twenty-five Peruvian laborers from the road to work on the construction of his private home. Donelson is now wanted by the Peruvian Government on these (and several other) charges of fraud, but he has vanished into the continent like Martin Bormann.

In December, 1968, Brown & Root fired Pettis after he refused to reassure the Peruvian Government in exchange, he says, for "any other job in Latin America." Peru had stopped payment on the road largely because Pettis would not tell the transportation ministry that the road was being constructed properly or the payroll figured honestly. Enormous psychological pressure was mounted against Pettis by the Americans to get him to recant. "There were a lot of little things that really add up to make you feel isolated," he says. "The contractor people's kids threw eggs at my kids and would have nothing to do with them. And the American Consul in Lima gave me a temporary passport—like visitors from the Communist countries—and then tried to dismiss it as a bureaucratic error. Stuff like that adds up."

Pettis has been without salary since December, 1968, and more than half a dozen job offers have been "suddenly canceled," he says. "Every firm in the business considers me a 'rat.'" When he asked his lawyer to talk with Brown & Root about a possible breach of contract suit, the attorney wrote back that the company's position "seems to be that your first duty was to the Brown & Root 'team' rather than to the Peruvian Government, and that by your actions you violated this duty."

Pettis and his wife are in the process of moving to Spain, where they hope to set up a small school. He is rather bitter about the whole conflict in Peru: "This is the kind of thing that's ruining the United States all over the world. We look like a bunch of crooks, and anyone who tells the truth about it is considered crazy. I feel that when an engineer takes a job like that highway, he has to protect his client. I hate this thing of costs being $8 or $10 million above the contract. You've got to stand up against the pressures to live with yourself. You sure won't make much money that way—I mean what the hell did I have to gain out of this?—but you have to do it. Looking back on it, I believe that I would do the same thing again. You really have no choice. But if you ask my wife, she would say no."

Meanwhile, construction on the highway has been halted, with a huge wastage of funds, and the Brown & Root image in Latin America has been tarnished—as has the reputation of AID. But this scrape has not prevented further partnership between the company and the government. For example, Brown & Root and Morrison-Knudsen head a construction consortium that obtained a contract in February, 1971, to upgrade the notorious "Tiger Cages" at Con Son prison in South Vietnam, where 288 "isolation cells" are to be built for $400,000. Profitability will be bolstered by a provision for the use of prison labor.

John McGee

John M. McGee, a middle-level engineer, went to Bangkok in May, 1967, to monitor the delivery of petroleum, oil, and lubricants (POL) to Thailand and South Vietnam for the Navy Fuel Supply Office (NFSO). He immediately began complaining to his supervisor, Arlie Rankin, that huge quantities of petroleum were being stolen for a well-organized black market because of a lax and corrupt system of invoice controls. "He told me that everything had gone smoothly before I arrived, and that he would have me fired if I caused any trouble," said McGee. "That's when we began to develop personality differences, because I wanted to get an investigation into the whole mess. The delivery system is so big and confusing that even the officials don't really know who's responsible."

Things deteriorated rapidly after McGee wrote the Navy Fuel Supply Office in Washington and requested (without success) that headquarters look into the monitoring system. Supervisor Rank finally took the highly unorthodox step of ordering McGee to stay out of his office (where the records were kept) and to communicate only in postmarked letters. "It's kind of funny looking back on it," says McGee, "but at the time I didn't think so. I mean here were two grown men working closely together on a multimillion-dollar operation and playing like little kids. We saw each other every day because our offices were almost next to each other, but business had to be conducted by mail, with big postal delays. One week he wrote me seventeen letters and I had to reply. Pretty soon I got fed up and complained to him, in a letter, that our communications system was 'gobbledy-gook.' Then he cited me for disrespect in an official letter of reprimand, on the grounds that I had slandered his correspondence system."

This document, known as the "gobbledy-gook reprimand," was appealed up through the NFSO personnel command, but was not acted upon. McGee appealed through grievance channels to the Commanding Officer of the NFSO, Captain Richard Jones, for an investigation by the Air Force Office of Special Investigations, which did probe the matter but classified its report and filed it away. He then wrote for help from the Civil Service Commission, which declined and termed the matter a "personality disagreement" after consulting—in standard procedure—McGee's supervisor, Arlie Rankin. Finally, McGee received a personal visit from an authorized representative of the NFSO Commanding Officer, who delivered a "resign or be fired" ultimatum.

"That was the real turning point," recalls McGee. "Resigning would have meant breach of contract, and I would have been required to pay for transporting my family and belongings back to the States—and to reimburse the Navy for sending me over. Getting fired would have meant that I couldn't expect to get another job. I would have had to buckle under and do what they wanted, except that I tape-recorded the ultimatum conversation, and the guy really hit the ceiling when I told him because he knew the ultimatum was illegal."

In March, 1968, John McGee, disabled war veteran with a soft country accent, who "just wanted to get to the bottom of this," wrote to Senator William Proxmire. The Senator demanded an investigation by the General Accounting Office. A preliminary report showed that 52 per cent of all petroleum deliveries to Thailand (about 5.5 million gallons) had been stolen over a ten-month period in 1967. The situation looked worse in South Vietnam. The GAO released a more complete report on July 28, 1970, which detailed the techniques of theft and the weaknesses of control. Although both the oil companies and the government agencies are required to keep records for inspection, the GAO study was limited and contained no precise estimates of the problem "because of the nonavailability of knowledgeable personnel and of pertinent records pertaining to POL activities in Southeast Asia."

The petroleum thefts were carried on by organized rings of truck drivers and others, who sold the goods on the black market. They did very well. So did the American oil companies, because the government was forced to step up its POL orders to make up for the stolen quantities. Everyone was getting along nicely except the public, a critical but distant party to the arrangement. And the public didn't seem to mind, which is why McGee looked so foolish when he rocked the boat on the taxpayers' behalf.

Having exposed a major scandal against the public interest, John McGee received the obscure whistle-blower's reward and was transferred to Washington, where he was filed away in the bureaucracy. "I didn't have any job or any duties," he said. "I just occupied a desk. I read the *Post* in the morning and the *Daily News* in the afternoon." After more than six months at these tasks, he was again transferred in June, 1969, to Pensacola, Florida. This transfer took place on the direct order of Secretary of the Navy John Chafee, reacting to severe pressure from Senator Proxmire and Senator Joseph Montoya. However, Pensacola proved a bureaucratic Siberia-substitute, where McGee was assigned to a nonexistent program that required him only to keep up with correspondence regarding its proposed birth. The program, which McGee believes is a good one, got under way a little more than a year later, but it is still in preliminary snarls, understaffed, and beset with all the problems of being low-priority, in a time of budget-cutting.

"I am still radioactive around here," says McGee. "I have been for more than three years. Once you go outside with criticism, that happens to you. The people down here are afraid that I'll find some small skeletons in their closet. No matter how much I try to explain the circumstances of the petroleum incident, they still think I'm a risk. And most of the people resent me, too. They know that Secretary Chafee put me down here, and they believe that I got my job because of political pull with senators—that I'm a privileged character. It's no fun, but your skin gets pretty thick after a while."

John McGee plans to stick it out with the government because he has so many years invested toward retirement and because he can't get a good job recommendation. He is discouraged that his actions and the GAO reports have not really cleaned up the POL delivery system in Southeast Asia.

McGee's controversy concerned a relatively major scandal, and the GAO reports actually took it to the back pages of some newspapers. Nothing at all is heard about punier fish.

"There is no telling the number of people who get quick medical discharges after they make waves or speak out," says B. B. Bray, associate staff director and federal employee ombudsman for the House Committee on Post Office and Civil Service. "They get sent to a psychiatrist and then out, or they get 'reorganized.' The personnel people say, 'Well, he's got a file this thick, which indicates that he has a poor personality, a bad disposition, and that nobody can get along with him.'

"Things haven't gotten a bit better in the last ten years, and may be worse," he continued. "The system is such that responsibility never gets pinned down to those people who hurt the public. Not only do they fire the complainants, but the others get promoted. There is a cancerous element in these things: The agencies are more interested in finding out who complained than in the substance of the complaint. The Pentagon will spend a thousand dollars to cover up a nickel error, and the other departments aren't much better."

Jacqueline Verrett

There are among the pure whistle-blowers a few people who have survived storms as violent as those that struck Pettis and McGee. Jacqueline Verrett, of HEW's Food and Drug Administration (FDA), is an example of an employee who has both won a case and survived—though not without scars.

For a dozen years, Mrs. Verrett has been pumping chicken eggs full of the molecular concoctions that are added to American food to make it look better, last longer, and, above all, cost less. A pioneer in the chick-embryo testing method for food additives, biochemist Verrett became disturbed when her tests showed that cyclamates, a widely used sugar substitute, caused substantial and grotesque deformities in the embryos. She began reporting these findings through FDA channels on March 7, 1968, and continued to bring them up with growing alarm in memos, meetings, and her semiannual research reports.

By the fall of 1969, when the FDA still showed no signs of acting on the matter, the cyclamate findings were being talked about in scientific circles—based on the Verrett research and parallel work elsewhere. Because of these discussions, Mrs. Verrett was not terribly surprised when NBC's Paul Friedman asked for an interview in late September, at the prompting of James Turner, author of the Nader report on food additives, *The Chemical Feast* (New York: Grossman, 1970). "The cyclamate publicity had been going on for some time," said Mrs. Verrett, "and I didn't think the NBC interview was any big deal. I kind of backed into the controversy by not anticipating the explosion here in HEW."

When she sought routine clearance for the taping session

with Friedman, Mrs. Verrett's office was suddenly besieged by about a dozen lab-coated scientists and administrative officials of FDA—an unprecedented gathering. They earnestly remonstrated with her, urging her to forgo the interview because of the "undue public alarm" that would no doubt ensue if her deformed embryos were to appear on the television screens of the millions of Americans who consumed cyclamate-laden diet drinks and food products. Although the nervous assembly based antidisclosure arguments on an abiding concern for the protection of the public, there was no comparable concern directed toward getting cyclamates off the market at that time.

The almost frantic fear of the adverse test results appeared to spring from a double standard within FDA on both tests and media policy. Mrs. Verrett contrasts the response to the cyclamate embryos with the warm welcome usually given even the flimsiest experiments that make food look safe. In the summer of 1969, for example, Mrs. Verrett produced a preliminary study of another suspect additive, monosodium glutamate (MSG), using only 180 eggs. Although she found no clearly harmful effects, she emphasized that the test was in no way conclusive. Nevertheless, FDA Commissioner Herbert Ley rushed to Congress and hailed the "exquisite, sensitive, new toxicological approach" that found MSG as safe as apple pie (homemade). The cyclamate data, in contrast, came from a thorough investigation that used about 13,000 eggs and established a definite causal relationship between the chemical and embryo deformities. Yet cyclamates remained officially safe, and no one rushed to Congress—only to Mrs. Verrett's office to head off the public panic. (The absurdity of this situation should reinforce the suspicion that something sour is afoot whenever measures "protective of the public" are advocated not by aggrieved members of the public but by people with a bureaucratic or financial stake in the operation. This suspicion seems as justified in the cyclamate controversy as it is in licensing and guild legislation or other public-spirited measures put forth by occupational associations.)

The FDA put great pressure on Mrs. Verrett not to go through with the interview, but it could not afford an outright refusal of permission. She went ahead. "It's taxpayer's money and taxpayer's research here," she said later, "so I believe that the public is entitled to know about the results—especially if you are careful not to overstate the conclusions. I give the American public credit for taking information for what it's worth. As far as I know, there was no harmful public alarm about cyclamates. The only great alarm took place in the Secretary's office."

Indeed, there was some commotion in the office of the HEW Secretary, then Robert H. Finch, after the chick embryos were shown on the Huntley-Brinkley show. Secretary Finch was soon visited by Donald Kendall, president of Pepsico, Inc. (which obtains it legal counsel from President Nixon's New York law firm), chairman of the President's council on industrial pollution, president of the Grocery Manufacturer's Association, and friend of President Nixon. Kendall sought assurances from higher authorities than Mrs. Verrett that cyclamates were safe enough to protect his company's enormous investment in cyclamate-filled diet drinks. Finch was also contacted by representatives of Abbott Laboratories, the major producer of cyclamates and a more or less regular participant in health disasters. (The most recent Abbott episode occurred in March, 1971, when some of its intravenous fluids were recalled from hospitals upon discovery of contamination. According to Morton Mintz of the *Washington Post,* a survey of twenty-one hospitals out of some 3,000 supplied by Abbott revealed 350 cases of blood poisoning, including nine fatal ones, connected with the fluids.)

The upshot of the cyclamate revelations was that the additive was removed from general use on October 18, 1969—not on the basis of Mrs. Verrett's FDA data, but on the basis of a coincidental, fortunate discovery of bladder cancer in rats by Abbott itself. (The use of company evidence, rather than public data, made consumer lawsuits against Abbott much more difficult.)

The upshot for Mrs. Verrett was that she was publicly censured for unethical conduct by Secretary Finch—twice within ten days, without an explanation of the charges. Also, during the period between the NBC appearance and the announcement of the ban, she was prohibited from granting interviews or even from answering her office telephone.

Such direct criticism from a Cabinet member is usually more than sufficient to focus bureaucratic antibodies on a low-level employee as if he were an offensive bacillus and drive him from the government. Yet Mrs. Verrett remains.

"I'm still kind of a leper around here, if you want to know the truth," she said. "I'm called to some meetings if it's absolutely essential, but that's about it."

Her bureaucratic afterlife probably stems from an odd combination of circumstances. For one thing, her rare skills are now almost indispensable to FDA because a large number of new additives are to be tested in the near future as a result of consumer pressure, and, ironically, the chick embryo method has been determined to be the best for rapid screen-testing. Also, her testing unit is unusual in its independence. Mrs. Verrett can work effectively even in bureaucratic isolation. Most other government employees at her level would become helpless without the active cooperation of many associates working toward group solutions. She works in a rare pocket in the government where talent and the skills of a small group can produce results without so much reliance upon the ability "to get along" that often assumes prime importance in both government and industry. She works, in short, in a job for which special talents are almost determinative, rather than in the more typical jobs in which talent or competence is more evenly distributed—where no one's skills are really indispensable and where personal associations and cooperative spirit become the key to one's success. Finally, Mrs. Verrett has survived because her widely publicized case has brought her support both in the press and in the Congress. Warren Magnuson, for example, the powerful chairman of the Senate Commerce Committee, is strongly in her corner.

None of these factors means that Jacqueline Verrett is guaranteed a position at FDA, of course. In fact, she may face danger in the current plan to expand the chick-embryo facilities and move them to Pine Bluff, Arkansas, the chemical and biological warfare center, when all of its nerve gas and toxins are swept out. That plan will require a reorganization of FDA, and reorganizations are notoriously useful for "streamlining" personnel.

In the meantime, Mrs. Verrett is still injecting additives into chicken eggs, without a great deal of chemical confidence in the American diet. "I can't say that I'm very optimistic about our effect here," she said. "There is a kind of tightening up and restriction that is proindustry and anticonsumer. In some ways, we are worse off than we were a year and a half ago.

"And one sad thing is that you have to get really dramatic test results to have any hope of making an impact. If thalidomide had caused mental retardation instead of birth defects, for example, I think we would still be using it. The same with cyclamates."

The twisted chick embryos packed a big wallop with the average tabloid reader, and the press attention that she got undoubtedly helped Jacqueline Verrett save the country from cyclamates and herself from unemployment. Although her actions may not rescue Americans from an artificial diet, they must be counted as a victory for whistle-blowing. That she did not pay a high price for her purity without something to show for it may not provide much consolation for Charles Pettis or John McGee, but it may encourage others who have to face similar decisions.

13 The Cost of Courage

Barbara Newman wrote about the career limbo of the man who set a dollar record by blowing a $2-billion whistle in the *Washington Monthly* for July, 1969, four months after Robert Benson's article on defense spending appeared and eight months after A. Ernest Fitzgerald exposed the cost overrun on the C-5A airplane in November, 1968, and thus helped make weapons spending and military waste an issue of wide public interest. Fitzgerald testified before Senator William Proxmire's Subcommittee on Economy in Government of the Joint Economic Committee on the C-5A contract between the Air Force and Lockheed. A debate regarding Lockheed's solvency and efficiency has continued ever since, with the latest step by the government being a $250-million loan guarantee that was provided by Congress in the summer of 1971, in the midst of great controversy.

Fitzgerald remained in the Pentagon after his testimony, but he was removed from his regular position as a cost management expert and given more clerical duties. He had become such a threat to the harmony between the Pentagon and its contractors that he seemed to be personally repellent to many colleagues as he walked the halls around his office. People would seldom speak to him, for he had taken on some of the scent of a traitor and a loner within the organizational team at the Department of Defense.

In her article "The Cost of Courage," subtitled "The Pentagon's Loneliest Man," Barbara Newman, Washington correspondent for New York's Municipal Broadcasting System, wrote:

> The career of A. E. Fitzgerald is in jeopardy. His sin: zeal and honesty in performing his job as a high-ranking Air Force management expert. In most worlds, efficiency experts who ferret out waste and sloppiness are rewarded. But Fitzgerald works at the Pentagon, where a cost expert can come upon hard times, especially if he tells the truth to Congress.
>
> No one in Washington had ever heard of A. E. (for Arthur Ernest) Fitzgerald until November, 1968. That was when he broke the news to a congressional committee that the giant C-5A military cargo plane would cost the government almost $2 billion more than it said in the original contract price negotiated with Lockheed. To the discomfiture of his superiors, Ernie Fitzgerald has been invited to appear at a number of hearings since that time. And one day in June, fifteen minutes before he was scheduled to discuss the costs of the Minuteman program before a joint committee of Congress, the Air Force ordered him not to testify. Although the Air Force reversed itself the next day—after the committee chairman, Senator William Proxmire (D-Wis.), complained to Secretary of Defense Melvin R. Laird—the story accurately suggests that the Air Force hierarchy would like nothing better than to have Fitzgerald leave the Pentagon forever.
>
> What sort of man would you expect a man like A. E. Fitzgerald to be? Perhaps an antimilitary zealot who infiltrated the Pentagon. Or a liberal abstractionist concerned about an imbalance between the military and domestic budget. Or a foe of the military-industrial complex. But he is none of these. He is, in his own words, "a parsimonious hawk." He does not suggest that the role of the military in American life is too large or that we are not paying enough attention to the central cities. Those are not the issues that engage him.
>
> Fitzgerald is a zealot in another direction: he can't stand the sight of waste. It appalls him. So do inefficiency, slack procedures, and incompetence. And now he finds himself the loneliest man at the Pentagon because he has accused the procurement hierarchy of all these things (and helpfully documented it with chapters and verses).

Looked at another way, A. E. Fitzgerald is a GS-17 bureaucrat with a salary approaching $30,000. His title sounds long and anonymous: He is Deputy for Management Systems in the Office of the Assistant Secretary of the Air Force (Financial Management). He is forty-three years old. He is a self-made man. He grew up in a part of Alabama where one had to work hard to make a living. He went to the University of Alabama on the GI Bill after World War II. Hard work is still his habit, although the Air Force has isolated him from major responsibility for the last eight months.

Before he went to work for the Air Force in 1965, he was president of Performance Technology Corporation, a tough cost-efficiency organization that has done extensive work for the Pentagon. A study it conducted on the engines for the F-111 fighter-bomber recommended that contract costs be cut by 50 per cent. Its evaluation of the Minuteman II program found that costs were too high and that the Minuteman's reliability was in doubt. The Air Force ignored the findings on the Minuteman, only to discover later that (a) it had cost $4 billion more than the Air Force had told Congress it would cost and (b) the guidance system had turned out to be unreliable.

Fitzgerald, after participating in his company's study of the Minuteman guidance system, concluded that if someone relatively high up in the Pentagon had known about cost control and performance standards the Minuteman situation might not have occurred. In the fall of 1965, at the invitation of Leonard Marks, Jr., Assistant Secretary of the Air Force for Financial Management, Fitzgerald agreed to join the Air Force staff. He took a substantial salary cut to do so; but he felt it was important work that he could do well.

He became actively engaged in promoting more efficient management techniques in Air Force procurement almost as soon as he arrived on the job. Some of his superiors in the Air Force hierarchy did not appreciate his efforts, particularly in the area of cost control. But Fitzgerald is the kind of man who bears up well under official displeasure when he is convinced that he is right.

He thought he was right last November, when he appeared for the first time before the Economy in Government Subcommittee of the Joint Economic Committee, headed by Proxmire. His testimony then—to the effect that the C-5A would cost the government $5.2 billion, rather than the $3.4 billion anticipated in the contract—set off the first significant stir over inefficiency in military procurement procedures.

If, as seems clear, his revelation helped to stimulate debate on a broad range of issues involving the military, it also caused the Air Force to start its program of massive retaliation against Fitzgerald. He was stripped of his primary duties —overseeing cost reports on the major weapons systems and working on performance standards for contractors; his transfer to tenured civil-service status, promised two months prior to his congressional appearance, fell by the wayside; President Johnson's Secretary of the Air Force, Harold Brown, asked for a memo outlining the different ways in which he could fire Fitzgerald. In the long months since November, Fitzgerald has retained his title but lost his principal functions. He would be long gone from the Pentagon by now if it were not for the array of senators and congressmen—from all over the political spectrum—who are convinced of Fitzgerald's value as an efficiency expert and who believe that the $2-billion misunderstanding over the C-5A deserved the public airing it got.

The C-5A is the largest airplane ever built. It is almost as long as a football field, and it is designed to carry great amounts of military equipment.

Its complex history, difficult even now to reconstruct, can begin, for the purposes of this article, when the government signed the C-5A contract with the Lockheed Aircraft Corporation in October, 1965, about a month after Fitzgerald went to work at the Pentagon.

This was the first major defense contract to embrace what is known as the "total package" procurement concept. Under the old method, contractors would compete with one another during the research-and-development phase, after which the Pentagon would choose the prototype it liked best and sign a production contract with the company that produced it. At that point, the company would become a "sole source" supplier of the new product. Thus, a contractor would set a low price for research and development, in hopes of competing successfully for the "sole source" production contract. But any contractor who ultimately won a sole-source contract could, in the absence of competition, set high prices for production, partly to recoup any losses he may have suffered on the R & D phase.

Total package procurement was the brainchild of Robert H. Charles, who was Assistant Secretary of the Air Force for Installations and Logistics. He presented it as a way for the government to save money by forcing a contractor to put a total fixed price for all of the stages involved in developing and producing a new article of hardware. Secretary of Defense McNamara described it as "a damn good contract."

And it well might have been, if it had gone according to the original plan. But mysteriously and suddenly a new element—which Fitzgerald calls "the dark at the top of the stairs"—entered the picture. This was a so-called repricing formula which completely violated the "total packaging" principle behind the new-style contract.

When the government signed the contract with Lockheed, it committed itself to buying only the first fifty-eight planes, known as the C-5A. If the government decided not to go ahead with a second order of fifty-seven planes (C-5B), its liability could not exceed the ceiling price of the original contract. The repricing formula—so mysteriously found in some copies of the contract later on—would allow Lockheed to recoup whatever losses it may have suffered on the C-5A by getting higher prices on the C-5B's.

It is particularly curious that the repricing formula did not appear in any of the copies of the Lockheed contract distributed to the Air Force Financial Management staff, where Fitzgerald works. Although the evidence thus far indicates that Secretary of the Air Force Harold Brown and Assistant Secretary of Defense (Comptroller) Robert N. Anthony were not informed of the formula, it seems clear that Charles, who devised the new total-packaging contracting method, must have known about it.

He was obviously concerned about Lockheed's welfare. When the Air Force informed Lockheed in early 1967 that its contract might be terminated unless it remedied technical deficiencies in the C-5A, Charles sent a thirteen-page memo to Secretary Brown indicating how unfair this was to Lockheed when the company was about to float a $125 million debenture in the market.

More dark appeared at the top of the stairs through alteration of official records of the program's costs. These involved what are known as "overruns"—the amount by which a government contract exceeds the target, or hoped-for, price. Such expenses cannot exceed the contract limitation, but when they occur the government shares the cost with the contractor.

In June of 1968, Fitzgerald was surprised to discover that the overruns on the Lockheed contract had disappeared from the official records. He asked for an internal audit and received it in October. It said that the overruns had been deleted at the order of Assistant Secretary of the Air Force Charles and Assistant Secretary of Defense Anthony. Anthony has subsequently said that he had nothing to do with it. Charles has acknowledged that it was done on his orders and has insisted that it was justified. The Department of Justice is exploring the legality of deleting cost overruns to determine whether it amounts to falsification of government records, a criminal offense.

In a vastly oversimplified way, these are some of the facts that Fitzgerald shared with the Proxmire committee in the fall of 1968. Early in 1969, in the last week of the Johnson Administration, the Air Force gave Lockheed the go-ahead on the second batch of planes (the C-5B's), even though the cost estimate had risen from $22 million per plane to $40 million per plane. The House Defense Appropriations Subcommittee, however, contends that the Air Force exceeded its discretion in placing the order, since no funds have been appropriated for the second batch.

A. E. Fitzgerald believes that most military men should not be involved in procurement; because they lack expertise in costing, they are too often putty in the hands of canny company negotiators. Another reason that some tend to be malleable, he feels, is that the Pentagon has an "up or out" policy, which forces officers to retire if they are passed over twice for promotion. Thus, if an officer faces the prospect of such forced retirement—or even of regular retirement—he has little incentive to be tough with potential employers on the other side of the negotiating table.

For telling it like it is, A. E. Fitzgerald has been stripped of his duties and assigned to investigate the cost overrun on a twenty-lane bowling alley in Thailand (his first question: "Why was it built?"). Whether the Nixon Administration

> restores him to effectiveness by reinvolving him in cost and performance studies of major weapons systems will indicate the depth of Secretary Laird's public assertion that he intends to get tough with contractors and cut costs. Not long ago, at Laird's invitation, Fitzgerald met with Laird and Deputy Secretary of Defense David Packard. Although both were cordial, neither Laird nor Packard indicated that Fitzgerald has any future at the Pentagon. After all, Fitzgerald has done more than any man in Washington to encourage a close look at waste in the Pentagon budget. But, like the subjects of most other profiles in courage, Fitzgerald has no regrets. He is well aware that he who makes waves may drown in them.

After the Newman article was published, Fitzgerald continued to be ostracized within the Pentagon, and he was subjected to a background investigation by the Office of Special Investigations in the Department of Defense. The probe, under Brigadier General Joseph Capucci, resulted in a thick file of unfavorable comment from informers identified only as T1, T2, T3, and T4. (One of these said that Fitzgerald's old Rambler marked him as a "penny-pincher," a comment roughly indicative of the kind of material Capucci dug up in the Pentagon's version of a loyalty screening.) Jack Anderson ran a special report on the Capucci file in December, 1969, but it was not widely seen in Washington because the *Washington Post* refused to print the column. Meanwhile, Fitzgerald was isolated among his colleagues for his efforts at cost-cutting—because those efforts had entailed making the Pentagon look bad in public, and thereby vulnerable to budget cuts that placed all employees in jeopardy. "I just wasn't invited to meetings any more," says Fitzgerald. "Isolation is the standard treatment. I can't think of anything that was invented just for me. Maybe a half dozen of my close friends kept up contact, but their careers haven't gone anywhere either. Everything changed very quickly."

Four months after the Newman article, and about a year after Fitzgerald's original testimony before Proxmire, Fitzgerald's office underwent a reorganization and his job was abolished.

Air Force officials defended this severance before Congress as an economy move (even though Fitzgerald's post was refilled almost immediately) and kept straight faces when incredulous congressmen laughed or inquired why the Air Force had focused its budgetary scissors on Fitzgerald rather than on his disclosures regarding the C-5A. The flap over the dismissal was rough, but the Air Force survived, and those who handled the affair were promoted.

Fitzgerald himself appealed the Air Force action to the Civil Service Commission (CSC) on the grounds that the Air Force had no just cause to fire him, and that he was merely doing his job as an efficiency expert by testifying truthfully before Congress without breaking any Defense Department regulations. When the CSC hearings began in May, 1971, the hearing examiner insisted that they be closed to the public. Fitzgerald's lawyers went to Federal District Court seeking an order for open hearings. The Fitzgerald case would be helped generally by the presence of the public and reporters, but particularly by the presence of Clark Mollenhoff—now a reporter for the Des Moines *Register*—who handled the Fitzgerald firing for the White House and who now supports Fitzgerald's request for an open hearing. If attorneys for Fitzgerald were to ask officials like Air Force Secretary Robert C. Seamans whether politics motivated the firing, straightforward answers might be encouraged by Mollenhoff's presence in the hearing room, with memories in his head of many phone calls over to the Department of the Air Force.

Judge William Bryant issued an injunction ordering open hearings on June 25, 1971, which the Justice Department appealed on behalf of the CSC in August. The appeal process is likely to take more than a year, by which time many of the principal witnesses from the Air Force may no longer be in office. Effective delay may therefore deprive Fitzgerald of the opportunity to prove that his former superiors had broken the federal law against the harassment or intimidation of witnesses before congressional committtees, but the government appeal is likely to be decided in his favor—which would establish for the first time a government employee's right to an open hearing if he thinks his case is strong enough to hold up under public scrutiny.

Although such a precedent would be important to future Fitzgeralds, the right to an open hearing seems such an obvious and minimal part of due process that the striking aspect of the case is the effort by the CSC to preserve closed hearings by appealing up through the federal courts. Its effort is indicative of the Commission's laxity in protecting employees when they are right by all submitted evidence and proper in their conduct, but out of line politically. Generally, the CSC will protect someone who is incompetent as long as he is not hot, and the time that is supposed to go for the protection of people like Fitzgerald is taken up with the gray and pasty questions of bureaucracy—such as whether a master's degree is required for a data analyst or whether a GS-15 can function without a conference table or private coffee table in his office.

Fitzgerald himself is amused at the irony of being fired by an Administration under Richard Nixon. "He used to be for the protection of government employees," says Fitzgerald wryly, "but now I guess he's decided it's more important to keep food in the trough for those huge corporations that feed off the public like fat horses."

This reference to the President's history of support for government employees stems from the bill introduced by Senator Richard Nixon on April 26, 1951, stating that it would be "a violation of law for any officer of the Federal Government to dismiss or otherwise discipline a Government employee for testifying before a committee of Congress." Senator Nixon went on to say that it is essential for each witness to have "complete freedom from reprisal when he is given an opportunity to tell what he knows," and that without such freedom "hearings will amount to no more than a parade of yes men for administration policies as they exist." But the Senator's political purposes were different from Fitzgerald's, as evident in the cosponsorship of the bill by a group, including Pat McCarran, Kenneth S. Wherry, John W. Bricker, Robert A. Taft, and Joseph McCarthy, who apparently feared that military witnesses favorable to General MacArthur would clam up at the congressional inquiry into MacArthur's recall from Korea out of fear of retaliation by the Truman Administration.

Fitzgerald is now a part-time consultant to the Joint Economic Committee, with a decidedly dim future in his career field of cost management for manufacturers. "In fact, my consulting career out there is over for good," he says. Still, he calculates that he is better off than Henry Durham, the Lockheed production-control engineer who issued a detailed statement of the gross inefficiencies at Lockheed when the Congress was considering the $250-million loan guarantee. This statement, coming from a knowledgeable inside source, clashed with the official Lockheed position that its troubles came from general market conditions and from the red tape spewed out by all the bureaucrats in Washington. Durham was declared Public Enemy Number Two by the newspaper in Marietta, Georgia, the location of Lockheed's C-5A plant (the Number One spot was reserved for Proxmire), and he has received so many threats against his life that six federal marshals have been guarding him night and day since he released his statement. Fitzgerald thinks his own lot has been soft in comparison.

Although he was not surprised that the majority of the uniformed Air Force and Lockheed personnel despised him for his testimony, Fitzgerald was a bit dismayed by the response of what he calls the "defense liberals" and the Whiz Kids left over from the McNamara days. "They didn't really attack the substance of what I said," he remembers, "but they disagreed in principle with my methods. They said it wasn't the proper way to act—going outside like that. They argued that my testimony made it harder for them to operate inside, and that I should have built or joined a coalition to maneuver on the issue gradually. I think they're wrong, though. Nothing I talked about before Congress had not already been thrashed out in the Pentagon.

"These people also contended that excess costs came from a deliberate policy of achieving goals other than efficiency," continued Fitzgerald. "They said that you have to consider the survival of a community like Marietta and the human problems involved in reordering priorities. They felt that such considerations could be sold to Congress only when disguised as weapons systems. Those goals are all right with me, but I don't think social reform should be accomplished by constructing a vast, highly-paid, middle-class WPA through the Pentagon. Nor should you do it with concealment and lying before Congress."

One former high-ranking Air Force official reflected the disenchantment with Fitzgerald's methods: "I think the sense of annoyance with Fitzgerald really came from the complexity of the C-5A issue. Those matters were obviously complicated, and his charges of overrun were so blunt that his motives were called into question. I'm not suggesting that he was wrong, but I do think you should make every effort to work things out internally before you blow the sides out of an organization like that."

Fitzgerald's initial decision to speak before Congress was not preceded by lengthy soul-searching like Jim Boyd's when he was contemplating blowing the whistle on Senator Dodd. Part of the difference, of course, may be ascribed to Fitzgerald's lack of personal ties to his bosses; Boyd was paralyzed by a long and very personal association with Dodd. Also, Fitzgerald may not have foreseen the virulence of the Air Force's reaction. And at least some of Fitzgerald's relative nonchalance about the decision seems to follow from his rather old-fashioned, homespun nature. It seemed to him natural to tell what he knew when asked, and rather devious and sneaky to consider doing anything else. A more modern cost manager might readily have found ways to protect himself by obscuring the issue without really lying, but Ernie told it straight.

The tactics of the Air Force retaliation, especially the Capucci investigation, hardened his resolve not to back off from the correct figures. "They suggested that I use 'more balanced' numbers on the C-5A, and then someone would doctor my figures when I sent testimony through channels. Also, I was urged to emphasize the outstanding technical aspects of the C-5A design," he says.

Although Fitzgerald was not specifically successful in cutting costs on the C-5A, the $2-billion figure involved did earn him the distinction of having blown the most expensive whistle yet recorded in the new tradition of muckraking from the inside. More important, he was very influential in stimulating a renewed interest in defense spending and waste.

The results of three years' efforts to curb military spending have been mixed. The ABM was approved in the summer of 1969, but the vote was far closer than it would have been without the C-5A's damaging impact on the sacrosanct status of weapons programs. Weapons like the B-1 bomber cannot expect to sail through appropriations fights without strong justification for the expense. Military spending remains high, of course, in the $80-billion-a-year range, but it has at least become an issue —with close votes and the possibility of curbing programs when the preponderance of evidence shows them to be unwarranted.

14 Fitzgerald on Fitzhugh

A. Ernest Fitzgerald believes that the statistical complications, the nooks and crannies, of weapons procurement present one of the most formidable obstacles to an intelligent review of defense spending. These intricacies, partly contrived by those who push through appropriations behind the screen, conceal cost overruns even from responsible congressmen—who miss things by not asking precisely the right question or by asking questions that can be deflected into an area away from the flaw. If this is a tricky problem for congressmen, it is usually a baffling one for the working press, whose thin knowledge of the procurement game cripples any effort it might make to generate public excitement over weapons spending when covering any single program under consideration.

In November, 1970, Fitzgerald wrote an article for the *Washington Monthly* describing how the Defense Department conned the press into misreporting the work of the panel commissioned to study Pentagon waste in the midst of the controversy over the C-5A. The panel, headed by Gilbert Fitzhugh, recommended ways to end the waste problem and control the Pentagon, and its ideas were applauded by the media. In fact, says Fitzgerald, recommendations having the opposite effect are buried in the boring technical language of the thick report. Fitzgerald says that diligent reporting could have ferreted out the deceptions in the

Administration's claims for the Fitzhugh Report, but it would have required a great deal of time, which reporters usually don't have, especially before deadlines. Whistle-blowers can cut this time short, which is why they are sometimes needed.

Gilbert Fitzhugh's Golden Fleece

On July 27, 1970, an elaborately staged news conference took place at the Summer Palace in San Clemente. Emerging from a ninety-minute meeting with the President, Secretary of Defense Melvin Laird had good news for the assembled reporters. As reported by the newspapers, the Secretary, his deputy David Packard, Henry Kissinger, and others had met with the President to discuss the then secret Fitzhugh Report. Mr. Laird's message to the newsmen was that the report, a year in the making, would be released the next day, and that it would recommend changes in Pentagon procurement designed to prevent massive losses to taxpayers because of cost overruns on weapons programs.

After the San Clemente press conference made the news by announcing what would be reported, the report was issued with another press conference and the appropriate fanfare —followed by analyses and personality profiles, which kept alive the good news that the Pentagon was to be brought under control.

The Fitzhugh Report itself covered a broad range of Pentagon management problems, but the best-publicized items dealt with big weapons procurement and civilian control. The costly, overrun-producing procurement practices of the McNamara era were to be replaced by a careful, conservative, step-by-step procurement approach, popularly called "fly before you buy." Civilian control would be strengthened, with the Joint Chiefs of Staff put in their place through reorganization.

All this was handled masterfully, with the appearance of great toughness on the part of the Administration and Fitzhugh, the chairman of the board of the Metropolitan Life Insurance Company. Fitzhugh held a press conference in which he expressed wonder that the Pentagon works at all, which gained him the reputation for having smitten the Pentagon. The *New York Times* and other leading journals hailed the "new critic of the Pentagon." The press, TV, and radio consensus was that the Fitzhugh Report was not a whitewash after all and that those who had said it would be should take it all back and be ashamed of themselves.

The Fitzhugh panel grew out of controversies in the spring of 1969, when the Department of Defense was beset by trouble from all sides—including embarrassing probes into the Pentagon's sordid procurement mess and the enormous waste of military spending programs. Secretary Laird was hopping mad about the bad press which the big procurement programs were receiving. On March 27, he wrote a letter to his assistants: "I am increasingly concerned about allusions in the press and elsewhere to runaway costs on such key or major programs as the C-5A." He then went on to ask for suggestions: "What sorts of actions on DOD's [Department of Defense] part can be taken to thwart or ameliorate the continuing adverse commentary on program costs and suspect technical effectiveness?"

Soon the decision was made to employ the hoariest trick in the bureaucratic book. A panel would be appointed to study the problem, and all the trimmings of the study commission syndrome were used. The establishment of the group was announced with flourish by the President himself. The panel was to have a year to complete its work, which would buy valuable time to mend fences and dim the public memory of the then fresh horror stories (the current White House staff is generally believed to be dedicated to the proposition that the public memory is about three weeks long). The scope of the panel's study was broadened to include the structure of the entire Defense establishment, which helped dilute the attention given to the spending control issue. Finally, the panel was composed of individuals who either knew nothing about military procurement or were beneficiaries of current practices.

Let's consider what we obtained by waiting for the report's recommendations, beginning with those on the organization of the Pentagon. This section was highly advertised as strengthening civilian control of our military establishment. Its salient feature was the recommendation to remove the Joint Chiefs of Staff from immediate control of military operations. Presumably, this responsibility was to be assigned to an individual "drawn from civilian life." Political and press reaction to this feature was overwhelmingly favorable. Many liberals were ecstatic, forgetting for the moment that we already have civilian control in the persons of Senator John Stennis and Representative F. Edward Hébert. They will be disillusioned to learn that the new post of chief of the Pentagon's military operations section has been filled by the chairman of the Joint Chiefs of Staff. This possibility was suggested by Fitzhugh himself.

So the most widely heralded organizational recommendation has amounted to exactly nothing. Admiral Rickover, among others, has been predicting this for months. Speaking of the Pentagon's civilian and military bureaucrats' propensity to fake corrective actions by reorganization, he said, "Every time they have trouble, they change the organization. Generally, they change the telephone numbers." The admiral, a long-time bureaucrat-watcher, recognized early that the Pentagonists would not even alter the historic pattern or sequence of bureaucratic protective reactions. He knew that nothing would really change.

However, in the present instance, this is not quite the case. Things are not the same, for the Fitzhugh Report contains many other organizational recommendations, some of which actually make things worse.

One example affects the principles of internal control in procurement. Sizable businesses usually keep separate the functions of generating requirements for purchases, placing purchase orders, certifying satisfactory delivery, approving invoices for payment, and issuing checks. This is done to minimize the possibility of collusion and defalcation. These functions have tended to be drawn together in the Pentagon's big weapons development programs, supposedly for speed in handling contractual matters. In those few instances in which reductions in weapons costs have been made, the government contracting officers, or purchasing agents, have been independent of the government program offices. Program offices, the government's focal points for day-to-day management of military systems, generally view the government-industry relationship as a partnership rather than an arm's-length buyer-seller situation. In several cases these contracting officers have used their independence and their considerable legal powers to very good effect.

In any event, it has long been an article of faith among the larger military contractors that government contracting officers should be placed under the direction of the program offices, where they would be more "responsive" and would be more "understanding of industry problems." Key industry associations, especially the AIA (Aerospace Industry Association) and the CODSIA (Council of Defense and Space Industry Associations), have long favored this arrangement.

The Fitzhugh Report recommended giving the government program manager directive authority over the contracting officer. This was an incredible recommendation for a businessman to endorse.

Most of the Fitzhugh Report's favorable publicity was focused on the recommendations for acquiring big new weapons systems. "Fly before you buy" was the keynote recommendation. This "breakthrough" was trumpeted around the world. This was more than just a recommendation, according to news releases. The press accounts said the panel had simply confirmed a policy already adopted by Secretaries Laird and Packard. The *New York Times* wrote:

> The panel's recommendation of procurement was, in fact, somewhat redundant, since the Pentagon, under Mr. Laird's direction, had already adopted the general policy of developing prototype weapons and making certain they worked before going into production.

Indeed, the panel's recommendations in this area do appear to be closely related to Packard's policy guidance memorandum of May 27, 1970. In turn, Packard's memo was a restatement of his general guidelines issued shortly after his arrival in the Pentagon. It said: "The most important consideration before moving into full-scale production on a new weapons system is to have assurance that the engineering design is completed, that all major problems have been resolved, and this has been demonstrated to the extent practical by actual performance testing."

Now, as far as this goes, it is hard to argue with. It is particularly attractive if coupled with a further objective of retaining competitive options as long as possible. It's neither a new idea nor an untested one, but it's a good suggestion nonetheless. If this had been the report's only recommendation, and if the Pentagon had followed it in good faith, the taxpayers would have gotten their money's worth from the Fitzhugh panel.

Senator William Proxmire tested the Pentagon's sincerity when he introduced an amendment calling on the Pentagon to report on its loudly announced policy—just to report after the fact on whether the policy had been followed.

Laird, Packard, Stennis, and company opposed Proxmire fiercely. They said that his proposal was "premature," despite the fact it supposedly had been their *de facto* policy for more than a year, and formal policy for almost three months. Laird said that "it would eliminate flexibility in acquisition strategy," notwithstanding the fact that Proxmire's amendment required only an after-the-fact report. In short, the Pentagon had no intention of really following the practice if it could be avoided.

This was not news to Proxmire, of course. For one thing, he had the hard evidence of the Pentagon's recent, past and future commitments to buy before flying in almost every big program. Furthermore, his subcommittee for economy in government had heard testimony on the subject from the three assistant secretaries of Installations and Logistics (procurement) in May, 1970. Two of the three dismissed fly-before-you-buy (FBYB) as impractical. Why? Because it did not provide adequate contractor employment during the interval between completion of the prototype and beginning of production. As most of us know by now, providing employment is a major objective in most cases. In some cases, it is the name of the game.

The Fitzhugh panel did not address this question except in its vague endorsement of the old industry chestnut of "maintaining a viable industrial mobilization base," whatever that is. Since the procurement chiefs' objections to FBYB were well known long before the panel's report was issued, it seems the panel should have dealt with the objection if it really anticipated adoption of FBYB.

It is also strange that the panel, while giving lip service to improving the engineering definition of new weapons with FBYB, summarily dumped the Pentagon's established procedures for contract definition. These procedures call for thorough studies of proposed new weapons systems aimed at ensuring that big, expensive systems do not involve undue technical uncertainties. Most students of the process would agree that contract definition as carried out under existing procedures is too laborious and too dependent on paper studies. However, these procedures contain good features, too, and the chief problem has been a lack of enforcement. Fitzhugh has thrown out the baby with the bathwater. With existing contract definition procedures abandoned and with FBYB revealed as a public relations ploy, the Pentagon is left bankrupt with regard to advance definition of contract baselines.

But then, the Pentagon has long advocated what used to be called "the rubber baseline." This permits plans to be progressively modified to approximate actual performance, a comfortable operating mode.

A look at the Pentagon's recent history and future plans for FBYB should have tipped off a prudent man not to place heavy dependence on such documents as Packard's policy memo, as Fitzhugh apparently did. Last year, Congress and Secretary Laird vied for credit for "killing" the production program for the Navy's new F-14 fighter until the plane could be flown long enough to work out the bugs. Yet during the year, in closed hearings and before the plane had flown, Laird requested and received approval to begin spending production money. Similarly, the Air Force's new fighter, the F-15, is not following FBYB, nor is the ABM or any of the big new ship programs, such as Senator Stennis's Mississippi-built DD963 destroyer, or the larger tank programs, such as the Sheridan.

All this looks bad, until you read what the report *does* recommend. The report endorses level-of-effort contracting, which is another way of saying that the contractor's product is man-hours expended. Under this plan, the contractor has no real commitment to deliver anything, much less a necessity to excel. The same holds true for the present yearly $700–800 million of independent research and development (IR & D) grants for larger contractors. I can't think of any weapons system invented under these grants. Apparently, neither can Senator Stennis's committee, which, along with Senator Proxmire, has questioned the size and wisdom of the grants. The Fitzhugh Report is vague on the handling of the IR & D subsidy, but it is critical of congressional questioning and appears to endorse the present no-strings-attached grants.

Fitzhugh also endorses parametric cost-estimating for procurement. This approach builds in, and indeed amplifies, mistakes and inefficiencies of the past in establishing prices for new procurements. While the parametric, or "will cost," approach to estimating has some application in projecting funding requirements, the "should cost" approach is infinitely better in procurement if one is interested in saving money. (A distinction should be drawn between saving money and eliminating overruns as such. In theory, at least, overruns could be eliminated by making initial estimates fat enough to accommodate shoddy engineering and bad management. This would not save money. On the other hand, demanding but attainable estimates are a first step in the series of management actions needed to cut costs.)

The "should cost" approach, which seeks to identify and eliminate "fat" in cost estimates, has had considerable publicity of late. In a good move, the Army rediscovered this old-fashioned, hard-nosed approach. According to testimony before a Joint Economics Committee subcommittee in May, 1970, its first "should cost" study identified about 34 per cent of the contractor's proposed cost as "fat," or potential savings. Based on my own experience, this is about what should be expected on small weapons programs, such as the Army's pilot program, the Hawk missile. Large weapons programs are usually much fatter. Naturally, the large contractors and industry associations oppose "should cost" and endorse "will cost" pricing. The latter approach is, of course, a comfortable, congenial, and gentlemanly approach. It is also ruinously expensive. Under the "will cost" approach, even increasing prices are mathematically justified and everybody wins except the taxpayers, who are generally ignorant of the process and consequently do not complain. Fitzhugh's endorsement of "will cost" or parametric pricing delighted the military spending coalition.

Despite acknowledgments of "poor management" in weapons contracts in public statements by Packard, Fitzhugh does not mention this unpleasantness. He says nothing about overhead increases, declines in labor efficiencies, or the like. He ignores the fact that the Pentagon does not know whether its giant contractors are overrun or underrun on work done through a point in time, nor does it know the specifics of any deviation from plan. That is, it doesn't know whether overruns are traceable to increases in labor, material cost, or overhead expenses. Most hot-dog stand owners would know, but the Pentagon and its large contractors have barely a clue.

These omissions are apparently the result of the panel's assumption of a trend toward fixed-price contracts in which the contractors would have more responsibility and in which the government's need for monitoring would be reduced. The report states the assumption boldly: "During the past decade, the trend in government contracts for developments has shifted markedly from cost-plus-fixed-fee toward fixed-price contracts, many of which have embodied incentive features." They are simply dead wrong here. The C-5A airplane and Cheyenne helicopter contracts are to be converted to cost reimbursement. The new programs such as the F-14 Navy fighter, the F-15 Air Force fighter, and the B-1 bomber, are starting out as cost reimbursement (cost-plus) contracts. The trend is in the opposite direction from fixed-price contracts.

Even if the Administration were serious about its fly-before-you-buy policy, the effect of other new policies could dissipate any possible savings. Starting with a cost-plus development contract, then negotiating the follow-on-production contract without competition and with pricing based on past actual cost rather than "should cost," prices of weapons will be even more bloated than at present. True, the *appearance* of overruns will be avoided by having contract prices adapt to actual costs, but the taxpayer will have to pony up additional money just the same. He'll feel better about it, though, because he won't realize what's happening to him.

Another of Fitzhugh's recommendations is to abandon the Selected Acquisition Reports (SAR), the quarterly reports on status of weapons systems programs. The Fitzhugh panel comments that the SAR's "measure subsequent events in the development against the standard of the original estimate." Deviations from the plan require explanations and, according to the panel, this produces further ill effects:

> These explanations in turn generate further detailed examination of deviations by the Department [of Defense] and especially by the Congress. All this has led to an understandable

> but nonetheless undesirable rigidity on the part of the project manager to stay as close as possible to the cost and schedule as originally estimated.

Clearly, this will never do. If this kind of factual exposure is allowed to continue, the taxpaying natives may get restless.

The most serious omission, perhaps the most serious shortcoming of the entire report, is the failure to deal with the problem of the motives involved in arms procurement—motives which often lead to lucrative but dishonest collusion. It must be hard for the panel members to understand that Pentagon managers work hard at devising ways to take a dive, to throw the game, in contract negotiations with giant firms. Anyone who has any doubts about this should go over the Air Force's plan for making Lockheed well again, which was outlined in a set of twenty-five "Official Use Only" briefing charts dated August 31, 1970. After hiding the C-5A overruns, admitting they falsified government reports to protect Lockheed stock prices, and juggling figures to "avoid the appearance of excess profits on Run B" (the second order of C-5A's), the Air Force came up with a masterpiece. In summary, here's what they proposed to do:

1. Lockheed would agree to accept a "fixed loss" (an indefinite amount but a fraction of their loss otherwise), which would be lent back to them with repayment to begin in 1974 *if* the Pentagon should choose to ask for repayment, and *if* the Pentagon wouldn't choose simply to give Lockheed more money.
2. The Pentagon would remove contractual ceilings on Lockheed's expenditures.
3. Lockheed would be absolved of guaranteeing the performance of the airplanes and of managing the program.
4. Penalties for substandard performance and late delivery would be removed.
5. Lockheed and the Pentagon would agree to circumvent the normal legal procedures designed to protect the taxpayers.
6. The Air Force would get whatever number of C-5A's Lockheed chose to produce.

To me, the Air Force's bail-out plan is evidence of the Pentagon's collapse of will in dealing with its giant contractors. If the Lockheed bail-out precedent is established, how can the Pentagon *ever* hold a large contractor to his commitments? What is the significance of any procedural or organizational reform if the over-all intent problem is not solved? If the government's policy is to accept whatever the giant contractors produce and give them whatever money they need, why should managers of these big firms concern themselves with making quality products, with meeting specifications, and with holding costs down?

In justice to Lockheed and the C-5A project, I should acknowledge that other large recipients of contract funds generally get the same kid-glove treatment in dealings with the Pentagon. The F-111 airplane, the Mark II avionics system for the same machine, the Minuteman II missile, the SRAM, the MBT-70 tank, the Mark 48 torpedo, and numerous other projects failed about as badly as the Lockheed C-5A program. None met its original specifications, and all were vastly overrun. Nevertheless, none of the large prime contractors has suffered unduly as a result of their failures.

Lockheed is just unlucky. Usually the bail-out is accomplished routinely, though somewhat clandestinely, through the simple mechanism of contract changes, known in the trade as "contract nourishment." Publicity, along with the enormous sums of money involved, is making the Lockheed bail-out more difficult.

I am at a loss to explain the Fitzhugh panel's failure to deal with the problem of intent. It is completely beyond me how any reasonably intelligent group of experienced businessmen could spend a year studying the Pentagon's contracting mess without even speculating about the possibilities inherent in enforcing contracts with large firms. One popular theory is that the panel missed the major causes of the Pentagon's procurement mess because the study was planned that way and was staffed to guide the report to its bland outcome.

The business connections of the panel's members do not inspire confidence in their objectivity, to say the least. Shortly after the panel was formed, Senator Proxmire let loose a blast at the panel, charging that there were apparent conflicts of interest on the part of panel members. The specifics are worth reviewing.

The chairman, Gilbert W. Fitzhugh, was not only chairman

of the board of the Metropolitan Life Insurance Company but also a director of the Singer Company. Metropolitan Life held over $34 million in common stock of 24 of the 100 largest Pentagon contractors, and had outstanding loans of $1,325,000,000 to 24 of the top 100 military contractors. The Singer Company also held military contracts. Fitzhugh resigned his positions with these companies, temporarily at least. He is now back in harness at Metropolitan.

Next on the list was Robert C. Jackson, chairman of the board of Ryan Aeronautical Company. At the time of Jackson's appointment, Ryan held military contracts worth $293,158,000. Jackson also held memberships in the Air Force Association, the Navy League, the Army Aviation Association, and the Defense Orientation Conference Association, all of which are self-interested and outspoken supporters of Pentagon activities.

After listing the defense work of six other Fitzhugh Report associates, Proxmire concluded that eight panel members, representing a majority on the fifteen-member panel, had official positions with twelve different companies that held a combined total of at least $1,021,902,963 in military contracts.

Further objectivity was lent to the panel by such members as Joseph Kirkland, secretary-treasurer of the AFL-CIO when appointed, and Hobart Lewis, president of Reader's Digest.

J. Fred Buzhardt was the administrative officer of the staff. He is a graduate of the United States Military Academy. He spent eight years as a staff member with Senator Strom Thurmond. During that time, his biography stated, he was "assigned largely to work with staff of Senate Armed Services Committee and Military Preparedness Sub-Committee." At the time of his appointment he was on the Pentagon payroll as a special assistant, and he is now General Counsel to the Pentagon.

The apparent domination of the panel by individuals with Pentagon-contractor viewpoints makes the suspicion of bias unavoidable. This suspicion is heightened by the fact that most of the actual work of the panel's review was done by Pentagon employees or by the Stanford Research Institute and other Pentagon contractors. So far as can be determined, the Pentagon paid all the bills.

When Senator Proxmire revealed the business connections of the panel members last year, he predicted a whitewash in the report of weapons acquisition activities. According to the *Washington Post,* Fitzhugh responded with the hope that the panel's report "would be judged on its own merits" and not on the makeup of the panel.

They have flunked the course on both counts, at least in the procurement area. The report is a whitewash written by whitewashees. Defenders and beneficiaries of the mess are still trying to cure it by pouring money on it, then scratching dirt over it. Once the slogans are disposed of (fly-before-you-buy and civilian control), the Fitzhugh panel's report amounts to just such a nonsolution.

With all this, it is tempting to write off the whole Fitzhugh panel effort as just another of the endless series of bureaucratic anesthetics for the taxpayers. From my point of view, there is only one reason to reserve judgment on the final outcome of the whole episode. That reason is the man himself, Gilbert Fitzhugh. He seems to have great integrity, and certainly has a fine reputation to protect. It is possible that he was used by the self-serving authors of the incredibly bad weapons acquisition recommendations. After all, he did state early in his review that he knew little or nothing about the process. He has now been educated by some of the country's most successful participants in the Pentagon's ongoing procurement swindle.

If I were in Fitzhugh's position and had not been a knowing party to the whitewash, I would be extremely annoyed. I would take a hard second look—and consider things like the hustle factor and the problem of honest contract enforcement with large corporations.

It would be most refreshing to see a businessman make some businesslike recommendations for a change, like objective evaluations of true need for the weapons in the first place; like writing sound, well-defined, binding contracts, with improved definition resulting from competitive prototypes where possible; like enforcing the contracts, even if some of the lodge brothers lose money occasionally; like finding ways to get more competition, both in initial awards and continuing programs; like negotiating tough prices, based on what the work should cost with the fat squeezed out; like keeping track of program status, and insisting that problems be fixed before they become national disasters; like controlling spurious get-well contract changes; like setting difficult, specifically quantified cost reduction goals for Pentagon managers; like fixing the Pentagon's rewards system so that those who underrun are promoted and those who overrun are disciplined (has *anyone* ever been fired for overrunning?).

The report wouldn't be hard to write. Let's hope Gilbert Fitzhugh writes it.

Ernie Fitzgerald did not go far in the media with his critique of the Fitzhugh Report, because any treatment of that report had to be dull in comparison with the stark simplicity of what he had had to disclose earlier: a $2-billion overrun. Although the report, if implemented, may finally be more important than the C-5A controversy, it will not be so thoroughly followed in the press.

One of the whistle-blower's chief problems with the press is the possibility of being ignored, but there are others. Often, he may have nearly the opposite difficulty, that is, he may receive so much attention that he has trouble keeping the press commentary focused on the evidence he has brought to light. There are always side issues involved in whistle-blowing, since the employee must at least break solidarity with his organization and thereby invite the "rat fink" label, and may even have to break the law to expose his material. So his action usually injects so much passion into antagonists and observers that all kinds of arguments—procedural, *ad hominem,* substantive, philosophical, nonsensical, and so on—can be thrown into battle, and out to the media, with high-voltage assurance. In short, the whistle-blower will be a figure of controversy, and the facts of his case will be in danger of getting lost in the fight over the propriety of what he did.

The whistle-blower has to walk a very tricky tightrope while newspaper columnists and readers and assorted officials are determining what they think of his case. He must constantly point to the evidence, to the fact that the significance of that evidence made it imperative for him to disclose it in spite of regulations or laws to the contrary. If that evidence is left unsifted (as it often is, simply because the sifting is tedious), the whistle-blower loses. Attention will be focused on some side issue, such as his own personality. Consequently, the whistle-blower has to make every effort to rub the nose of the press in the facts and force it to make a judgment on their merits. Moreover, with the press and commentators, who tend to be hostile, he has to try to avoid the *ad hominem* argument by stressing the point that the validity or invalidity of his evidence has nothing to do with his character. Conversely, with representatives of the media who tend to be favorable, the whistle-blower has to stress that celebration of his heroism is not terribly useful to the task of convincing people that he was right. Neither of these messages to the press is easy to get across.

15 The Odd Couple*

The public reaction to two whistle-blowers, Otto F. Otepka and Daniel Ellsberg, clearly illustrates the disorienting spells cast upon fervent observers by the spectacle and drama of exposures from within—especially in cases that involve national security, as these two did. Otepka violated national security by slipping classified documents to veteran Red-hunter Julian T. Sourwine of the Senate Internal Security Subcommittee. He was fired for his transgressions in 1963, lost his position as chief of the State Department's security-evaluation division, became a martyr of the right wing, and is considered by some to be the first whistle-blower in the modern period. Ellsberg violated national security by slipping classified documents, later to be called the "Pentagon Papers," to numerous senators and newspapers. He is being tried for his transgressions in 1971, has lost his security clearance at the RAND Corporation, become a martyr of the left wing, and is considered by many the capstone contemporary whistle-blower.

Although these two men are ideological opposites, there are unmistakable similarities between their respective exploits, viewed on a suitably high plane of reflection after all the human

* This chapter, written especially for this book by coeditor Taylor Branch, appeared in a shortened version in the *Washington Monthly* for October, 1971.

juices and interesting particulars have been drained away. Ellsberg and Otepka operated by the same laws of motion in some ways, following their higher instincts regarding the public interest as they saw it, exposing treachery in places of power on questions of life and death. These similarities suggest that anyone who wants to fight institutional *rigor mortis* by encouraging people to speak out from within government is obliged by honesty and consistency to take his Otepkas with his Ellsbergs, and vice versa—to take a man like Otepka, who thought his bosses were ruining the country by being too sweet to Communists everywhere, with one like Ellsberg, who thought his former colleagues were ruining the country by killing people and lying about it.

Similarity hardly comes across as the theme of the public comment on the two men: Most people who are roughly "for" one of these prophets are decidedly against the other. The comment shows, rather, the extraordinary heights to which eloquence can soar in matters of national security, and the number of contradictory but self-evident truths that can be found to be at stake upon diligent inspection of such cases. The debate also shows that any self-interested position can be cloaked in a lofty principle passed down from the eighteenth century, that indeed such principles are in such ample supply that used ones can be discarded like banana peels when a fresh gut position, in need of altogether different packaging, comes along. These standards for human behavior can be invoked in security questions from the grand to the banal with all the flourish of the Ecuadorian Navy in defense of its tuna waters or a Florentine prince defending his honor, eyes glazed with true conviction. Only a question of loyalty can cause a man to thrust out his chest, stand ten feet tall, and thunder ominously over issues like whether the AO-143 class oiler in our Mediterranean fleet should have more freon 12 in its deck load, or whether a security officer who eats supper with a Communist or a Klansman is tainted enough to be fired.

The facts of the Ellsberg case—half of the question needed to point out this flexibility of principle—are fairly well known owing to their recent occurrence and the wide publicity surrounding them. The Otepka affair bears review.

Otepka had been in the government for twenty-seven years and in the State Department's Office of Security for ten years when he was fired on November 5, 1963, on charges of "conduct unbecoming an officer of the Department of State." President Kennedy, setting a precedent for dealing with criticism from the Right, assuaged a Calley-like tide by announcing, "I will examine the matter myself when it comes time." But he was killed before the review process got under way. It seems that Otepka, described by the *Reader's Digest* as a "tall, quiet, darkly handsome man"; by *Newsweek* as "a sad-eyed, introverted man"; and by the *New York Times* only as "stocky" (descriptions showing the effect of politics on the eye of the beholder), had been running afoul of important people for some time. In 1955, for example, he had refused to dispense with formalities and thereby hindered the clearance procedure for Walt W. Rostow at a time when Secretary of State Dulles wanted Rostow on State's Committee on Operations. Subjecting Rostow to a full-dress examination of his character was considered an affront to his dignity. When President Kennedy wanted Rostow on the team in 1961, Otepka again refused to waive security proceedings, which, some say, is why Rostow ended up in the White House while Otepka was at State, rather than going through the State security mill. (Apparently, Otepka was a bit troubled by the internationalist leanings of Rostow's writings on economic development, unwilling to be taken in by possible ruses like Rostow's "non-Communist manifesto," as he subtitled *The Stages of Economic Growth.* Also, because Rostow was a professor, his commitment against Communism was suspect *a priori.* (Subsequent events and the Pentagon Papers were to show that Otepka was dead wrong in his doubts about Rostow; in fact, some beneficiaries of hindsight have wished Otepka had possessed more clout in his efforts to keep Rostow out of the government.)

Otepka had also nettled the new Administration by locating

and firing the State Department employee who had leaked a secret survey of U.S. prestige abroad to the Kennedy campaign forces in 1960. The survey, showing a dip in America's standing in international esteem, had been used with telling effect by John Kennedy in the campaign to show that the Republicans were blowing things in foreign policy, partly by following what seemed to be a deliberate path toward national weakness. Otepka had also been critical of the lax security procedures for the Cuba desk officers at the State Department, one of whom, William Wieland, was considered by the Republican Party almost single-handedly responsible for delivering Cuba into the enemy camp. Otepka testified before a Senate committee that he had dissented from the decision to clear Wieland without further study of his inner proclivities, and so much stir was created over Wieland that President Kennedy was forced to defend him publicly in a press conference.

Finally, Otepka had refused to waive security investigations for six men of decorum whom Secretary Rusk wanted in 1962 for the Advisory Committee on Management Improvement to the Assistant Secretary of State for International Organizational Affairs (ACMIASSIOA, which may be Washington's very best acronym). The six—among them Harding Bancroft, Sol Linowitz, and Andrew Cordier—had been chosen for that august and rather useless body to study whether American employees of international organizations should be required to pass U.S. security investigations. The issue itself was one of some controversy, spurred on by a letter to the *New York Times* on July 30, 1962, that attacked the security regulations as a dangerous legacy of the McCarthy era. The letter was from one of the few consistent people on the entire security battlefield, Leonard Boudin, who is now the chief attorney for Daniel Ellsberg. In any case, Otepka refused to waive security clearances for men who were going to study the need for security clearances, and that kind of zeal for checking out the private leanings of prestigious persons had long since aggrieved the Kennedy Administration. Though it was not said for public consumption, it can be guessed that the New Frontier found it absurd for establishment personalities to be subjected to the paranoid probes of a man like Otepka—son of a Czech blacksmith, immigrant messenger boy, career bureaucrat, who, while not a friend or even an acquaintance of Joe McCarthy, obviously shared the witch-hunting Senator's logical perspective and his concern for purity of blood in the Department of State. The idea of Harding Bancroft, Executive Editor of the *New York Times,* being sniffed for disloyalty by an old Red-hound like Otepka was too much to bear—as silly, say, as the idea of J. K. Galbraith being examined for the Harvard economics faculty by some car-washing budget-balancer from Nebraska. The Otepka problem was a common one for an age of caring: that, while one strives to avoid derogatory comments about disadvantaged or plainly unsophisticated people, one also strives to avoid spending a great deal of time with them and certainly to avoid being in their control. Or so it was with Otepka.

John F. Reilly, Assistant Secretary of State for Security, was so intent upon getting rid of his anachronistic subordinate, the unstylish rough rider on the New Frontier, that he bugged Otepka's telephone and set up an elaborate system of surveillance to catch him in an act of shame that would stand up as grounds for doing him in. Reilly's sleuths scoured Otepka's "burn bag," a receptacle used to mark for instant destruction items like doodle pads and carbon paper and other parts of the afterbirth of state secrets that might leave telltale signs. They finally scored one day when they found classification stamps that Otepka had clipped from classified documents. Thus declassified informally, it turned out, the documents were being sent by Otto over to old J. T. Sourwine at the Senate Internal Security Subcommittee, where they could be used to surprise and embarrass Otto's bosses by showing how lightly they took the Red menace right here at home. The burn bag also contained a once-used typewriter ribbon, an instant replay of which revealed that Otepka had worked up a primer of questions for Sourwine that he could use to catch State Department officials in factual errors regarding the Communist question. (For some time, conservative senators on the committee—men like Thomas Dodd, John McClellan, and James O. Eastland—had been asking Otepka's superiors if they had been using hurry-up security procedures. Otepka's documents showed that their denials were incorrect, put forth no doubt to avoid hassling with members of Congress over what a Communist was. It was far easier for the State Department to strike a pose of militant but responsible anticommunism than to suggest to the likes of John McClellan that scrutinizing the personal habits of employees was dangerous nonsense. Otepka caught them in falsehoods that resulted from trying to take the easy way out, and conservatives interpreted this as a cover-up for a policy of coddling softness toward Communists.)

When the State Department used the burn-bag evidence to dismiss Otepka, the fireworks and oratory began. The *Chicago Tribune* skipped over the declassification problem to define the issue as a test of the principle of patriotism: "There can be no doubt that this case reflects an intention by the Kennedy Administration to conduct a purge of patriots." The Charleston, South Carolina, *News & Courier* agreed: "To reprimand a U.S. citizen for doing his duty would be a shame and an outrage." The *Reader's Digest* later published an article called "The Ordeal of Otto Otepka" with this lengthy subtitle: "Why have State Department employees been using the tactics of a police state to oust a dedicated security officer whose only sin seems to be loyalty to his country?"—which pretty well summed up the conservative presentation of the problem.

The "police state" argument followed a tactical guideline: It is easier to attack the process by which the opponent operates than the substance of what he says. However, it also bore some risk of the "corner problem," wherein people paint themselves into a corner by citing principles whose future application might haunt them. In this case, the *Digest's* forthright position against a police state was quite risky. It not only made it tougher to argue in subsequent tirades that the State Department was undisciplined and namby-pamby, but it also would require a redefinition of the issues when J. Edgar Hoover's wiretapping and surveillance came up for debate. Most conservative journals ignored the classification question and the he-broke-a-rule point of view, except perhaps to note in passing that classification was nonsense in general and that Otepka's leakage of secret material did not hurt the national interest anyway, but rather struck another blow against the pinkos in the State Department.

Meanwhile, in the Senate, members surveyed the Otepka affair and concluded that the main issue at stake was, as it so often is, the dignity of the U.S. Senate. Conservative Senator John Williams of Delaware remarked, "In this instance, all that Mr. Otepka was guilty of was cooperating with a congressional committee." Senator Peter Dominick of Colorado, addressing Senator Dodd, thanked him for having "pointed out the very difficult position Senate committees would find themselves in if it continued to be held that the executive branch could prevent any of its employees from coming before Senate committees, either by threatening them with dismissal or by verbally preventing them from testifying under that threat." Dodd, a foreign policy buff, defined the question in terms of national survival: "If those forces bent on destroying Otepka and the no-nonsense security approach he represents are successful, who knows how many more Chinas or Cubas we may lose?" But Dodd, too, was anxious about the powers of himself and his colleagues, and he entered a long discourse with Senators Strom Thurmond and Frank Lausche of Ohio on November 5, 1963, the day Otepka's dismissal was consummated, which Thurmond climaxed by declaring that the Kennedy Administration's action would "nullify our system of government by tending to destroy the constitutional system of checks and balances." There was no Commander-in-Chief talk on that day, no talk about how the President's powers were essential to survival in a hostile international environment. The conservatives were safe from the corner problem, however, because the war in Vietnam had not yet begun. The doves in the Senate would not really discover the checks-and-balances principle until about 1968, leaving the conservatives ample time to switch over to the Commander-in-Chief line without undue embarrassment.

The liberals in the Senate were exceedingly mousy about Otepka (perhaps according to the rule that supporters of the screwee, as underdogs, generally have the floor in loyalty scrapes), while the supporters of the Kennedy Administration sought to ride out the storm in public silence. This does not mean that they were necessarily apathetic, for some Otepka supporters claim that there was great pressure to let the Otepka fervor die out as the groundswell for General MacArthur had. Clark Mollenhoff, then a straightforward, very conservative reporter for the *Des Moines Register* (who later would serve Nixon in the White House and is now again working for the *Register*), made a speech about the obstacles to coverage of the case in which he said:

> I realize the broad range of direct and indirect pressures brought to discourage a defense of Otepka, for I met most of them at some stage from my friends in the Kennedy Administration. One put it crudely: "What are you lining up with Otepka and all those far-right nuts for? Do you want to destroy yourself?"
>
> There were also the hints that I could be cut off from White House contacts and other high Administration contacts if I continued to push for the facts in the Otepka case.

Liberal newspapers made slightly more noise in the dispute than the liberal senators: their editorial writers swept aside all the chaff about higher loyalty and patriotism and the dignity of Congress to focus on the principles at stake with a fixity that is born of discipline. The *Washington Post*, for example, zeroed in on the law-and-order question (it is always best to attack on matters of procedure): "For all of Senator Dodd's sputtering, he must know that what Otto Otepka did was not only unlawful but unconscionable as well. Mr. Otepka certainly knew this himself—which is no doubt why he did it covertly instead of candidly. He gave classified information to someone not authorized to receive it." The *New York Times* took a similar line, with slightly more emphasis on propriety:

The disturbing aspect of the case is that both Mr. Otepka and members of the Senate subcommittee have defended their actions on grounds of "higher loyalty." . . . Orderly procedures are essential if the vital division of powers between the legislative and executive branches is not to be undermined. The use of "underground" methods to obtain classified documents from lower level officials is a dangerous departure from such orderly procedures.

The *St. Louis Post-Dispatch* minced no words: "The State Department acted forthrightly and courageously in firing Otto Otepka, its former chief security risk officer, on charges of unbecoming conduct." And the *New Republic* magazine editorialized as follows against Otepka's argument that "every government official enjoys the right to furnish information to Congress":

That was answered some years back, and by Senator Dodd's colleagues. The Senate Select Committee which examined the censure charges brought against the late Senator McCarthy stated that the President could prescribe reasonable regulations to safeguard information "notwithstanding that the regulation might indirectly interfere with any secret transmission line between the executive employees and any individual member of Congress." . . . As for Senator Dodd's suggestion that every government employee should stand ready to tattle on any other before any Congressional committee involving itself with security, he merely is attempting to subvert every other espionage system to that of his own.

The *New Republic* piece foreshadowed the main fallback argument for the liberal press from the law-and-order attack on Otepka's propriety, which was a kind of smear tactic that involved using words like "controversial," "McCarthyism," "tattle," and "infidelity" as often as possible in connection with Otepka's name. This strategy, following from the rule that it is often useful to adopt your opponent's principles and turn them back on him in verbal counterinsurgency, as Marx did to Hegel, amounted to McCarthyism turned on its head, or guilt by association with McCarthy. Thus, when Otepka defended himself by citing the government employees' Code of Ethics (which charges employees to place loyalty to conscience, country, and the "highest moral principles" above "loyalty to persons, party, or Government department"), the *Washington Post* news story stated that "the last time that issue was raised with public prominence, it was raised by Senator McCarthy in sweeping form." A *New York Times* story by Neil Sheehan in 1969 continued this motif of the beat-them-at-their-own-game campaign: "The enthusiastic pursuit of 'subversive elements' in the government loosed by the late Senator Joseph McCarthy slowed to a desultory walk in later years, but Mr. Otepka . . . did not change."

Closely related to the McCarthyism tactic is the motives angle, by which an opponent in a loyalty brawl is accused of being in the whole thing for himself—for publicity, money, or some other mortal craving—which automatically invalidates anything he or his supporters say. Thus, Senator Stephen Young of Ohio called Otepka a "witch-hunter" and "a petty, self-seeking bureaucrat" as late as June 24, 1969, the day Otepka was confirmed by the Senate, sixty-one to twenty-eight, for appointment, by President Nixon, to the Subversive Activities Control Board. Young's charges were reminiscent of the early Ralph Nader days, when Nader was impugned as a "self-styled safety expert" by General Motors and other critics. (The sting of this barb is indicative of the decline of individualism: It implies that it is better to be styled by someone else, like Harvard or Helena Rubenstein or the U.S. Army, than to go with your own styling.)

So Otepka returned to the public spotlight in 1969, when President Nixon made good on his campaign promise to review the case "with a view to seeing that justice is accorded this man who served his country so long and well." The Subversive Activities Control Board seemed like an appropriate resting spot for a seasoned personnel-sniffer, who could spend the rest of his days scrutinizing political groups for loyalty blemishes. Actually, the SACB was a secondary choice for Otepka, who really wanted to go back to the State Department but was frustrated in his desire by Secretary of State William P. Rogers, who did not want him. The late Senator Everett Dirksen, claiming Otepka as a constituent and as an ideological brother, had suggested the SACB spot, and he went to work with the other conservative senators to give the Board and its $36,000-a-year members something to do. They knew that Otepka would be an additional burden in the annual appropriations battle with the liberals, who never fail to notice that the SACB members are so inert as to appear strikingly like welfare recipients, but at ten times the poverty standard. Conservative senators regularly approach the SACB problem with a three-pronged attack: by legislating more functions as a reason for more work, until the Supreme Court rules them out; by excoriating the court for crippling the board; and by appropriating more funds on the grounds that the SACB would do more if it had more money (organizational failures get more money because they need it; organizational successes get more money because they deserve it). The senators have to sail fairly close to the wind for their SACB arguments in order to avoid the corner problem when a *real* welfare bill comes up, but they almost always succeed.

The task of selling Otepka himself was undertaken with the old principles of patriotism and higher loyalty. Representative John Rarick (D-La.) set the conservative tone in the House, overlooking the classified-documents question in favor of the partisan-politics question: "Why must Otto Otepka continue to suffer for placing his country above partisan politics? His last remaining appeal is to the American people—by telling them the full story. Otto Otepka has kept faith with his fellow countrymen. Let us hope the American people will not abandon this dedicated civil servant." In the Senate, the four hoariest members of the Judiciary Committee—Eastland, McClellan, Dirksen, and Roman Hruska—assembled for a confirmation hearing to pay homage to the SACB nominee. "You have been punished because you attempted to protect your country," said Chairman Eastland to Otto, and the four senators respectfully declined to ask the witness anything but his name.

Senator Dodd led the fight on the floor of the Senate and helped organize Otepka Day, on which patriots around the nation celebrated his resurrection. Every time Dodd took the floor to wax eloquent about Otepka's higher mission against international Communism, he represented the largest collection of loyalty contradictions ever assembled in one place—a veritable focal point where all passions on the morality of exposure intersected. For, since Dodd had first praised Otepka for exposing the State Department with pilfered documents and denounced the State Department for penalizing the higher patriotism of Otepka, he, Dodd (as Chapter 2 in this book tells), had himself been exposed for pocketing campaign contributions and other financial misdealings. At the same time the Senator was praising the patriot who exposed corruption in the State Department, he fired the infidel who exposed corruption in himself—his administrative assistant of twelve years, James Boyd. To compound the irony, Boyd's medium of exposure, the Drew Pearson–Jack Anderson column, in the Otepka affair exposed the exposer, Otepka, because of his leanings to the right. In this vortex of confusion, with half of each player's face painted traitor and half hero, it was not surprising that Dodd would resort to arguments tinged with the *ad hominem*: "The press campaign against Otto Otepka has been spearheaded by Drew Pearson, the lying character assassin and his trained jackal, Jack Anderson."

In the end, however, Dodd returned to loftier ground, joined by the honeyed tongue of Senator Dirksen—who read to the

Senate a moving letter from Mrs. Otepka describing the hardships the family had faced since Otto had been demoted in 1967, while his dismissal was still being appealed, to a $15,000-a-year job that was so "demeaning" that Otto protested by taking a leave without pay and forced her to go to work to support him. What is $36,000 for a patriot? asked Dirksen and Dodd of their fellow senators, and the two crusaders went to their graves knowing that the world would be better for having Otepka on the SACB. Otepka, for his part, called the Senate confirmation "my vindication," and a well-deserved one to boot, because, as he later wrote: "I have disagreed only with those who quarrel with the truth. I shall continue to disagree."

The vindication did not come easily, for during the period when Senate confirmation was pending, the *New York Times* practiced an enthusiastic brand of beat-them-at-their-own-gamism. Reporter Neil Sheehan was dispatched to check up on Otepka's acquaintances and began his story on April 4, 1969, as follows: "A fund with John Birch Society ties has paid about 80 per cent of the $26,500 in legal costs incurred by Otto F. Otepka in his four-year fight to win reinstatement as the State Department's chief security evaluator." The story went on to pin down Otepka's "ties" to the Birchers by declaring that "last summer he attended the four-day annual God, Family, and Country rally in Boston, organized by Birch Society leaders." Sheehan also tracked down James M. Stewart, chief fund-raiser of the American Defense Fund, which channeled money to Otepka's lawyers. Stewart looked and acted like a Bircher, although Sheehan wrote that he "would neither affirm nor deny whether he was a member of the Birch Society," saying, like Pete Seeger, "I am not answering the question because it is irrelevant." Beyond such waffling about his affiliations, Stewart further hanged himself with his reading matter, because Sheehan found out, after a hard-nosed inquiry, that "he does subscribe to a number of Birch Society publications."

Having established that Otepka's legal defense was being solicited by a man who might as well have been a Bircher, if he were not in fact a bona fide one, and that Otepka himself was hanging around in right-wing crowds, the editorial board of the *New York Times* concluded that Otto was ineligible for membership on the SACB. According to the April 8, 1969, editorial:

> The disclosure that Otto Otepka received $22,000 from a fund with extreme right-wing associations should be enough to kill his nomination to the Subversive Activities Control Board. After this, senators of conscience cannot vote to confirm Mr. Otepka in a $36,000-a-year job, where his work, if any, will be to judge the loyalty of American citizens and organizations.

Thus the *Times* staked out a principle that compelled it to oppose Otepka—a principle that, like the orderly procedures imperative under which it supported Otto's firing, rested on the ground of process and form rather than substance. For, with the premise that anyone who displayed rightist quirks should be disqualified from the position of oddball-sniffer and extirpator of subversives, the *Times* itself ventured onto the turf of subversive-hunting and declared Otepka ineligible by the very standards that the SACB uses to ferret out dangerous organizations. Rather than taking the political view that the whole SACB concept is unconstitutional and therefore should not be supported—or the resigned view that the SACB is a useless bit of welfare doing nothing, but that it was a shame for the President to use his discretion to appoint, in the *Times*'s view, a schmuck like Otto—the editorial board rested its case on the assertion that Otto was too tainted to do the job right and that a neutral mainstreamer would be more efficient.

An average newspaper might have rested its case there, but the *Times*, not being an average newspaper, possessed a "wait-a-minute" person on the board whose job was to step back and take the long view of responsibility. Apparently, that person noticed that the Otepka editorial might look like McCarthyism to some readers, and told his colleagues that such an impression, left uncorrected, would be detrimental to the *Times*'s historical commitment against Joe McCarthy's methods. So the argument was sealed with the addition of the following mop-up paragraph:

> The far right doubtless will cry "guilt by association," the charge made long ago by civil libertarians against the likes of Mr. Otepka, but there is a crucial difference here. Mr. Otepka's link to Birchites is no youthful indiscretion of many years ago but an activity carried on as recently as last summer.

Having taken the precaution of protecting its flank by recalling and then beating down the best case against McCarthyism—the telling point about the unfairness of using "youthful indiscretions," which the *Times* itself had once made so forcefully—the editorial board rested. It had at least as strong an indictment against Otepka as McCarthy would have had against his victims, had he not ruined it all by rummaging through their old college notebooks.

The fact that Otto's sins did not fall in the "youthful indiscretion" category probably did carry some weight with a liberal readership—with people who remembered going to the verbal barricades for Alger Hiss and others like him over whether their doings on the Left were permanent blemishes of character or merely the wanderings of callow youth. Those people who (perhaps for tactical reasons) had said that what was really wrong with Joe McCarthy was his reliance on outdated evidence, his once-a-subversive-always-a-subversive line, would be relieved to learn that Otepka, unlike Hiss, was still at it. "As recently as last summer," the *Times* editorial concluded, in an apparent reference to the God, Family, and Country rally that Sheehan had uncovered. (Some sources suggest that the freshness of Otto's blight could have been established also by the subscription dates on Stewart's magazines.) Anyone who bought essentially all of McCarthyism except for the Senator's attacks on people for what they did in the past would be sympathetic to disqualifying Otto from the SACB for associations that persisted well into his maturity.

When Sheehan wrote another story for the Sunday *Times* on April 20, emphasizing Otepka's right-wing associations and his likeness to a bureaucratic version of Joe McCarthy, Senator Strom Thurmond strode to Otto's battlements with a declaration on the Senate floor that the *Times* had deliberately smeared Otepka. He charged that *Times* Executive Editor Harding Bancroft had commissioned the Sheehan investigation in order to get even with Otto for the vexations caused back in 1962, when Bancroft was examined for loyalty before going on ACMIASSIOA. The *Times* had no comment on this countersmear, holding to its position that its interest in Otepka sprang from the logic in the youthful-indiscretion editorial.

Whatever the motivation behind the Sheehan articles, their spirit caught on in the Senate, culminating in Senator Stephen Young's speech against Otepka's nomination on June 24, minutes before the vote. Senator Young avowed that James Stewart, who raised money for Otepka's lawyer to use in Otepka's defense, had, on June 16, 1969,

> Attended a fund-raising party at the home of Julius W. Butler . . . an admitted fundraiser for the John Birch Society and active in several John Birch front organizations. . . . The guests at Mr. Butler's home last week included Robert Welch, founder and head of the John Birch Society, who spoke at length spewing forth the usual John Birch lunatic obsessions. Mr. and Mrs. James Stewart, I am told, were in charge of the refreshments that were served at the meeting and were introduced to the crowd and received applause.

Young also hit Otepka for "trying to smear Walt Rostow, the Kennedy-Johnson national security adviser, as a security risk," and added, "Now, I take a dim view of a man like Otepka, who seeks to play God with other people's patriotism."

All this failed, and the Senate confirmed Otepka. The *Washington Post* emphasized the fidelity question in its editorial lament: "Otto Otepka's long and unfaithful service to the State Department certainly entitled him to some reward from those on Capitol Hill who were the beneficiaries of his peculiar form of infidelity." The *New York Times,* as is its custom, resorted to the who-are-you? argument to bewail Otto as a "living symbol of some of the worst days of the McCarthy-McCarran era."

Two years after his investigation of Otepka, Neil Sheehan was ensconced in a New York hideaway as head of a *New York Times* writing team that prepared stories based on the top secret Pentagon Papers—slipped to the *Times,* the *Washington Post,* and other parties by Daniel Ellsberg. Instead of investigating Ellsberg's left-wing associations (such demented pariahs as Noam Chomsky, some SDS leaders, the staff of the *Harvard Crimson,* and the editors of the *Washington Monthly*) or noting his glazed eyes and Martin-Lutherish manner when he opened speeches by confessing himself a war criminal, Sheehan stuck to the material at hand and exposed the deceptions perpetrated by Ellsberg's former bosses. It is possible that Sheehan's views on classified material had changed over the two years since 1969, as had his views on the war in Vietnam. As late as 1967, Sheehan had chronicled his footprints in the long path from war support to war opposition in a *Times Magazine* article entitled "No Longer a Hawk, but Not Yet a Dove." By 1971, he had progressed far enough to write a piece in the *Times* speculating on the possible criminality of people behind him on the path and, with Ellsberg, to decide that the issue of classified documents paled in significance compared with the overriding injustice of the war.

Of course, the decisions regarding publication of the Pentagon Papers were not made by Sheehan but by the managements of the *Times* and the other papers involved. By 1971, the editors of the *Times* had decided that the real issue involved in the exposure of classified documents was not orderly procedures but the people's right to know as embodied in the freedom of the press. A June 15 editorial in the *Times* stated that the paper felt it had an obligation to publish the Pentagon Papers "once these documents fell into our hands." The *Times,* almost as disposed to see conflicts in light of its own powers as the Senate is to see them in terms of Senate dignity, defined its position so narrowly as to leave Dan Ellsberg out in the cold. Rather than present the Pentagon Papers as a joint venture between Ellsberg and the newspaper, the *Times* argued that retribution for "declassifying" the Pentagon Papers was a matter between Ellsberg and the government. The *Times* took responsibility for the papers only when they fell on its doorstep out of nowhere, after which their news value insistently required publication. (There is considerable circumstantial evidence that the *Times* was not as passive in the matter as it implies, and that the newspaper more or less agreed to receive the papers after some preliminary negotiations.)

It is easy to imagine that the *Times*'s forthright exposition of press duties in matters hot enough to be classified must have convinced Otto Otepka that *he* could in the future slip classified documents to the *New York Times* and expect to see them published. Surely he must have been heartened by the *Times*'s objectivity—by the fact that the editors took no overt political or moral position regarding why the war papers should be read in spite of their classification—indeed, there was no editorial at all on the war series until the government stupidly tried to suppress it after three days and introduced the freedom-of-the-press question. The editors then said that the people should have a chance to read the papers, that neither the government nor the press should stand in the way of such breakfast-table enlightenment, and that no one but the people can really tell what they mean. Otto must have reasoned that the people could also decide what his documents meant—that they could supply the political judgment if the press would only give them the chance, as the *Times* said it should. Still, Otto is no fool, at $36,000 a year, and he might have concluded that the *Times*'s opinion on the war really did have something to do with its willingness to publish the Pentagon Papers, despite appearances and words to the contrary. He might have guessed that the *Times* would not have published material like the Pentagon Papers in 1961, in 1968, or even in 1969, when he joined the SACB. Even so, the newspaper's changing views on the war would also help get exposure for Otto. His previous efforts to sully the reputations of war criminals like Walt Rostow and McGeorge Bundy had not been appreciated at all, but now the *Times* seemed to have come around enough on the war that it might again go for a batch of documents on such persons. Both the *Times*'s increasing readiness to examine the doings of war criminals and its agnosticism about the import of the Pentagon Papers should logically work in Otto's favor—and get his documents at least in the back pages. Nevertheless, Otepka must fear lest the strictures about orderly procedures reappear, rising even above the freedom of the press to leave him out in the cold again.

The need for orderly procedures was identified as the central issue in the Pentagon Papers controversy by such newspapers as the Richmond *Times-Dispatch,* a journal that had been all defiant courage and patriotism and Paul Revere when Otto was riding but might well have reached into the *Washington Post*'s Otepka file for an editorial on Ellsberg that declared: "If each clerk, administrative assistant or under secretary could ignore departmental policy and decide for himself how information should be classified, nothing would be safe." Senator Gordon Allot, a supporter of Otto, chimed in with his attention similarly focused on the rules as he felt they should apply to the *New York Times*: "The point is that the *Times* has neither the right nor the duty to decide which classified documents should be classified in which way." Meanwhile, supporters of Ellsberg in Congress took a line something like the following from a House speech by Representative Margaret Heckler of Massachusetts: "What is basically at stake is the right of a free people to know the actions of a government they have chosen to represent them. This is the touchstone of our national philosophy." The political Left, in other words, talked about freedom, while the Right talked about rules. Nobody talked much about the war.

The State Department has been one of the few bastions of consistency in the Otepka and Ellsberg matters, opposing both men on the procedural grounds of loyalty and classification rules. The tight-lipped secret-keeper is so vital a part of the myth and operation of foreign policy that the department's hard line on squealers has, not surprisingly, produced people in accord with nontattling values. Many State Department employees also deride the actions of the two men on the grounds that they are fundamentally unsound people—excitable, passionate, moralistic, unstable, visionary—precisely the kind of unfortunate person that the security processes are designed to protect against.

One dovish foreign-policy veteran sat in my office a month before the Pentagon Papers came out and told me that our mutual friend Ellsberg was crazy, that he was so obsessed by the grossness of the war that he had lost good judgment, that he was a psychological "plunger" who was ill at ease with murky situations and had to be either 100 per cent for the war or 100 per cent against it. He said Dan had now plunged so completely on the dove side that he was consciously changing his life-style to make it more hip. That view is widely held in the foreign-policy field. But conversations about the state of Otepka's or Ellsberg's mental balance have nothing really to do with the charges the two men were—and are—trying to make stick, and more than one foreign-policy-maker dove has been accused of dwelling on Ellsberg's character to avoid facing Ellsberg's arguments and to protect his own skin by staying instinctively with safe, cocktail party talk. And all this begs the question of whether Ellsberg and Otepka might be somewhat shaken up because they are right.

While the State Department, in its concern for its own procedures, has seen both the Ellsberg and Otepka cases through a monocle, most of the rest of us have been so walleyed on the matter that we have seen no parallel between them at all. When columnist Carl Rowan suggested that Otepka was "a sort of Daniel Ellsberg in reverse," most of his readers were shocked. One reader, Otto Otepka, scoffed the analogy in an interview with UPI reporter Marguerite Davis, who wrote that he "said he gave no classified documents to newspapers, but merely provided senators, at their request, with information to support his own sworn testimony." Thus, even Otepka—convicted by the *New York Times* on a technicality—distinguishes himself from Dan Ellsberg on a technicality, and a misleading one at that, since part of the "information" he gave to the senators was a batch of classified documents.

It is highly ironic that the cases of these two men, whose purposes are so far apart ideologically that it is probably dangerous to suggest a similarity at any level, have been argued on virtually interchangeable principles. None of them—the Senate's right to know, the people's right to know, freedom of the press, orderly procedures, or national security—went to the heart of the matter. Both men made an essentially moral choice, much like those made in civil rights sit-ins, to take a specifically taboo step in order to dramatize an injustice that they felt transcended the classification system. Otepka thought that the classification system was important, but that the Administration's spinelessness in the cold war was more important. Ellsberg thought that classification, if bad, was important (which is why his decision produced such personal anguish), but that the history of the Vietnam war was more important in its lessons about the past and the nature of that war. Both men made their decisions in the midst of ethical conflict, and any evaluation of either decision demands that you take a position as to why it is or is not worthy of support. In other words, given that it is possible for something to be important enough to transcend the classification regulations, you have to make a political judgment about the purposes of Otepka and Ellsberg—whether, in essence, you are happy with Rusk's firing of Otepka, or would lean toward Otepka's firing Rusk; whether you lean toward Ellsberg or toward Melvin Laird.

Most politicians and newspapers have shied away from taking a political stand on either Ellsberg or Otepka—choosing instead arbitrary principles that seem to pop up here and there like prairie dogs out of their holes. People's judgments about the moral strength of the Otepka and Ellsberg decisions determines which of these principles *will* pop up—orderly procedures or the public's right to know—but these judgments themselves seldom come into the foreground, or are even admitted. They lie beneath everything, like hidden rudders, while the debate actually takes place over surrogate questions. Without these rudders, without the enormously different perceptions of the importance of what Ellsberg and Otepka were trying to do, the passion collapses out of both cases, leaving shells. Then the only differences between them are that Otepka is trying to stay on the job while Ellsberg is trying to stay out of jail, and that Ellsberg's documents carried a much higher classification than Otepka's.

It is too bad the debate about Ellsberg and Otepka has focused on these principles that are really side issues, because they squeeze out discussion of the moral choice. Even Ellsberg's supporters try to make his decision antiseptic by arguing that all classification regulations should be scrapped, or are void, meaning that his action should be taken like a normal magazine article. Such talk misses the point of what Ellsberg did, as if civil-rights supporters had dwelt on the weakness of laws against disturbing the peace rather than on the moral force of the sit-in (which was actually strengthened by the legitimacy of such arrests in other circumstances). Instead of talking about what in the Pentagon Papers gives Ellsberg a strong case for making them public—instead of convincing people that the documents offer new perspectives on the war that justify their publication—most people's energy has gone into the classification debate, or into making Ellsberg a folk hero, or into self-congratulatory editorials on the courage of the press. Similarly, instead of offering reasons why Otto Otepka's "higher loyalty" was deluded, or a politically unjustifiable loyalty that didn't even warrant breaking classification regulations, most people have tried to come up with some rule that would avoid the uncertainties of political choices. These rules, such as orderly procedures, would produce contrary decisions in the Ellsberg case—if the hidden rudder were not there to guide things to another rule. More important, there is some danger that people may come to believe in the rules. If, for example, the *New York*

Times editorial writers actually believe that the youthful-indiscretion rule, which was invented in the 1950's as a tactical ploy against Joe McCarthy, truly marks the point where McCarthyism went out of bounds, then evading the issue has taken a heavy toll.

On a lighter side, these pseudo-debates may serve as relief for the frustrations and difficulties of the real moral issue. Otto's supporters probably knew they weren't going to hype up the cold war as in the old days, that people were too tired of it to swallow the line about how the symps in the State Department mailed Cuba to the Commies. But Otto gave them a smaller cause to fight for, and they didn't spoil that fight by trying to spell out too specifically what Otepka was seeking to prove before he got fired. That might spoil the debate, which was better left no-holds-barred for Otto.

Likewise for Ellsberg: The real war had tattered every spirit that cared about it long ago. The most important political message in the Pentagon Papers—that the President lied—seemed powerful at first, but public fervor died down quickly. The deeper historical lessons seemed too vague for political application in the near future. So a lot of signs pointed to the idea that Ellsberg was not so useful any more in the cause of ending the war, his flare effect having played itself out—but that the Ellsberg phenomenon itself would provide a worthwhile battlefield against the hawks, a symbolic diversion from the depressing inertia of the war, a substitute skirmish for righteousness's sake that still might have some impact.

There is probably a reason why principles seem so clownishly shuffled in and out of different loyalty debates. The issues are serious, like the war in Vietnam, involving life and death. The opposing sides are therefore very combative, but the converts are being won out on the edges and among the uncommitted. Things are exceedingly vague and undecided on those fringes, where principles are in conflict and nothing seems self-evident (the very idea of political self-evidence having gone downhill since the Declaration of Independence). There is great strain involved in staying out on the fringes, and a great temptation to go to the center of the camp, where principles matter less as debating tools than as slogans. People can wax eloquent about principles when not worrying about points of contention with the other side. Logical absurdities are overlooked, and real debate is suspended. Here principles serve the need to rally, to strut, to score rhetorical successes with flourish, and to bathe in hot-buttered self-satisfaction. Some dignity has been given to the ancient process in recent years by the invention of the necktie and other emblems of prestige and reason.

It is well for those of us who support what Ellsberg did—because the Pentagon Papers did change some minds on the war—to keep the Otepka episode in mind. Thinking of his arguments and the furor around him should keep us from being opportunists in debate— from latching on to the arbitrary rules that surface around any such controversy. These rules, and the sonorous platitudes that editorial writers and politicians trumpet in their names, provide ludicrously poor guidance in evaluating as serious and complex a matter as the Pentagon Papers. By themselves, the rules make ungrounded compasses, pointing east for Ellsberg and west for Otepka in a spectacle that is tragicomic.

Arguing in support of Dan Ellsberg on any such basis as the obvious weaknesses in the classification system is shaky, because it runs headlong into opposite impulses regarding Otepka. But, more important, such an argument misses the point—like speaking out for a sit-in because of improprieties in the disturbing-the-peace laws, when the real issue is race. Whatever positive force there is in what Ellsberg did comes from the nature of the war and what the Pentagon Papers really say about the war—from political and moral issues that have no simple ground rules. When the debate strays from that central question, it loses both its passion and its logic, leaving a dusty bag of principles and counterprinciples that Otto Otepka can use just as well.

16 The Man Who Leaked the Pentagon Papers

(This interview with Daniel Ellsberg, which Taylor Branch taped in Washington, D.C., in late September, 1971, appears here in print for the first time.)

BRANCH: We want to focus in the interview on your decision to take decisive action to make the Pentagon Papers available to the public, and on the psychological process you went through in deciding to do so. I think the best way to get started is to review briefly the chronology of your actions regarding the war. You were basically a hawk on Vietnam through about three years of high-level involvement with the policy from inside the executive branch. You decided that we should get out of the war when you returned in 1967 from two years with the State Department in Vietnam. After rejoining the RAND Corporation, you worked on the Pentagon Papers in late 1967, read the last batch of them in September, 1969, and first delivered them to the Senate Foreign Relations Committee in the fall of 1969. Is that basically correct?

ELLSBERG: Yes, but you should realize that after the papers had been given to the Senate Foreign Relations Committee, it turned out that they had not become available to the public, so there was a series of later decisions that finally brought the papers to the public almost two years later. During 1968 and 1969, I was also making suggestions to people who did have access to the papers that some way should be found to make them public. I thought that more people at RAND could be allowed to analyze the study or that Secretary McNamara could give a number of scholars some kind of limited access. Another thought was that those few of us who had read most or all of the study should make public at least some conclusions from it, distinguishing those upon which we agreed. But the impression I got, indirectly, was that Secretary McNamara was expected to be negative on any such proposal. And in light of that, no one was ready to take any initiative toward opening the papers for general study, much less declassifying them.

I also had the understanding from men close to Secretary McNamara that he regarded the study, based on what he had been told, as being biased and as giving a misleading impression of his own role. The attitude was that he would not allow any increased access to the study. Given his feelings, it seemed unlikely that his successor, Clark Clifford, would be willing to go into this. And it was not expected that either of them would do it in the absence of approval from President Johnson. Finally, the people who headed the study had made personal commitments of secrecy at the time this study was originated, in return for which they received considerable special access in the course of their work. They had the feeling that they had been specially entrusted with this study and with its safekeeping, and that therefore they would be breaking a personal trust if they were to do anything against the wishes of their superiors.

BRANCH: So it was not only a matter of classification regulations and the law, but also a sense of personal obligation to McNamara not to make known conclusions or inferences from the Pentagon Papers.

ELLSBERG: I think the personal discretion was far more important than any immediate thought of the security regulation in this case.

BRANCH: You have said that there was an enormous gulf between talking with your colleagues who had access to the study and going to the Senate Foreign Relations Committee. When and how was that gulf bridged?

ELLSBERG: As I remember, the decision came fairly suddenly in the fall of 1969.

BRANCH: Was there a precipitating incident or something that brought about this sudden resolve to go outside the executive branch?

ELLSBERG: Yes. A number of factors came together in the very late summer of 1969, all of which released earlier inhibitions. One was information from within the Administration that the war was not ending—that, on the contrary, Nixon's intention was to retain American presence there and to bolster it indefinitely with threats of escalation. I felt that a new approach had to be found to encourage him to change that policy or to force him to do so. Also, reading the study as a whole had increasingly impressed me with the need for Congress, at least, to share responsibility for our getting out of the war, and for the possibility of subsequent events that might be called a defeat. I felt that one of the important lessons of the study is that no President who felt sole responsibility for the consequences of final extrication would ever take steps to accomplish that. Third, I had come to believe—mainly from reading the Pentagon Papers—that the domestic politics of the issue were so critical to ending the war that I felt Democratic officials and the Democratic Party in general must be willing to share political responsibility for a possible "defeat," rather than trying to capitalize on it. Many of these impressions really came to me most sharply just in the late summer of '69 when I read the earliest parts of the history, because it's in reading the section dealing with '49, '50, and '51 that one sees most clearly the role of domestic politics. The pressures on the Truman Administration at that time, which arose from charges that they had lost China and were weak on Communism, were very well known in '49 and '50 and seemed to lead directly into steps to keep the Democrats from being charged with losing Indochina in addition to China. Then later, I think, the same incentives continued to apply to the Republicans under Eisenhower, and they continue to apply even now. No President feels that he can permit the Communists to assume power in Saigon while he is in office, and he will take the least costly, least visible course to prevent that final fall—troops, bombing, or whatever.

The fall of 1969 seemed a very appropriate time to release a history that made the responsibility of the Democrats very obvious. I felt that the first year of the new Administration was the promising time for a President to commit himself to withdraw, and that it seemed urgent that he do so before he himself became too committed to the war. And having decided in the fall of 1969 that some new measures were required, I came into personal contact at the same time with Americans whose own sense of obligation led them to accept prison rather than to cooperate with what they saw as a criminal war. The force of their example enlarged the kinds of alternatives that I thought I ought to be willing to consider.

BRANCH: Could you elaborate a little more on these contacts?

ELLSBERG: I had over the previous year and a half begun to read about Ghandian principles and had become interested in meeting some people who lived by them. I was invited to attend a conference of the War Resisters League at Haverford College. I went, wanting to see what these people were like, while not at all necessarily committed to their point of view. At the meeting there were people who had been conscientious objectors and draft resisters in World War I, World War II, and the Korean War—quite a range of ages represented, and people from all over the world, including Pastor Niemöller, who had spent 1938–45 in Hitler's jails for opposing the regime. There were also several very impressive young Americans who were on their way to prison for their refusal to cooperate with the draft. I talked to them and found that their reasons were conscientious and principled. They were very intelligent, thoughtful people, not neurotic or fanatic as they are often depicted by the media. Their example was very challenging to me; it made me ask myself if I were really doing all I could to bring this war to an end. That was a powerful thought, because anyone who has the experience in policy and clearance that I have, or did have, can tell unauthorized people like senators a great deal about the war if he is willing to break the security regulations of the Department of Defense.

BRANCH: I take it, then, that the prospect of prison was the chief obstacle that you had to overcome at that time in order to go to the Senate Foreign Relations Committee.

ELLSBERG: No, the main obstacle was the psychological one of even imagining that you might reveal such information, if you have worked in the executive branch for more than a decade as I have. It is instinctive there that certain other agencies of the executive branch are the primary enemy and that other branches outside the executive branch are enemies second only to one's immediate bureaucratic opponent in matters that seem of such importance that people become dedicated to agency doctrines and folkways. So that the very idea of passing information to Congress—whether classified or not, but information that could possibly harm the budget or the prestige or influence of your agency—would be a step equivalent to defecting to the Russians. You might even be more likely to imagine defection than leaking such information. In other words, the whole way of life in the executive branch is such that violating agency secrecy is not an option that you are constantly weighing in your mind, but rather an unthinkable move.

You see, with the kinds of information involved here, it's a tremendous change for the very notion of giving such information to anyone outside the executive branch to come to consciousness. I know that may sound strange, but it's true. We're talking about an area of foreign policy in defense decision-making that is not normally regarded as the public's business to make or the Congress's business to make, but rather the sphere of the executive branch. So the notion that the public has a right to know or Congress has a right or the need to know is not very high in the awareness of many Americans—least of all, of course, in the well-disciplined and indoctrinated members of the executive branch. So someone whose life has been spent that way is focused entirely on influencing the decisions of the executive branch by activities within it—such things as persuasion or analysis or wire-pulling or bureaucratic methods of various kinds. But the greatest heresy and betrayal, essentially, would be going outside to make pressure there. Interestingly, that's not true of the military services when it comes to their relations with Congress. They rely very explicitly on their relations with certain congressmen or certain committees to bring pressure to bear upon their own civilian superiors and bureaucratic hierarchy in the Department of Defense. But that is an exceptional case.

As I look back on my activities in trying to extricate us from the war starting in mid-'67, I find that they break down into several periods. The first period, from mid-'67 for two years till the end of the summer in '69, still entirely reflected the attitude that these issues were properly reserved for the President and that one could effectively challenge the current policy only by influencing the President and his agents more or less directly. This was both effective and the proper way to do it. So I was working with the Defense Department program. When I talked to people outside the executive branch, it was really to prospective Presidential candidates, in late '67 and through most of '68. In either case, it seemed that the way to change the policy was to change the President or to change the mind of the new President. And as late as early 1969, I was working in the Executive Office Building for the new Republican President Richard Nixon and for Henry Kissinger, still attempting to raise questions and analyze answers and improve the understanding available at the White House so as to affect policy. I gave little thought to influencing anyone else. But that changed abruptly in the summer of 1969 when I began to turn to Congress. For ten years—at State, RAND, Defense, and consulting at all these places at various times—all my efforts, information-carrying, and understanding had been directed to improving policy through high officials within the executive, ideally the President himself. For someone of my background, it is a radical shift from thinking that the President is the only man whose thoughts should be influenced, who counts, to becoming aware of and taking seriously other members in other branches of the government.

BRANCH: There are many *dovish* members of the foreign

policy establishment who disapprove of what you did on the grounds that foreign policy cannot be made outside of the executive branch. I suppose this is natural, because to say otherwise would reduce their own importance. In any case, they have not made that radical shift that you made, it seems.

ELLSBERG: No, they haven't. Since the papers came out, I have been trying to challenge the very widespread, almost universal conception among Americans that the government is equivalent to the executive branch. The use of these terms is almost synonymous, and it should not be. In reading the Pentagon Papers, I was convinced not only that Congress should have had a greater role in deciding whether we should have involved ourselves, but also that the public judgment in weighing the values that seemed to be at stake seemed to be much sounder than that of the government officials I dealt with. A relatively high proportion of women and black people have been right about the war for a number of years—before I was, and before a number of my colleagues in the government. Basically, I think the public in a democracy should have a great deal more information about decisions bearing on the lives of their sons and on the way they spend their own lives. The idea that the foreign policy should be left entirely to the President and his appointed officials seems to me one that has brought us a great deal of trouble in the last twenty-five years, and it is one that we should escape from.

BRANCH: Nevertheless, it is a very powerful idea among people who have spent the last twenty-five years building up the idea that only strong Presidents can get good done in the face of a retrograde Congress and state governments that are even worse.

ELLSBERG: And it's simply natural that people who regard themselves as experts in the foreign policy of the executive branch should have a fairly self-aggrandizing view of the way foreign policy should be made. They don't recognize themselves as an interest group. Beyond that, they are often individuals of a background and social status very frankly elitist, and their attitude of foreign policy is part of a general contempt for the opinions and judgments of most of the people in the country, before whom the foreign policy professionals never have to go for vindication of their policies.

BRANCH: Several others who appear in this book have mentioned an apprehension of losing their way of life, the circles they moved in, and the whole career that they had spent their time building. Did you believe at the time that making the Pentagon Papers available to unauthorized people would effectively cut you off from the whole foreign policy world? Don't you consider it highly unlikely that you will get government employment in the future?

ELLSBERG: Absolutely. It's essentially impossible.... But to put this in perspective, there were two activities that I happened to be engaged in at about the same time and pretty much for the same reasons. One was covertly preparing to reveal this information to the public or the Senate. And the other was working with some RAND colleagues on preparing a letter to the *New York Times,* simply calling for unilateral withdrawal. Now, that letter was essentially almost as final a step to be taken in respect to one's relation with the executive branch as what I personally was doing by releasing 7,000 pages of top secret material to the Senate. As a matter of fact, I'm not sure at this moment that the shock over my doing the latter is any greater in the executive branch or among my former colleagues at RAND than the shock over the letter.

BRANCH: Could you describe the nature of that shock? Were people afraid to associate with you? What would they say to you after the letter appeared in the *New York Times*? How did it manifest itself that you had done something that was essentially taboo?

ELLSBERG: Well, in that case, there were numerous memos written at RAND expressing shock and outrage at what we had done, almost exclusively because of—and this surprised me—the risks that were imposed for *their* employment at RAND, which depends on government funding. Although the letter stated that we were expressing our own personal views and that there were others at RAND who disagreed with us, RAND was mentioned in the letter. This was partly misleading because the RAND management had actually asked us to mention RAND in the letter. They felt that to do otherwise would make it look as if RAND had censored the letter or was trying to hide our association, which was bound to come out in the stories anyway.

BRANCH: Before you signed the RAND letter, much less released 7,000 pages of classified documents to the Senate Foreign Relations Committee, you effectively had to decide that you were going to leave the foreign policy way of life, those associations, those people. How did you bring yourself to accept that?

ELLSBERG: Well, the letter and the documents came pretty close together, so it's difficult for me to disentangle them. I really expected at that point that the government would be seeking to put me in prison. So the issue of my future employment by the Department of Defense or by RAND was somewhat submerged.

BRANCH: How did the letter affect your relations with your colleagues at RAND?

ELLSBERG: It essentially destroyed my relations with several of them, including some superiors and some very close friends—and it made a number of people with whom I had not been particularly close very hostile.

What the reactions to the letter within RAND revealed very strikingly was a pervasive fear of the loss of job. One saw it in similar institutions as well. The fear was not very deeply buried, coming to the surface among the employees at RAND in the belief that their jobs would be immediately threatened along with their whole way of life, which on the whole was a quite good one. It was very striking that the objections to our action were almost entirely based on the threat that we posed to that way of life—as opposed to professional considerations regarding the credibility of RAND in its ability to influence the government. That was mentioned occasionally but not with very much emphasis and not often. RAND's self-image was that of a very independent-minded organization, capable of thinking creatively about problems in the general area of national defense and the national interest. RAND considered itself very free of any coercion by any agency or by the government in the kinds of solutions they proposed and the analysis they undertook. So independence, and I could even say fearlessness in an intellectual sense, was at the heart of RAND's institutional self-image and even of the self-image of most of the individuals with RAND, too. Their sense of themselves was that, by accepting a discipline of discretion or silence with regard to the world outside the executive branch, they paid the price for great access to information within the executive branch, within the national security agencies, and for freedom to analyze. Thinking and seeing themselves in an intellectual context, they regard themselves not only as free thinkers but as courageous, and could easily point to many disputes with the Air Force on matters that were in fact very sensitive and raised a good deal of temper, say, within the Air Force. Despite RAND's independent self-image, the significance of the letter was related in the press to the fact that RAND derives most of its income from the Defense Department and, in fact, mostly from the Air Force. In other words, it was regarded as striking and ironic that someone whose income came from the Air Force would be willing to take this position. This view was fairly definitive proof that RAND's image to the outside world, far from being that of an independent organization, was that of an obviously kept organization, and thus the news value which the name RAND gave to our letter was not that of the weight of independent objective scholarship. Even a former RAND consultant like Paul Samuelson made the point in his *Newsweek* column that the significance of the letter was that when even Air Force lackeys come out against the war, things must be very serious. Now, he always claimed that he was using that phrase ironically, and possibly he was, but it wasn't read that way at RAND and probably most of the readers did not take it that way.

Now most people at RAND were certainly unaware, I think, of this universal image of it and would have regarded it as extremely unfair. I would myself, until this episode—but there we were, surrounded by fellow employees who feared for their jobs and, indeed, feared they would lose their jobs merely by virtue of the fact that a colleague—a few handfuls of colleagues—registered agreement with the position that the Gallup polls had already revealed was held by a majority of the American public. This had to mean that they regarded their jobs as very much on the line—subject to loss by very delicate disturbances.

BRANCH: Did you have any indication that people who reacted in fear for their jobs were aware of what that reaction said about their own freedom?

ELLSBERG: I think few people were confronted with this because few felt strongly enough against the war to feel some impulse to join us and thus be brought face to face with their own inhibitions against doing this. One person did say, "I would have signed that letter with you if I were willing to give up the high alimony I had committed myself to with my former wife, and if I were willing to take my sons out of an expensive school where they are going, and to give up this house. I have to admit that I am just not willing to do that." He went on to say, "Perhaps what I ought to do is sell this house and put the money into a Colonel Sanders fried chicken concession, and then be free to say just what I think." Now, this is just one example of the kind of thinking that I've come across a lot recently, which seems greatly to magnify the inevitable material losses that would accompany doing something that one has decided for whatever closely calculated reasons not to do. In other words, it's very convenient to think that there really is no reasonable possibility of taking this somewhat risky action because the consequences surely would be disastrous.

BRANCH: A risky action that the people felt in principle they should take?

ELLSBERG: Yes. When people have decided that they're not willing to take the risk involved with the action they think is the right thing to do, they then proceed to recalculate that risk to make it look almost suicidal, so that no reasonable person could really be expected to accept it.

BRANCH: And therefore anyone who does take such risks must be unreasonable or crazy.

ELLSBERG: Or else highly courageous, but at any rate so different from a normal, decent person that the example poses no threat to them. I see this attitude, for instance, right now behind the widespread perception in the media and also in establishment circles that I am to be regarded as a fanatic. I think the basis for this is clearly a strong desire to perceive that only a fanatic could have done such a thing.

BRANCH: What you're saying is that the people who dismiss what you did as the work of a fanatic are not necessarily the people who disagree with you strongly about the war, but in fact that a number of doves on the war may feel a need not to have to ask themselves why they are not taking similar risks.

ELLSBERG: Sure. I think there's a very basic psychological mechanism at work here—that when people are questioning their own reasons for not spilling something, they really have to come up with satisfactory reasons to continue to withhold some information or to refrain from taking some decisive action. And those reasons cannot be that they're cowardly or not very patriotic or inhumane or excessively concerned about their careers. Those are just not satisfying over a period of time. And if it's your children or your wife suggesting that you act, you are anxious to counteract the pressure from them with a more satisfactory reason. And that is by saying that the risks are enormous, and/or that the gain is likely to be tiny, if anything—and that any good effect is counterbalanced by various bad effects that are likely to follow. You conclude that in those circumstances only a madman would do it. Thus if you see someone else do it, the first way to defend against the force of the example is to say that he's a madman, to imagine that he's totally deranged.

BRANCH: How did you handle one problem that stumps a lot of potential whistle-blowers, the fear of losing income and financial security?

ELLSBERG: Unlike most whistle-blowers perhaps, I thought—

not knowing then as I do now that the administrative rules on classification had no statutory basis—that my future involved the possibility that the government might attempt to send me to prison, with the corresponding notion that I would not be financially dependent on my credentials any longer. So I didn't really dwell on that consideration. My wife brought money to our marriage, but we didn't get together until some months after the documents went to the Foreign Relations Committee and we were not engaged until half a year later.

BRANCH: But surely you must have given some thought to the possibility that you would not be in prison. How did you think you would live?

ELLSBERG: Well, I would see a very austere life ahead, but it so happened that the very same people who had impressed me with their dedication and willingness to go to prison in past wars, and some in current wars, were also people who had lived most of their lives very austerely and who showed by their example that it is possible to live a very committed and useful life in a style that involves very little money.

BRANCH: One of the other obstacles that has been very strong in deterring some exposure of things within the government is the general confusion expressed by people about how complicated things are, and not just foreign policy but domestic policy as well, and the amount of presumption involved in going public in a matter like this. How important was it for you to have formed a theory that made the war fall in place to some extent in your mind?

ELLSBERG: Well, my own ideas about the war are as confused as anyone's in so many respects, and they involve a great deal of uncertainty and speculation. Even where I think that I see certain patterns, parts of those patterns are very clear and parts are very conjectural. It wouldn't surprise me at all if other people studying the same documents come up with some hypotheses that I haven't considered, and, on the other hand, I'm sure there's a great deal more evidence yet to be brought to bear on the war which would turn a lot of my current hypotheses around. . . . Now, it was very important that one of the things I learned was that the war was most unlikely to be ended by pressures within the executive branch or by better informing the President. The Pentagon Papers reveal that over four different administrations the President had been told very realistically what his prospects were from the course of programs he was actually choosing. This was always accompanied by, naturally, some uninformed advice, but the fact is that he did have available some realistic advice at any given time. So one had no basis for hoping that an accurate, realistic, and persuasive paper would be a new influence to bear on any given President that never existed before, one that might end the war. It seemed clear that the only thing that would change the President's policy was a change in his political environment—Congress and the public at large—and that had to be done by informing people other than the President.

BRANCH: So, while that particular conclusion helped in building the resolve to make the Pentagon Papers public, you don't think it's necessary to have built a complete theory or anything like that—it is possible to act without being able to explain every nook and cranny of the war?

ELLSBERG: It certainly would be possible for me. The image of me in some accounts as a person who manages to be certain about the future at any given point is just totally inaccurate. I can't think of a time when I have been certain about the future course of events, and like most people I don't require certainty. If I waited for a thoroughly satisfying theory of the war, I'd still be waiting.

BRANCH: We've been talking mainly about how you approached or handled the potential cost involved in taking the documents to the Senate Foreign Relations Committee. But that step did not produce anything in the way of making the documents available. What options did you consider then?

ELLSBERG: I won't say all of them because they involve in some cases people who have not yet been visited by the FBI, and I don't want to complicate their lives. But I did, for example, speak to a number of lawyers who were experienced in civil liberties or constitutional or international law about the possibility of court cases that might bring the information to light, or might actually involve subpoenas of the Pentagon Papers or of myself as a defendant or witness. I did speak to other congressmen to see if individual representatives or senators might be willing to introduce the material into the *Congressional Record*. And, as I say, there were some other possibilities. So, really, I turned to the newspapers as something close to a last resort on this.

BRANCH: The best avenue being the Congress?

ELLSBERG: Yes.

BRANCH: It must have been terribly disappointing to have made this decision to take the documents to the Senate and then have them sit there.

ELLSBERG: It was very disappointing, but at the same time it was possible to see the shifts in public mood that had led to their inactivity on this. In other words, their reluctance to hold hearings did clearly correspond to decreased public interest involving the President's speech, for example, following the removal of the troops from Cambodia and so forth, so I couldn't entirely quarrel with the political judgments that were being made, but having made the personal commitment myself, I did want to see it bear fruit.

BRANCH: So after the Foreign Relations Committee obtained the documents in the fall of 1969 you didn't seriously consider going to the press until more than a year later?

ELLSBERG: No, because actually there was a series of occasions when the hope of hearings loomed in the middle distance. In other words, it was clear that they weren't being held in the short run but there often seemed occasions a couple of months away when they were likely to be held. That happened several times. It was only after the final disappointment in the summer after Cambodia that I finally began to approach others.

BRANCH: That would be in the summer of 1970, after they had the documents for about eight months or so. So you started approaching other resources, but when did you begin taking seriously the press as an alternative?

ELLSBERG: The early spring of 1971. And even when I was investigating the newspapers as an avenue, I was still pressing for some other channels. For one thing, I had no reason to feel sure that the newspapers would accept them. I wasn't sure that was a viable channel, either. I wasn't at all sure that specifically the *New York Times* would take the risks or the political pressures. So I constantly had to be thinking of a variety of ways up till the last moment.

BRANCH: Did you get any legal advice before you went to the Senate?

ELLSBERG: Yes, I did, but it was relatively informal, from the lawyers that I know.

The lawyers I spoke with were, naturally, very cautious about in any way underestimating the risks of the course of action that I might choose. And, in retrospect, I think they clearly erred on the side of exaggerating the risks. So I couldn't be said to have gotten any encouragement in the sense of being told this was a relatively safe enterprise.

You see, no leak has ever before been prosecuted, so none of the lawyers I questioned had ever really studied the legal status of the classification rules. They started by taking the Defense Department's references to the Espionage Act at face value, as I had. But the fact is that the Espionage Act is intended to apply to espionage, that is, to foreign spies and people who give information to them with intent to help a foreign power or harm the interests of the United States. Obviously, my intent was the opposite of that, and the Justice Department hopes to avoid discussing intent at all. The Espionage Act has never been applied to a person, in government or out, who gave information, classified or not, to the Congress, press, or public. We have no Official Secrets Act, as in England, applying to the sort of classified information that is in the Pentagon Papers; Congress has always refused executive branch proposals to pass one. Of course, any official leaking information can be fired, or be subjected to other administrative penalties, and might never again be hired by government. But Congress has repeatedly judged, in effect, when this issue has been put before it, that criminal sanctions are not appropriate.

So the legal picture looks very different to me now from the way it did when I revealed the papers.

BRANCH: Were you getting any encouragement from other sources at all, or was this a pretty private decision on your part, with you on the advocacy side and everyone else emphasizing the risks?

ELLSBERG: Well, I had to be careful as to who I discussed it with, and one problem that I faced both in Congress and with lawyers, and with anybody else, was the same problem I had in the executive branch—and that is that it was extremely hard to get anybody to read or even show any interest in a large part of this massive amount of data. So inevitably people were giving me judgments that did not reflect their knowledge of this material or even their imaginative guess as to what might be in it. On the contrary, most people imagined that it couldn't reveal much in the way of startling information. At any rate, the public would never take time to read very much, and hence its influence couldn't be more than very limited. That was certainly, I think, the attitude of the Senate Foreign Relations Committee. And of Senator Fulbright. It was true, really, even of most people I dealt with on a personal level. It was hard for them to imagine the risks could be justified, and I was aware listening to them that they might well be right. But, on the other hand, I was aware that I was the only one who had read the material, that their opinion was not an informed one in that sense.

But they could, of course, make the judgment that nobody else was about to read them either, and that's plausible. I could hardly contradict it from my own experience. I would say that I've often been asked whether I was very startled by the coverage that they did get from the newspapers or the public, and the answer is that, of course, I didn't really foresee the injunction process, which built up the drama and the public interest. But even so, I was not very surprised by the amount of space the newspapers gave them or by the public reaction. I know there could well have been less, but the actual events were within what I thought was the reasonable range of expectations. And that reflected my own knowledge of the contents of these things, which did in fact excite nearly every newspaper that got a look at them. But I'm not sure I know anyone that I dealt with in the two years previous who had come close to imagining that the publicity could be that great.

BRANCH: So you thought the benefits in terms of public reaction were likely to be pretty large in the sense of coverage of the lessons in the Pentagon Papers.

ELLSBERG: All of what I've just been discussing is not benefits so much as leadership, publicity, but that's a necessary element, of course, for having effect. And I'd always figured from the beginning that the basic effect, that the major effects to aim for were effects that would only be felt over a long period, at least one to two years, and possibly longer than that, with consequences I hope to be felt over decades. But I didn't feel that much effect would appear before a year or two in that it will take that long once the material is out to go through it and to compare and analyze and argue about it and to have it in the public consciousness. After all, hardly any long, difficult book on an important subject has much impact for at least a year or so, because it takes that long for people to get around to reading it and discussing it, and this is an extremely long book on a very controversial subject. I also felt that these effects depended upon the entire study's being available, because you had to see patterns that emerged in a number of administrations to draw what seem to be the most important conclusions about the foreign policy and military policy and the current role of deception by the executive.

BRANCH: Sometimes you speak as if the impact of the Pentagon Papers were going to come from a rather scholarly analysis of the entire paper—or at least from people thinking about and weighing what the history says about our foreign policy. Other times, it seems the chief political impact of Pentagon Papers toward ending the war is a far simpler message: the mere documentary evidence that the executive branch lied, which upsets voters who are not likely to read the entire Pentagon Papers very carefully. Do you separate out these two effects of the Pentagon Papers? Which one is more important to you? You do speak of many people reading them and drawing their own conclusions, but obviously that's likely to be a very small fragment of the population. Don't you think?

ELLSBERG: Yes and no. I do think that members of the public will read some of the actual documents and get a feel for the tone of them, the point of view of what they express, or what they don't say as much as what they do say, and the way alternatives are used, and so on. I never really counted on this having much effect on ending the war, although it worked out as a major hope. That clearly depended on factors that were hard to predict. It wasn't easy to predict just how much attention people or newspapers would give them. Obviously, they might not get much immediate attention. I felt the release of them was justified even if, contrary to my hopes, there was essentially no effect within the next year or two, because I felt that these benefits from this unprecedented comprehensive study were definitely worth the costs which were involved in this.

BRANCH: So you say it really wasn't a strategic decision to end the war—you didn't do it based on a calculation that the study had a great potential impact for ending the war immediately.

ELLSBERG: Well, it was a strategic calculation all right, but it did involve more than the immediate prospects of the war. I thought it was justified even if the effect on the war were to be very small. As for the war, there was one kind of effect that I hoped it would have—and I think it probably has had that effect—and that is to make it much more difficult for the President to carry out escalation and, in particular, to do it with the cover of deception and secrecy that this current President has used in the past regarding, for instance, Cambodia and Laos. I think the newspapers would be very much less likely to accept the kinds of lies that accompanied the statements made with regard to Cambodia and Laos—for example, the lie that the North Vietnamese troops in Cambodia were massing for an attack east into Vietnam, when in fact our intelligence showed they were moving west, if anything, to escape from our expected invasion and to secure logistical routes in Cambodia. And I don't think the press could easily accept the kind of secrecy regarding the Laotian invasion. I know they accept the escalations once they occur. Now this could be very important—because I think that Nixon has thought of the threat of escalation as a good kind of negotiating tool, which is very foolish and is shown to be so by the whole history of the conflict. And I hope he now believes that he no longer has that card in his hand and he now concludes that he has no good cards left with which to get the kind of settlement that five Presidents have sought—and that he will simply have to cut loose and present it as a local setback in the context of an over-all Asian peace-making settlement with China. It may even be that the timing of his acceptance of the Chinese invitation was itself brought about by the pressure caused by the Papers. And the future course of events might reflect the surprisingly warm public acceptance of that experiment.

BRANCH: I think one of the other potential impacts on the war currently is the documentary evidence in the Pentagon Papers of deception—already widely believed by most doves, who consequently see nothing terribly new in the Pentagon Papers. But the documentary evidence to prove it may have had an enormous impact on people who had been in the middle before, saying that in a dispute between the President and the doves over whether he lied or not, I have to believe the President. I think one potential political impact of the Pentagon Papers is to hit those people in the middle with hard evidence that the President had, in fact, deceived the country through the executive branch. This seems to me one political impact that has already been felt. Do you think that's true?

ELLSBERG: Certainly. I felt for a long time that one of the

strengths of the government in this process of news management was that almost no reporters had any conception at all of the degree to which they were deceived in this land by the executive branch. So that their skepticism and news-probing still fell far short of guessing at the degree to which policy was being concealed from them. They were content with vague, evasive answers and contradictory answers to questions. They were content with situations in which they were blatantly lied to and accepted conditions where they would not name the sources of their stories and thus make them accountable for the lies. They simply didn't adopt a very critical point of view, and I doubt if there is any newspaperman who has really read the papers who can honestly say he was not surprised by the extent of the deception. Certainly I have talked to some very experienced and cynical newspapermen who were frank to say they were amazed by the papers. And I hope that will be reflected in their own probing behavior in the future.

BRANCH: What do you think would have happened, when the Pentagon Papers were printed in the *New York Times*, if the Nixon Administration, instead of trying to seek an injunction to prohibit further publication, had calmly announced that the documents should not have been leaked because it was against the law and they were going to prosecute the source of the documents, but that they weren't going to try to stop publication? What if the Administration had said that the *Times* had a right to bring it out and that the papers were only contingency plans from the past administrations, anyway? What if they had really downplayed the whole affair?

ELLSBERG: Well, I didn't expect that. On the contrary, I expected them to do pretty much what they did—not in terms of injunctions, necessarily, but in terms of outcry and a great search for sources and so on. Your question implies a kind of perfect flexibility on the part of the Nixon Administration—similar to the criticism of Diem, for example, for not managing to be conciliatory with the Buddhists when they first made their demands in 1963. That was simply an extremely unlikely reaction from Diem, as the Buddhists themselves were well aware. And in this case we are talking about an Administration which, like its predecessors, relies tremendously upon a secrecy system in order to conduct a policy, or a great many policies, for which they could not honestly win public support. Thus, when it sees that secrecy system challenged in the most spectacular way, it's quite unrealistic to think they could size up the particular situation so quickly and to decide it would not be wise to fight it. So they were in a terrible bind, even if they had known the contents of the document well enough to feel sure it wouldn't hurt them if this particular information got out. They still would have been terribly challenged to meet this threat to the secrecy system lest their larger policies suffer from it and get to be public knowledge. And also you have to keep in mind they didn't know the contents of those documents—not because they hadn't had access to them, but because they didn't bother to read them. I knew what this thing revealed, and a few newspapers did by this time, but the Nixon Administration didn't know. There probably wasn't one member of the Nixon Administration who had read those documents.

BRANCH: Was there any specific incident in the spring of 1971 that led to or precipitated going to the press and making contacts with the press? Were there any specific things that happened, or was it just a gradual decision on your part?

ELLSBERG: Yes, the second invasion—Laos—took place since my initial decision to reveal the documents to the public. In other words, for all the reasons in any given month that could be brought forward why either the Foreign Relations Committee or I should postpone publication, the fact remained that almost 10,000 Americans had died since I started that process. Hundreds of thousands of Vietnamese, Indochinese, had been killed or wounded, and two invasions had taken place by the spring of '71. So it seemed no longer justifiable to wait until some better opportunity came along.

BRANCH: You once said you were probably the only civilian that served at a high staff level who was subsequently exposed to the realities of the war in Vietnam close up. How important do you think that dual role of being on both ends of the war was to your ability to make decisions?

ELLSBERG: Well, I think, probably quite important, in making me willing to make such an abrupt change in my own career and my own way of life and professional allegiances, as well as risking prison. Many people, of course, have seen the war much closer than I, and longer than I. But essentially none of them—certainly none of them—have literally read all of the Pentagon Papers, and particularly have not read those sections that clearly separate the legitimacy of our actions in Vietnam from memories of World War II, or Korea—where even greater brutalities and devastation took place in a context that most Americans accept as having been legitimate. On the other hand, at least a couple of other people have read all of the Pentagon Papers and survived. To this day, it's still an extremely small number. It may possibly be no more than Les Gelb, Mort Halperin, and myself—unless one or two people on the Senate Foreign Relations staff and one or two people on the *Times* or the *Post* have read them. Now, of these two others that I know have read all of it, neither of them has ever been in Vietnam. And although I know very well that their feelings are against the war and very strong, it's hard to have the same degree of human concern for people damaged by war if you have never met them face to face. And I don't say this invidiously at all. But I can't pretend that my feelings about a situation like Biafra or Pakistan, however anguished, are as immediate to me as what I know is happening in Vietnam. So the combination of a sense of immediate concern for what the war is doing to the people in Indochina plus the historical and analytical knowledge of the illegitimacy of our involvement gave me a sense of great urgency which it would be hard to have otherwise.

BRANCH: I'd like to discuss the loyalty question for a bit. How did you justify the release of the Pentagon Papers in light of the obligations you felt to RAND or the Defense Department or the executive branch in general? The distaste for traitors, and for being seen as a traitor, or some milder variant on the disloyalty theme, has been perhaps the greatest obstacle for whistle-blowers.

ELLSBERG: I think the principle of "company loyalty," as emphasized in the indoctrination within any bureaucratic structure, governmental or private, has come to sum up the notion of loyalty for many people. That is not a healthy situation, because the kind of loyalty that a democracy requires to function is a somewhat varied set of loyalties which includes loyalty to one's fellow citizens, and certainly loyalty to the Constitution and to the broader institutions of the country. Obviously, these loyalties can come into conflict, and merely mentioning the word "loyalty" doesn't dissolve those dilemmas that one faces. The Code of Ethics of Government Service, passed by both the House and Senate, starts with the principle that every employee of the government should put loyalty to the highest moral principles and to country above loyalty to persons, parties, or government department. Now, that concurrent resolution, if it weren't identified as such, would I think be perceived as a hopelessly idealistic amendment or as a subversive and radical notion by almost any governmental agency. And yet it points directly to the considerations that led me to do what I did and probably to most of the other decisions in your book. So it was a decision that reflected very much a sense of loyalty. To believe that the government cannot run unless one puts loyalty to the President above everything else is a formula for a dictatorship, not for a republic.

BRANCH: So you think that the way most people have come to resolve these conflicting loyalties—which is to give the highest loyalty to the immediate boss in the organization for which they work—is not always going to be a satisfactory and is sometimes going to be a harmful way to resolve those conflicting loyalties.

ELLSBERG: Sure. By the way, you've put it in the right way, because very few people think of their highest loyalty in practical terms as being to the President, but rather as being to their immediate superior, and that's what determines practical behavior. In other words, they are very often led, and feel very righteous in doing so, to lie to a superior several ranks above for the benefit of their immediate agency. So I think that I was somewhat unusual for having a very strong sense of demands made by loyalty to the President in opposition to the interests of intervening levels of authority. I felt that the greatest sin that one could commit was to mislead the President, whatever the interests in the particular agency.

BRANCH: What that means is that because most people feel conflicting loyalties at various points and varying degrees of strength, they feel torn as to which way to go.

ELLSBERG: I don't think they feel it as often as they should. The sense of the overriding loyalty given to one's superior, or let's say to the man who appointed you to the job, I think, keeps most people—many people—from perceiving these serious conflicts when they ought to.

BRANCH: But when they do perceive these conflicts, it's really going to present a situation where people have less easy rules to follow. I mean always doing as the boss says is a very easy rule, don't you think?

ELLSBERG: In my own case, there was a serious conflict in my own mind regarding my personal loyalties to friends who would be jeopardized in their careers by their past association with me or by the fact that they had given me access to documents that I was about to reveal. And I can sympathize with people feeling that under no circumstances should one jeopardize a friend that way. I say I sympathize, and yet at the same time I can't possibly come to the conclusion that it is absolutely ruled out. Certainly, I would feel extremely uncomfortable if I were jeopardizing them without putting myself into jeopardy as well. But even so, we're talking about issues of war and peace here, which I have to feel ultimately go beyond any individuals, especially when it is not their lives that are at stake but their careers.

The notion that one can properly act as a citizen while giving unquestioning loyalty, total loyalty, to one's immediate superior has an implication something like, "What's good for your agency is good for your country." And people who might find that ridiculous in the case of General Motors don't at all find it ridiculous to say that what's good for the President must be good for the country, that what accords with the President's wishes and interests must be good for the country. The Pentagon Papers, I think, reveal that that's not reliable—that to serve the President alone can be a very inadequate fulfillment of one's obligations as a citizen.

BRANCH: You mentioned the difficulty of hurting the careers of friends who were past associates. Did you feel the same thing about personal ties to the people who were damaged by the Pentagon Papers?

ELLSBERG: In a couple of cases, yes. I knew my former boss, General Lansdale, for whom I felt and still feel great respect and affection, would be unhappy in many ways because of the kinds of revelations made. And I regretted that. I would say the same about my late boss, John McNaughton, who died in '67. So much of the material came from John McNaughton—and I was close to him—that I think it would have been harder for me to consider revealing these without his consent, had he been still alive. In other words, I think I would almost surely have felt compelled to go to him and try to get his consent.

BRANCH: And if he had refused, do you think you would have been in a more difficult situation?

ELLSBERG: More difficult, yes. But I think I would have come to the same conclusion. I should also cite the case of one man, by the way, for whom I had a great deal of respect. He had been my superior and friend, working within the government and at RAND, and I was totally regretful of what this was likely to mean for him, in the sense that I didn't want it to hurt him within the government. I also thought it would hurt him personally that I had done this. And yet, I could see no alternative that would spare him, and it seemed to me that the historical situation required this to happen. That isn't to say that I could have brought myself to do something, let's say, that would have resulted in his death, even in matters that involved much greater death. In other words, I don't think I could make that kind of decision. But it did seem to me that I would not be justified in perhaps sentencing many thousands of people—Americans and Vietnamese—to die because of constraints put on me simply by friendship.

BRANCH: Did you talk to Lansdale before releasing the papers about what his personal reaction would be?

ELLSBERG: Oh, no. I didn't come close to revealing to any of those individuals what I had in mind, lest they be suspected of conspiracy later.

BRANCH: Put yourself for a moment in the position of Secretary of State. How would you handle a situation in which an employee of yours went public—with information that was truthful but which you did not wish to be out? How would you handle violations of the classification regulations?

ELLSBERG: I think that should properly be judged only in the context of a very different attitude from what now prevails toward the right of the citizens to know. Now, to perceive that a subordinate has given out classified, or even unclassified, information is to see him as having done a totally unjustified, dangerous act. I hope that situation would change, so that the burden of proof is on the government—on me, the Secretary, in your hypothetical case—to justify the concealment of information. And an accurate revelation by a subordinate would normally be seen as a step to correct some lapse among his superiors.

BRANCH: How would you go about causing such a change, which has not been advocated by many Cabinet members?

ELLSBERG: I think the reaction of the public goes far to legitimize what I've done so far, as have the reactions of some members of Congress. Moreover, if I'm acquitted in trial, it would certainly have the effect of delegitimizing the concealment that has gone before. The next step, I think, is for Congress to be far more aggressive and active in its demands for information from the executive in contrast to its general posture of the last ten or twenty years. In other words, I think that the Congress must educate both the executive and the public as to the constitutional requirements for information if Congress is to perform its constitutional role, and one of the roles of Congress is to protect the public from an overweaning executive. That's why we have a Constitution. I think that in any circumstance the public needs protection from the pretensions of the executive to exclusive control of various policies.

BRANCH: So it seems that, whenever there is what we call successful whistle-blowing, you really have a dual effect. You affect not only the particular policy that you're talking about but also the public's impression of whistle-blowing in general.

ELLSBERG: I think that the act itself is crucial, but that it probably doesn't speak clearly enough and needs explication by the actor, by members of Congress, by commentators, and so forth. You can count on the act being countered quickly by people threatened, who will raise all kinds of considerations that would put its propriety in question—whether the person had a right to do that sort of thing, whether it would lead to anarchy, whether it was the work of an unbalanced person, and so on. This can considerably reduce the positive effects of any whistle-blowing, unless people counter those arguments articulately—something I've only begun to do, and which I hope this book will do.

BRANCH: Do you think there are other people in the government now, agonizing over whether to follow your path or to do some other kind of whistle-blowing?

ELLSBERG: I hope so. There certainly is a great deal more information in the government that should come out. It is even possible that some people are waiting to see what happens to me. If I am acquitted, maybe that will lead to quite a bit of imitation. But I do think it would be wrong to think that there would be a flood of revelations of classified information just because I'm acquitted. I think the inhibitions against people's revealing this information have always been much more professional and career considerations than fear of criminal prosecution. In other words, such things as fear of losing a promotion or losing clearance have always been adequate to keep most people from revealing this information, and it will continue to be adequate in the future. On the other hand, the revelation that the classification system has no force of law, which seems to be the case, should have a considerable effect on demystifying of secrets. Now the rituals that surround the protection of classified information have a somewhat religious effect and make them very important symbols of important status for the keepers of the secret. I think that my act on the one hand communicated some loss of awe on my part for these pages of manuscript, and that the revelation of their contents led many to ridicule their status as high "secrets." So I think that it will be very hard for people in the classification system to look at a page of information that happens to be marked "top secret" and see it as quite so magical in character as they probably did before. And that magic was possibly the greatest part of the protection.

The very fact that, in this case, my judgment regarding the contents of these papers has already been considerably vindicated by the public—and, for that matter, by the government, which has declassified virtually the whole study—must have given some encouragement to people that revelations would not be inevitably followed by public revilement. It would not have surprised me if Congress had reacted fiercely to plug the leaks in the security system and to denounce me as an untrustworthy person. But that didn't happen, and I think that's the kind of thing many people would have expected to happen.

I'm not conscious at this point of many people who say flatly that the information should not have come out. I don't think there are many who would say flatly that I should not have done what I did if that were the only way to do it. A lot of people insist that there must be some better way. But I've never heard a suggestion of a way to get this information out that I did not actively try. I think that a great many of the negative interpretations can be understood as answers to the question, "Why haven't I done more than I have?" The answer is that I'm not a madman, and the acts that I could have taken wouldn't have made any difference. In fact, even the Pentagon Papers haven't made any difference. The risks are enormously great, and it is simply unacceptable to have jeopardized fellow employees or friends or superiors. Those are very widely held attitudes, and I don't think they bear very close examination if you understand the issues of this decision, which do involve war and peace, life and death.

BRANCH: What do you say to the person who is a potential whistle-blower, but who has access to knowledge or information that has much less significance than the Pentagon Papers have?

ELLSBERG: Well, just that his opportunity is less and his obligations may be less.

BRANCH: And his risks are less, I guess.

ELLSBERG: No, his risks to his career may not be less at all.

BRANCH: I guess that's one of the problems. The risks are fairly constant for doing almost anything, whereas the benefits may not be so earth-shaking.

ELLSBERG: You could say that the risks are nearly constant up to the point at which there is a heavy chance of prosecution or prison. I think that's why the reluctance of a HUD employee to give an honest answer to a sidewalk reporter on a matter of current policy may be hardly less than the reluctance to reveal the Pentagon Papers.

17 The Future of Conscience

Like 1984, the future of whistle-blowing will become more important to ponder as we see more signs of it. In the decade ahead, whistle-blowers may fall prey to a period of negativism and confusion similar to that which overtook muckrakers at the turn of the century. Many of the old sharpshooters traveled the road with Lincoln Steffens from exuberant exposés and reform proposals to despairing criticisms of the we're-all-guilty, it's-the-system variety, which, while possibly accurate, had little concrete meaning for—much less capacity to arouse—the average citizen. Those muckrakers then became a sagging weight around the neck of their old ally Theodore Roosevelt. Perhaps sensing that the self-denigration vote was pitifully small, Roosevelt moved to separate himself from Steffens and his colleagues in a speech at the Gridiron Club in Washington on March 17, 1906. He cited a passage from John Bunyan's *Pilgrim's Progress* to warn his listeners against

> the Man with the Muckrake, the man who could look no way but downward with the muckrake in his hand; who was offered a celestial crown for his muckrake but who would neither look up nor regard the crown he was offered but continued to rake to himself the filth of the floor.

Roosevelt is widely credited with introducing the term muckraker into popular usage with that speech, incorporating a kind of nihilist overtone that really took the steam out of the early crusaders by guaranteeing them a hostile or nettled audience.

The reform movement in the post-Roosevelt period did not ride on the quieted muckrakers, but on Wilsonian moralism, a precocious auto industry, and vibrant economic progress. But if the whistle-blowers and muckrakers of the 1970's fall into the Jeremiah trap, their cause may stagnate for want of outlets like Wilson or truly exciting economic inventions. There is no progressive era visible on our horizon. It is therefore especially important that whistle-blowers of the next generation sharpen their wits to avoid the pitfalls of universal guilt and the intractable morass. (Even a touch of self-righteousness may be preferable to general despair—witness the deflation of the civil rights movement after Newark, Detroit, and Pontiac had quelled the fervor of Northern newspapers.) Whistle-blowers can make broad, systemic criticisms, but these do not promise reasonable hope for support or survival in their jobs. The greatest challenge in whistle-blowing is to devise solutions around which people can rally—little nuggets of politically useful hope to raise spirits when despair seems well warranted.

The Role of Naderism

The influence of Ralph Nader has unquestionably operated as a kind of antidote to all-out pessimism. Nader himself is not a whistle-blower—having always been an outside muckraker—but he is often considered one. The wiretapping and other persecution he suffered at the hands of General Motors gave him, like a whistle-blower, a fully justified image as an embattled loner fighting against almost absurd odds. Also, his explicit espousal of whistle-blowing values has linked him to the new tradition and tied the practice of internal exposure so closely to Naderism that any speculation about the future of whistle-blowing necessarily involves speculation about the future of Nader.

Thus far, Ralph Nader has avoided the quagmire of the "ultimate solution"—as well as the negativism that might be expected to follow when people discover that he has none—but not by putting forth a successful new model or a generalized system of how things ought to be. Indeed, most of his proposals for reform are curious mixtures of old doctrines, based simultaneously on ideal socialism and market capitalism. The logic of proposals like federal corporate charters, a consumer voice in corporate decisions, and greater federal regulation of industry tends toward socialism—inasmuch as economic decisions are to be more politicized than they have been and determined less by property rights. The vision behind Nader's antitrust campaign, however, is the free market—with the consumer protected by competitive efficiency. These two strains indicate a seeming ambivalence. Nader would probably nationalize the railroads while breaking up the auto industry. He would probably decrease the regulation of the airlines, because that industry violates market principles, but he would increase regulation and compensatory legislation in agriculture precisely because the market has unleashed its curse on the small farmer as well as on the quality of the food we eat.

This is not to say that Nader would be wrong in any of these proposals, but there is no consistency, no summary model, behind them. (The key ingredients in most Nader pronouncements are honesty and a nearly fierce candor. Nader's long journey on such good but old ethical horses is a measure of how badly the country needed him.) With his record and the sensible measures he does call for, Nader so far has avoided demands for a grand scheme. He may continue to do so for some time, with energetic campaigns that avoid even a hint of defeatism. But if Nader loses his shine, like the old muckrakers, he will be called on for a theory or doctrine to sustain his supporters through lean years. If, for example, Nader's reports and operations become so extensive in scope and familiar in tone that they start to look like pop records (similar tunes, similar beats, to the top of the charts for a short time and then filed away routinely as the next hit release appears), he will have to face the problem of a general solution more squarely. So far he has licked it with *ad hoc* successes, and he has managed to keep his gaze upward even with the muckrake in his hand.

Ironically, Nader's future contributions to whistle-blowing may be more jeopardized by his successes than by his occasional failures. For one thing, his power and relative security in fame may make it increasingly difficult for him to encourage whistle-blowers; it was far easier to call on others to risk all when Nader himself was a blood-brother "little guy." Also, Nader's now rather large and certainly powerful organization faces the obvious threat of decay of moral purpose that inevitably confronts any establishment. If there is a central lesson in Nader's line of work, it is that public-minded purposes tend over the long haul to erode in the face of parochial interests. Just as his raiders have shown this to be true of government, so it is a potential hazard for Nader's multiple groups—which, like the government, have themselves begun as nonprofit bureaucracies devoted to the public interest. And if his public advocates ever become reduced to the call that the public interest can be served *only* by more public advocates like themselves—falling in time to the bureaucrat's metronome—the signs of decay may be showing.

There is no certain danger that Nader's position of strength will erode his influence on whistle-blowing, or diminish his credibility as an advocate of the art, but whistle-blowing is a maverick practice that on the face of it is incompatible with the acquisition of power. Unlike crime, whistle-blowing loses some of its punch when organized. Because it is a necessarily unstructured, spontaneous profession, the preservation of independence is critical for the individual's readiness to take the whistle-blowing step when prudence counsels otherwise. Although there is now only a tiny fissure in Nader's truly remarkable independence, his current campaign for Public Citizens —modeled after John Gardner's Common Cause and selling shares of Ralph Nader for $15—may tie him down if his supporters, like the new breed of corporate stockholders, demand a voice in future decisions.

These caveats about Nader as an active supporter of risk-taking whistle-blowing are perhaps premature, as signs of erosion in Naderism are not yet plain—only to be feared. More important, Nader's future contribution to whistle-blowing is not likely to lie in the encouragement of individual whistle-blowers. His contribution has in many respects already taken hold, as he has helped bring about a value change in which people assume greater responsibility and loyalty to the general public at the expense of old loyalties to the immediate boss. His impact doubtless will continue to be felt around the country even if he retires, provided that tomorrow's whistle-blowers can overcome certain concrete, traditional obstacles to the exercise of conscience beside which the Man-with-the-Muckrake syndrome or the theoretical decay of Naderism pales.

Obstacles to More Whistle-Blowing

Take job vulnerability, for one. Always a critical psychological roadblock in the mind of the potential whistle-blower, it will probably become even more devastating as large organizations dominate an ever larger portion of the nation's employment. To return to Monticello was never easy. To become a self-made husbandman with ease is no longer possible. Even the small, independent business of twenty years ago is today an increasingly obsolete proposition. And if an employee becomes a damaged good, tainted by a reputation as an organizational squealer, he may find so many doors locked that a drop in station or a change in profession will be required for grocery money.

The legal rights of the job-holder, including the public employee, are meager in this regard, because the courts generally hold that employees are not protected for public utterances that impair the "special relationship" in the office, or promote "disharmony and inefficiency." Basically, this means that the employee may not make remarks or charges that injure the atmosphere of cooperation at work. This is a broad area, of course, but the courts have interpreted it to mean that the employee's criticism becomes less protected as he speaks publicly about matters more closely related to his job responsibilities. The whistle-blower will be the last to be afforded license on this scale, because he flies right into the teeth of the storm. Contemporary litigation to obtain more political freedom for government employees focuses on political activity *outside* the sphere of work—on the HUD worker's right to speak out on the war, for example—rather than on his own duties. And even if litigation establishes a broader base of protection, whistle-blowers must anticipate that the employers will find some way to make them scramble for a living—and pay—after their treachery.

Beyond job vulnerability, future whistle-blowers, like those of the recent past, will worry about their prospects for effectiveness after exposing a scandal. Calculations of potential impact if one remains on the inside are especially seductive for people on the rise in their careers. It is no accident that most of the pure whistle-blowers in this book had reached a career plateau—a point at which they could no longer stifle their urge to speak out in the honest hope of attaining a pinnacle of influence someday from which they could *really* clean things up. One of the most powerful weapons of organizations is their encouragement of the young person's hope that he can do more tomorrow and tomorrow if he'll just hang on—by which time he usually has so much invested and is so dependent that principled impulses are forgotten or dismissed with a sigh. In a fundamental sense, whistle-blowing takes a man or woman out of the stream and closes off options, and employees have demonstrated a remarkable ability to invent future strategies and comforting rationales to hold on to opportunity by refusing to take the leap.

This effectiveness trap is woven together with job vulnerability and the instinct of group loyalty to produce a powerful blockade against whistle-blowing. Finally, there is something deep in the temperment of decent people that is revolted by the thought of exposing an employer's failure. Most of those who have done it say that even when you are certain of your position, the shrill of the whistle sounds unseemly, the act pregnant with hero-delusions. At the last moment, it seems to reek of theatrics, like a loud shouting in a hushed museum, or of grandstanding. It is associated with scandal sheets, zealots, people who oversimplify the world into good and evil without room for the murky truth, who lack the quality of self-effacement in their enthusiasm for their own views. The attitudes that counsel against such standout aggressiveness and moral self-assurance are epitomized in the organization man, but they are real. They are so powerful, in fact, that many government employees have fought to the wall and bitten back their consciences without giving a thought to going public. Not a single member of the foreign policy firmament resigned in *public* protest against the Vietnam war or Pentagon waste, for instance, nor did any domestic government employees on the conservative side protest publicly against any policy like busing or deficit spending.

All the attitudes that work against whistle-blowing are strong, in short. They are well illustrated by the stories of people who came close but backed away.

After the invasion of Cambodia in the spring of 1970, word slowly seeped around Washington that three top members of Henry Kissinger's National Security Council staff were leaving the Administration because of basic policy disagreements. They left—without press conferences, statements, background conversations, or letters of their reasoning leaked to the press. The only publicity consisted of a few isolated "insider" columns that praised the courage of the men for leaving and marveled at the decorum, mutual amicability, and grace with which the separation was accomplished. It was, in short, the way one should resign.

The three men—Anthony Lake, Roger Morris, and William Watts—decided to go quietly for various reasons. Watts, who sat in on most top-level policy meetings concerning the war as staff secretary to the NSC, emphasized the need to protect the President's capacity to govern without fear of mutiny.

"I have an enormous respect for the office of the President," he said recently, "and I just think that man has got to have enough confidence in his staff so that he doesn't have to worry that they will betray secrets or attack him in the press. Presidents are paranoid enough already without having to worry about the staff. All the problems of running the country converge in that Oval Office, and I believe you should make every effort not to make those problems more difficult. The whole country was about to fall apart after Cambodia, anyway, so all we really had was a potential, an irresponsible potential, to create greater discord. We could have built up some public brownie points with self-serving publicity—and made a lot of money, too—but we would have been playing God with some of the very basics of how the society runs itself.

"Besides, the possibility of our influencing the Cambodia decision or the war in general was absolutely minimal," he continued. "If we had been Cabinet members or even sub-Cabinet members, our resignations might have had some impact—but not staff members, no matter how important we like to think we are. I suppose we might have made a slight dent in the public belief that the President must be right because of superior information by saying that we had seen virtually the same intelligence that he had and could not in conscience support the policy, but that came out in the stories, anyway. I mean the press got the idea that we were leaving mainly because of the war. I think there are only two ways to leave: quietly, or full blast complete with sordid detail. We chose the former, and a kind of middle ground finally leaked out.

"I have no regrets about how it came out publicly. In fact, I never gave more than a passing thought to really going public, having made up my mind about publicity before I took the job."

The three staff members informed Kissinger of their decision to leave almost simultaneously with the beginning of the invasion, but they did not actually leave their jobs until more than a month later, and they made a great effort to avoid the impression that they were leaving in a huff over the war. According to a *New York Times* story, Roger Morris went so far as to refuse to say that the war had anything to do with his exit. Morris now emphasizes a personal loyalty for Henry Kissinger as the principal reason for his discreet departure.

"I have an intense admiration for Henry," he said. "I think he is head and shoulders above anyone else at that level. He had been kind to us and very open about things. When you've lived with the complications and personalities of a policy, it's hard enough to totally disagree with it—much less make a personal break with friends on the other side. We were in the anomalous position of being inside the Administration writing statements for Richard Nixon, while our wives and friends were out demonstrating against his policy. And I guess if you can't resign from the Nixon Administration, you can't resign from anything. But making a personal attack out of it is different, because you've seen the reasoning and the agonizing behind a man's public stance. We were in a position of trust, and I really didn't want to make life harder for Kissinger.

"My main motive in leaving was not to change the policy anyway. If I had wanted to do that, I would have stayed on and fought inside, because the chances are that I would have been more effective there. But the price was too high personally to retain that effectiveness, and I really wanted to dissociate myself from the Cambodia decisions. There is a gradual, insidious process of erosion that takes place in government, until you don't want to fight any of the step-by-step issues any more."

Watts and Morris are slightly ambivalent about whether whistle-blowing is a selfish act of pure gratification or a principled sacrifice of one's career. On one hand, they tend to see public exposure as a self-serving play for the quick headline, and yet they also recognize that it generally means professional disaster.

"If we had gone public, we would have lost our credibility," said Morris, "and that's most of what you have. The foreign policy establishment punishes people whom they consider disloyal. It's more clubby than most others, and the members shun controversial, outspoken people."

"I'd look very closely at a guy who walked out of there and shot his mouth off," agreed Watts. "If he did it once, he could do it again. It's really not a good thing to do in the long run."

Going public is taboo for the organization man because it appears far too openly self-seeking for a time in history when aggressive self-effacement is a principal key to success. This is an increasing dilemma for the whistle-blower, for an effective siren has to be sounded so *loudly* to get attention that the ego will appear to have taken over and gone wild.

Personal loyalties present one of the most genuine, perplexing problems of the whistle-blower. A friend who provides someone with a job and gives him his personal confidence is not easy to denounce in public discourse, where you must be crudely for or against him. These complex human strings kept Jim Boyd paralyzed for seven months between his break with Senator Dodd and his pilfering of Dodd's records. And Boyd acknowledges that Dodd could still evoke almost a campaign spirit in him with tales of past experiences shared. When you understand someone (as Dostoyevsky understood Raskolnikov), with his foibles and weaknesses and jumbled motives for every decision, it's difficult to classify him as a public enemy and act accordingly. Boyd was helped over this threshhold by Dodd's malevolence toward him. Kissinger's staff members were not.

Advanced personal loyalty may help explain why high-level employees provide so few exposures. The average whistle-blower comes from the middle levels of the bureaucracy—high enough to have an over-all picture of some pillage against the public interest (as opposed to the view seen by highly specialized or clerical workers) and yet low enough not to have truly close ties with those responsible for policy.

There is yet another unique factor in the decision of the Kissinger staff members: However violently they disagreed with Administration war policy, they did not believe it to be a *crime*. This differentiated it from Boyd's reaction to Dodd's corruption, McGee's to petroleum theft, or Pettis's to fraud in development contracts. "Nixon wasn't getting any kickbacks in Cambodia," said Morris, "and Kissinger certainly wasn't in anybody's pay. It was a disagreement." Whistle-blowing is essentially a conservative action, in the sense that the facts brought to light should on their face provoke indignant public reaction. John McGee was not trying to change people's minds about theft—he was merely exposing a situation that he found self-evidently wrong and harmful to the public. The Kissinger staff members would have played a more political than moral role had they gone public, seeking to persuade rather than simply to provide evidence. This distinction is another element that bodes ill for future whistle-blowers, because there is scarcely any action by a recognized organization that most of the citizenry will agree is wrong enough to be the kind of thing to get agitated about. Even the cover-up of the C-5A overrun that Ernest Fitzgerald exposed was presented as a policy disagreement, and everything tends to slide toward the disagreement side of the scale as relativism prevails. Also, the assigning of responsibility for errors is becoming so diffuse and cloudy that many exposures die a natural death for lack of a clear target. The John McGee petroleum scandal, which hung in confusion until the outrage (and McGee) faded away, seems typical. It looks as though the trend toward complexity and interdependence in public affairs will continue, making it more difficult for the whistle-blower to find ground he can stand on firmly.

Liberalism appears to be a real villain in this onslaught against the whistle-blower and against the old yardsticks of homespun right and wrong. It invented relativism and the concept of broad social responsibility to soften competition and harsh individual accountability. It invented the team player and the group ethic and the T-group to take some of the sting out of social Darwinism. But bedrock conservatism played an equal role by sanctifying the vested interest. All organizations mix these two brews. Businesses are increasingly run by team players (although the leaders do not like to acknowledge the passing of the self-made man). And more liberal organizations, such as universities, foundations, and magazines, have become vested interests by their dependence on dividends, advertising, and taxes, although they often avoid dwelling on these materialist sources even more sedulously than businessmen avoid contemplating their friendly, cooperative management. So the rise of the organization and the loyalty instinct transcend ideology, and most people are suspicious of most turncoats. As a vested interest, the organization man dislikes the whistle-blower only when he strikes home—when his own job is threatened. As a team player in general, he dislikes Judases all the time.

Whistle-blowers of the future can expect many ordeals, most of them descended from trial by fire. All the difficulties of keeping a job and making the decision will be compounded by the general social stigma, the organizational halitosis that has plagued those whistle-blowers who have managed to hang on to their employment. Jacqueline Verrett calls herself a "leper" at FDA, and John McGee says that he is "radioactive" in Pensacola.

New Forces at Play: The Might of Right

Despite all the obstacles to whistle-blowing, it seems safe to predict that there will be more of it. After all, the barriers have existed throughout the past ten years, at the same time that the country has experienced the first rash of an astonishing defiance of institutional control. The whistle-blowers have cut across the grain—scraping across raw feelings, provoking hostile reactions from the powerful interests they stick, and losing some very demoralizing battles—but their very emergence proves that the barriers are not insurmountable.

When one stands back and looks at whistle-blowing historically, after searching futilely for a tradition or even a serious group of practitioners before the 1960's, it is the very existence of the species that is remarkable, not its tribulations. The reasons and forces that brought the whistle-blower into being are more interesting than the counterforces. They are newer. They are also more positive, because the strengths on which whistle-blowers have relied is basically that they have been judged *right* by most of the people who have studied the conflicts from outside the battle area. (Inside, it's a different matter. Few Air Force employees have appreciated Ernest Fitzgerald, and few Capitol Hill veterans respect Jim Boyd. They struck home, and whistle-blowers are not popular where they hit. Their colleagues don't like the danger of falling debris.) Most of the whistle-blowers have at least been supported by the majority of people who knew of their cases. And any measure of support for employees who rat on their employers or former employers is surprising in the context of the historical cold shoulder for those who tell.

The acceptance of whistle-blowers as not only correct but, in many cases, highly courageous and principled is a step toward redressing a twisted irony in the use of the word "traitor" for those who break organizational ground rules. The traitor was always hated, because he was the enemy, but there was a special edge on the scorn that historically made traitors hated everywhere—a special venom in the term that sustained an extra measure of emotional force. For the traitor was excoriated as a person without honor of any kind, who, among people willing to die for cause or principle or survival, could shuffle back and forth between opposing camps, sniffing for the highest bidder, unmoved by higher loyalty or human bond or ideal while fixated on the basest medium of exchange, cold cash. Benedict Arnold was hated for defecting to the British in the American Revolution, but he was despised as a real traitor because people found out that he had bargained at length over the pension he would receive—and even the number of calico dresses his wife would obtain—for switching sides.

The whistle-blowers have actually reversed the operation of the classical traitor, as they have usually been the *only* people in their organizations taking a stand on some kind of ideal. They have stood firm on some ground other than profit-making, while their colleagues have quaked and inveighed against them in the name of job security—or of some elaborate professional tradition designed to produce job security. In this light, it was grotesquely ironic for Air Force employees to scorn Ernest

Fitzgerald as a traitorous oddball while they themselves were clinging to the contracts and employment the Air Force provided, to the vital but ignoble currency that has historically purchased treason.

Resentment of people like Fitzgerald can be traced back through most of history: The assumption has usually been that anyone who spoke against his fellow breadwinners was a turncoat. Now, however, loyalties are broader, and old instincts may be so parochial that they lead to a backward perception as to who is really betraying the interests of the country. Fitzgerald and similar whistle-blowers have been so clearly right in their charges that they have shattered some assumptions about who is patriot and who is sniveling opportunist. This is no mean achievement, for the whistle-blower has only his work and a few facts wtih which to do battle with a huge organization. An institution not only has public respect, money, and hundreds of thousands of kept constituents, but often, as in the case of the Air Force, it also relies on the citizenry's *need* to believe in it. (Since people reason that we have troubles if a vital organ like the Air Force is corrupt and a single Rambler-driver like Ernest Fitzgerald is right, there is an understandable predilection to believe that Fitzgerald is wrong.)

The successes of the whistle-blowers in winning a measure of public admiration—leaving aside for the moment the questionable potency of this admiration in protecting them from retribution or in putting their reforms into effect—is in some sense a testament to the morality of the positions they have taken. This judgment by parts of the public is important, because it is the only lasting source of strength that the whistle-blowers have. More important, if the whistle-blowers of the future continue the record of being considered fundamentally right in what they do, building on the acceptance of their predecessors, then the essential truths in their messages will gain in force and may even in time have considerable impact on the policies they criticize. This is not to say, of course, that there would be no more John McGee's, no more broken and dispirited whistle-blowers, or that might would not continue to prevail in many cases over valiant stances—but the John McGees will continue to stick in people's throats until adjustments are made that recognize the validity of what they do. It will be impossible in the long run to overlook the moral power of people like McGee; and this power, in addition to the forces that produced the whistle-blowers in the first place, is what the whistle-blowers will ride on. It is their accelerator for an uphill journey.

Looking at the problem through the eyes of future whistle-blowers, the dilemmas are likely to center not on the morality of proposed actions but on their utility. Some, like Jim Boyd and Dan Ellsberg, will agonize over their decisions because they will have to break laws and rules to make their point, to serve the right as they see it. The conservative, "do your duty" whistle-blowers like Fitzgerald and McGee face only the power to hurt of narrow institutional loyalties, but anyone who goes through these wringers will probably feel quite sure that he is on firm moral ground. Thus, as long as the costs, or the risks, of blowing the whistle remain high, those who take action are less likely to be worried about the justice of their course and more likely to be worried about whether the whole ordeal is worth it.

The Challenge to Press and Public

For citizens, the issues of right and wrong in whistle-blowing are more difficult than they are for the whistle-blowers themselves. As pointed out in Chapter 15, on Ellsberg and Otepka, whistle-blowing boils down to an attempt to suspend the rules that produce loyalty and cohesive behavior institutions. It is Jim Boyd's act suspending Senator Dodd's rights of privacy by pilfering documents that incriminated the Senator; Boyd thought the unconscionability of Dodd's actions of overriding importance. It is Ernest Fitzgerald's testimony on the C-5A, which suspended the code of loyalty to the Air Force team because Fitzgerald thought the testimony was more important. When a whistle-blower suspends the rules, he is arguing that extraordinary circumstances exist to justify what he is doing. In short, he throws the case open to debate from scratch—debating politics, objectives, and first principles—because he feels that the rules and guidelines for resolving disputes and failures within an organization have been insufficient.

There can be no guidelines for deciding whether to support whistle-blowing in general, because each case itself actually disputes the validity of general guidelines. One can't decide that it is always justifiable to Xerox the records of an employer, as Boyd did, in order to zap him in the press, or to make notes and contacts within an organization, as Chris Pyle did, in order to mount a campaign against that organization's existence after leaving. Whistle-blowing involves throwing out the rules, and it thus demands great discernment on the part of the public and press to evaluate the case without leaning too heavily on rules that serve for ordinary times and ordinary disputes. A whistle-blower asserts a claim of extraordinary wrongdoing and persistent malfunctioning by his organization, and any mere recitation of contending rules usually produces nothing more than a tap-dance around the issues.

But although each case of whistle-blowing demands individual evaluation, certain generalizations are possible for someone trying to decide how socially useful whistle-blowing has been or could be—assuming that the quality of criticism remains as high in the future as that of the activists in this book. Public exposure with an "insider" element of exposé drama is useful as a means of prodding an organization toward reform when all the traditional, institutionalized methods of reform have obviously failed. It is one form of Justice Brandeis's sunlight disinfectant, a stain-remover for public policy. Whistle-blowing is socially useful if the nation's employees can no longer afford to live as rigidly by the rules of employment, and the attitudes of team loyalty inspired by those rules, as they have in the past. Although any country would fall apart if the rules and loyalties were thrown out altogether—and if each dispute were judged by a nation of newspaper-reading public-opinion-makers, ruling on the validity of thousands of internal decisions each week—a good case can be made that we must tolerate and even encourage transgressions of these loyalties when they are made by high-caliber whistle-blowers.

The poor performance of American institutions during the last decade has already produced such a dire litany that it requires no elaboration. However, whistle-blowing is especially encouraged by a peculiar kind of development in the country —one that is not haphazard but in fact can be predicted to roll on. The development is centralization, spurred by efficiency and interdependence. Centralization breeds concentrations of power. In the economy, it takes the place of cutthroat competition for business and labor, meaning that the only real check on tyrannical economic power—a competitive market place— has been eroded. In politics, there has been a convergence of authority on the national government in Washington, and on the more centralized executive branch within the national government, so that most decisions drift toward the center. In the complexity of decision-making there, problems often break down into a battle somewhat like John McGee's petroleum scandal—in which the intensely felt needs of a special interest are matched against a public interest that is only marginally felt by the millions of people thinly involved. There is an almost inevitable tendency to accommodate the special interest or the narrow interest of the government agency involved, and that tendency produces whistle-blowers.

This is not to say that centralization is necessarily bad. Most of us want one federal standard on school desegregation, rather than fifty separate state standards. It seems far more efficient to have a national welfare program, rather than fifty state programs. There is a movement for people to demand participation in all the "decisions that affect our lives," which is a prescription for centralized decision-making. Many people are for regional, even national, planning for ecology and consumer standards, rather than more localized efforts. Centralization may be feared and despised as an idea, because it is a cramp to freedom and diversity, but it constantly emerges in practice, with various soothing disguises. In any case, the trend seems inexorable.

So power becomes more concentrated, as vested interests eat up the mechanisms that once tried to control them. We have federal elections to put people in places of sufficient authority to handle strong organizations, but we elect only one federal official every four years, the President—the same amount of formal public involvement at the center that we had 200 years ago. Each voter exercises his Presidential franchise during his few seconds in the voting booth. Between these whiffs of electoral citizen-power, the President must govern largely on the basis of rather informal give-and-take with the very centers of power that the whistle-blowers attack. The public as a whole gets gobbled up by its larger parts.

To make things even worse, many people—among them, some of the most talented—are not interested in creating new centers of economic power, new transportation companies, for example, to supplant General Motors. And there is little evidence that the current centers of power will be displaced by new ones, that their potential for the accumulation of influence will be checked by natural obsolescence. One of the most striking and widespread attitudes among the young is a distaste for the idea of striving to make new centers of power. Such striving seems like the same treadmill that created the problems. Young people want to puncture power and let it deflate, rather than take it over. This may be bad politics, but it is a strong attitude. They are, in a sense, interested in countervailing *non*power rather than countervailing power. (One of the important attractions of Eugene McCarthy and Ralph Nader for young people has been their appearance of fitting this mold: McCarthy seems bored by power, and Nader immune from its trappings. If they prove other-minded, their glamour may dull.)

There is little evidence that the concentration of power in the hands of existing organizations—businesses, labor unions, government agencies, and so on—will abate. As the power becomes coagulated, it becomes lazy and entrenched. From there, it is a short step to its becoming corrupt and predatory—as large organizations feel driven to use their influence to carve out a healthy share of the market, or of the government budget. In response to this process, and to the deep feeling that something is dreadfully amiss, some people have been reading up on their Marx. Others have scurried for their Madison on checks and balances and the inevitable corruption of unchecked power. And some have blown the whistle, in bold if often awkward reactions against specific examples of this malaise that has seemed too pressing for theory.

In this way, whistle-blowing has moved into a breach left by the failure of the traditional methods of institutional control —mechanisms like competition in business, government regulation, and political accountability, which are supposed to ensure that institutions are guided toward the public interest. These mechanisms theoretically guarantee that ironclad institutional loyalties are not only safe but desirable. Such loyalties were built on the conviction that society's time-tested gyroscopes would remain well oiled. But these days the invisible hand seems to rely more and more heavily on public opinion, and general public opinion misses an enormous number of scattered little atrocities. The whistle-blowers have added some *ad hoc* information to redress this imbalance of knowledge. The other mechanisms of institutional control are failing, and whistle-blowing is a kind of unprecedented call to the bull pen.

It is an important, but not a decisive, weapon for reform—especially for the Nader-like kind of reform that pressures corporations and government agencies to live up to their own neglected standards. Its direct effectiveness in obtaining quick redress for the specific wrongdoing exposed by the whistle-blower has not been spectacular so far. The lackluster record probably springs partly from the simple fact that whistle-blowing is an unpracticed art, filled with difficult tactical decisions. Does one leave the organization to become an alumnus whistle-blower, obtaining some maneuvering room but sacrificing the drama and immediacy of an inside exposure? Or does one stay inside, where the battle will draw more press coverage, but where there is great danger of being neutralized by a confusing barrage of emotion-filled loyalty and motive charges? The strategy of whistle-blowing requires some political savvy, and that is only slowly building in an art like inside exposure—where the odds usually appear so overwhelmingly negative that whistle-blowers find it all they can do to blurt out their version of the truth. Savvy and whistle-blowing are incompatible in the sense that once somebody starts calculating what will win he is likely to hedge bets and reject whistle-blowing in favor of a quiet and drawn-out internal reform campaign. The guts of McGee and the skill of Pyle are a rare combination.

The effectiveness of whistle-blowing for immediate reform has also been hampered by the growing complexity of the required solutions. It is easier to be convinced that the whistle-blower is right in detecting rottenness than to concur in a proposed solution. And even when the solution, or a part of it, is clear, there is a frustrating scarcity of means to implement a public consensus. Most of the public familiar with the Fitzgerald case, for example—both liberals and conservatives—believe that he should not have been fired for testifying truthfully about the C-5A contract. His reinstatement would solve only a small portion of the issues raised by the C-5A affair, but it would be a start—and it is favored by the vast majority of people who have expressed opinions on the matter in polls. Yet the Air Force, the Civil Service Commission, the Justice Department, and the Administration generally see things differently (as did the Johnson Administration, by all signs, when the case broke during the waning days of its rule). They are engaged, as of this writing, in a coordinated effort of litigation and delay toward keeping all inquiries into the Fitzgerald firing within closed procedures. These powerful government agencies have all the weight of inertia behind them, and it is highly unlikely that the Fitzgerald case will become an issue in a Presidential campaign. As in most whistle-blowing episodes, time is on the side of the offending organizations, which try to wait out public outrage. The public faces a filibuster without a cloture vote. Meanwhile, Fitzgerald's allies in the Congress apparently realize that he is only one man, whereas the offending government agencies, and Lockheed, will be around swinging weight for a long time. Fitzgerald is easier to forget.

A final reason for the relatively poor record of whistle-blowers in achieving reform regarding the specific issues they address is that their unfamiliarity with this new medium of exposure is matched by equal unfamiliarity on the part of the public and the press. We are just learning to deal with the phenomenon of reforms advocated by "disloyal subordinates." We are still sidetracked by the prestigious denials and accusations made by the wounded organizations. The conditions of whistle-blowing put a daft spin on debate at times, sending the discussion into hot contention over side issues. We are still learning how to judge cases of internal exposure on their merits, rather than on the strict application of various contradictory rules or on the personal characteristics of the whistle-blower (who, because of the pressure, may always seem a bit off balance to the public). Each "successful" whistle-blower—successful in that most people believe that he is right, that it was better for him to have acted than to have remained discreetly loyal to his employer—makes a contribution to the public's willingness to accept inside exposure as a legitimate means of reform. He helps the public and the press feel enough at ease with whistle-blowing to examine the case without being hopelessly biased against the whistle-blower.

In this context, it is important that the meaure of each whistle-blower is not limited to his effectiveness in changing the practices he exposes. He is part of a larger process of gaining acceptance for internal exposure in general—to help make it possible for future whistle-blowers to have more impact, with less suicidal effects personally. Each successful whistle-blowing has at least three good potential repercussions. First, it may change policy. There will be Chris Pyles and Jacqueline Verretts and Jim Boyds. Second, it may help convince people that they cannot automatically entrust the public benefit to organizations that profess to be its agents. All large organizations—public or private, OEO, the Pentagon, or General Motors—are vested interests, looking to their constituents first, and nothing ensures that their welfare is synonymous or harmonious with the public welfare. The society, in short, is muscle-bound—each organizational muscle being strong and proud, but the whole body being knotted and cramped, stumbling over itself in spasms of uncoordinated strength. Third, a successful internal exposure helps convince people that our ingrained attitudes of treason, loyalty, and distaste for whistle-blowers are not only unnecessarily rigid but often harmful. Each case helps establish that citizenship requires a difficult balancing of many loyalties, and that people must take a personal responsibility for the larger context of what they do and are involved in, not just for the little cog they polish. Balancing many contesting loyalties is harder, but narrow simplicity may be more perilous.

Whistle-blowing is thus both an act of reform and a part of a lengthy process of adjustment for a society that is so off balance that its major institutions are capable of contemptible fraud against the public, and of repression against the employees who try to protect the public from their own leaders. Every whistle-blower who is right contributes to a kind of education by example for the country, even if he is widely regarded as a failure or as an impotent martyr for his particular cause. The educational value of people like Bob Benson may, in the long run, be as important as the tactical successes of people like Chris Pyle. Each whistle-blower who is right helps to roll back a little flap of the country's sleepy eyelid to help us see how great the need is to reform corrupt power, how dead Madison has really become.

Whistle-blowing is part of a movement toward conscience by employees who have become more willing to take risks to press their point of view within their organizations—to be ready to leave or be fired for their beliefs. Although that trend alone will certainly not carry with it the strength or vision to keep power as accountable as it should be, it is a wholly positive development. It should be encouraged, even by the employers themselves.

This does not mean that whistle-blowing should become a riskless proposition or that the rules of loyalty and the sanctions behind them should be abolished. One would have to be a committed anarchist or a fool to believe that *all* whistle-blowers should be guaranteed success and job protection. Not all whistle-blowers are good, nor are all organizational loyalties bad. The risk in public exposures has thus far operated as insurance of quality—far too costly insurance, since whistle-blowing now has more of a *kamikaze* feeling about it than an atmosphere of calculated gamble for the public good. There should be more protection for the whistle-blowers who prove right—at least more than has been received by blacklisted Pettises and exiled McGees—without making whistle-blowing an automatic free ride. The risk must be preserved, for otherwise whistle-blowing would become banal, the country would be inundated with exposures, and the good cases would become uselessly lost in a sea of bad ones.

If one draws a rectangle with Jim Boyd and Ernie Fitzgerald and Chris Pyle and Dan Ellsberg at the corners and the others along the lines, it forms a window for a society that is struggling to make its institutions work when all of its devised means of control seem to have gone lame. Sporadic efforts of individual reform are a kind of collective signal that the country needs new ideas and courageous people to cope with the malaise that has turned ethics upside down in many parts of government and industry. There is no assurance that we will get the new ideas, but we will probably get more whistle-blowers. The impact of their courage depends on how strongly we support each call for reform that we judge to be right. What we make of the whistle-blowers altogether—and whether we can figure out how to diminish the need for them—depends on how well we see through the window.

Index